ETERNAL VALUES
FOR A VALUELESS AGE

Studies in the Ten Commandments

by Robert C. Walton

Planters Press ™
Brookhaven, PA

Other works by Robert C. Walton

Chronological and Background Charts of Church History
Zondervan, 1986; revised and expanded, 2005

Faith Reformed Baptist Church Sunday School Curriculum Project
Editor and Principal Author
www.rcwalton.com

Notes on Classic Literature for the Christian High School Teacher
www.rcwalton.com/Literature.htm

ETERNAL VALUES FOR A VALUELESS AGE
Studies in the Ten Commandments

ACKNOWLEDGMENTS

After thirty-five years of teaching Ethics to high school seniors, I still stand in front of the class with handwritten notes first prepared in 1975. One should not conclude from this, however, that the course has not changed significantly during that time. While the basic structure and content remain the same, the illustrations, discussion, and supporting information have evolved to such an extent that, if one of my students today were to compare notes with his father or mother who had taken the course a generation ago (a not unusual occurrence), he would find the content significantly different. One of the consequences of teaching the same material for such a long time, however, is that one easily forgets the sources of much of the material. Did I learn that in seminary, did I read that somewhere, or did that idea or argument somehow develop as a result of my own growing understanding?

As a result, giving due credit is not an easy task. But while I cannot trace the sources of everything contained in the following pages, I do wish to acknowledge two men whose contributions helped to provide the foundation of the course's structure. The first of these is John Frame, my Doctrine of the Christian Life professor at Westminster Theological Seminary. When I studied under him, Dr. Frame was in the early stages of developing the approach to Christian Ethics for which he has since become renowned. From him I have borrowed the basic organization of my course, along with some ideas that those familiar with his writings would easily recognize. In essence, my course constitutes an adaptation of part of his seminary class for Christian high school students, and I want to thank him for his kind permission to publish this material. The other formative influence behind the course was my pastor at the time, Will Varner, whose series of sermons on the Ten Commandments provided many of the titles of the chapters in this book. To these men, and to many others who must remain unnamed, I express my sincere thanks, and trust that their influence has been passed on to my students over many years in the classroom. I also would like to thank my wife Chris, who spent many hours poring over the manuscript and making helpful suggestions that served to clarify the language and ideas of the book.

In addition, I would like to acknowledge the kind permission of Crossway Books for the use of the English Standard Version, which is the source of all biblical quotations in the text unless otherwise noted.

Robert C. Walton
Brookhaven, PA
July 2011

THE TEN COMMANDMENTS FOR TODAY

Should Christians today study the Ten Commandments? Opinions on this subject have varied greatly, from extreme Dispensationalists who have argued that the Law is no longer applicable because we now live in the Age of Grace, even to the extent of rejecting the relevance of the Sermon on the Mount because it was given before the coming of the Holy Spirit at Pentecost, to the Christian Reconstructionists who want the Decalogue to become the law of the land. Given the extreme range of views in the Christian community over the years, how should we understand the role of God's law in contemporary life?

On the one hand, one must acknowledge that the Scriptures have much of a positive nature to say about God's law. The Psalmist tells us that "the law of the Lord is perfect" (Psalm 19:7); Moses told the Israelites in his final sermon, "You shall diligently keep the commandments of the Lord your God, and his testimonies and statutes, which he has commanded you" (Deuteronomy 6:17); Jesus said, "If you love me, you will keep my commandments" (John 14:15), responded to a lawyer's reference to the Two Great Commandments by saying, "Do this, and you will live" (Luke 10:28), and told His disciples, "Until heaven and earth pass away, not an iota, not a dot, will pass from the Law until all is accomplished" (Matthew 5:18). Paul tells the Romans, "It is not the hearers of the law who are righteous before God, but the doers of the law who will be justified" (Romans 2:13). James, dealing with the same issue in negative terms, says, "Whoever keeps the whole law but fails in one point has become accountable for all of it" (James 2:10), and John affirms, "Whoever says 'I know him' but does not keep his commandments is a liar, and the truth is not in him, but whoever keeps his word, in him truly is the love of God perfected" (I John 2:4-5). The writers of both the Old and New Testaments clearly placed great value on God's law.

On the other hand, John says, "The law was given through Moses; grace and truth came through Jesus Christ" (John 1:17). Paul speaks of the limitations of the law when he says, "By the works of the law no human being will be justified in his sight, since through the law comes knowledge of sin" (Romans 3:20), and later argues that "one is justified by faith apart from the works of the law" (Romans 3:28). He speaks even more strongly about the negative impact of the law when he says, "the law came in to increase the trespass" (Romans 5:20), affirms, "we are not under law but under grace" (Romans 6:15), and goes even further when he says Christians have "died to the law," that "our sinful passions [were] aroused by the law," and that "now we are released from the law" (Romans 7:4-6). His comments in Galatians are still more negative, of course.

What are we to make of all this? First of all, we should note that the law in itself is flawless because it is an expression of the character of God. Keeping the law boils down to Jesus' words in the Sermon on the Mount: "Be perfect, as your heavenly Father is perfect" (Matthew 5:48). Following the Ten Commandments is thus, at its root, searching after godliness. In the first chapter, we will address in more detail the questions of the permanence and applicability of the law, but of the perfection of the law there can be no doubt.

Secondly, we must note that following the Ten Commandments saves no one. The law was never intended to make man right with God. No one is capable of keeping it perfectly except the sinless Son of God, who was God in human flesh. We must thus be certain from the very beginning that our students do not come to the end of the course thinking that God will give them His approval if they carefully follow the life choices outlined in the curriculum. Outwardly moral unbelievers are every bit as much on the way to Hell as openly immoral ones. In fact, perhaps the worst way of giving students false assurance of their standing with God is to communicate the idea that "being a good person" and "following God's rules" makes one a Christian. No, one who teaches this course must always be careful to communicate the reality of what moral living does *not* do.

Thirdly, those who teach the course must be aware that God's law is intended to sting the conscience. If the subject matter is taught faithfully, students should come away from their discussions with a greater sense of the extent to which we all fall short of God's standard, and thus the extent to which we all need Christ. As was the case with the lawyer to whom Jesus told the parable of the Good Samaritan, and later with the Rich Young Ruler, those who are confronted with God's standard of holiness will often become defensive, wanting to justify their own behavior and picture as unreasonable any demands stricter than those by which they already live. If the course does not prick the conscience, the students have not yet understood the comprehensiveness and depth of God's standard of holiness. In fact, the attitudes taken by students toward the applications of God's Word presented in the course are often helpful indicators of where they stand spiritually and the extent to which pleasing God is really a priority in their lives. Thus this study can provide opportunities to challenge the reality of students' faith.

Fourthly, the way in which the course is taught should make plain to the students that godly living is every bit as much dependent on the grace of God as salvation itself - sanctification is as much a work of grace as justification is. Considering God's standards for holy living and the application of those standards to problems of daily life and controversial societal issues should lead all of us to cry out to God to strengthen our faith and give us a greater desire for obedience. We should all recognize that Christlike living is utterly dependent on the power of the Spirit of God in the believer, and that, apart from the Spirit, no man can please God.

Fifthly, the teacher who presents this material to high school students must always be careful to communicate that outward behavior in itself is never a sufficient measure of godliness. The teaching of Jesus, both in passages such as the Sermon on the Mount and in His controversies with the Pharisees, emphasized that true righteousness is a matter of the heart, not simply of observable behavior. Thus discussing right and wrong behavior will never be enough, and in fact can easily give students the wrong impression. Scripture drives us to examine the motives of the heart - not only what we do, but why we do it. We must lead our students to do the same.

Finally, the course is intended to perform an apologetic function. In an age that recognizes no fixed standard of morality, Christian young people must be "prepared to make a defense to anyone who asks [them] for a reason for the hope that is in [them]" (I Peter 3:15). Spending time discussing the controversial social issues of the day is intended, not only to enable students to apply the Word of God to hard choices they may face in the future, but also to equip them to defend biblical morality on college campuses and in a broader world where such moral standards are rejected as obsolete, scoffed at as puritanical, or even condemned as intolerant. Students who are not prepared to stand firm for what they believe and live it despite the pressures with which they are daily bombarded will easily succumb to the loose morality with which our society is saturated. Careful instruction and thoughtful discussion should help students to heed Paul's warning: "Let anyone who thinks that he stands take heed lest he fall" (I Corinthians 10:12).

The basic structure of the book is relatively simple. After an introductory first chapter that examines in a broad context the question of how to determine moral values, the chapters that follow deal with each of the Ten Commandments in turn, beginning with a section on biblical background, which is then followed by discussion of various practical applications and contemporary issues.

1

THE PROBLEM OF RIGHT AND WRONG

For a Christian, the question of right and wrong is at its root a simple one - God's Word provides "all things that pertain to life and godliness" (II Peter 1:3), and our task is to seek to understand and apply it rightly. But the problem of right and wrong is not only of concern to Christians. Since the dawn of philosophy in the Classical Age, great thinkers such as Plato and Aristotle have exercised themselves over the questions of virtue and justice, both individual and civic. Understanding the variety of answers at which such thinkers have arrived is of value for the Christian, both to gain clearer comprehension of the society around them and see why people do the things they do, and to appreciate the unique beauty, truth, and power of morality based on the character of God. We will thus begin our study with a survey of non-Christian ethical systems, concluding the opening chapter with a broad look at biblical ethics as a point of contrast.

How, then, does one decide what is right and what is wrong? Brainstorming on this question with my students always brings a variety of responses: some people do what feels good or makes them happy, others follow what they've been taught growing up, some simply go along with their peers, some imitate figures in popular culture, some do what they believe will produce the most desirable outcome, and others try to live by the law, or even some religious writing such as the Qur'an or the teachings of Buddha. For many people, despite what they may claim, morality is simply an *ad hoc* proposition, determined as each circumstance arises without any concern for consistency. Often many of the approaches listed above may play a role in an individual's ethical decision-making. For purposes of study, however, we should note that non-Christian approaches to morality tend to fall into three broad categories - those that seek the foundation of morality in the Self, those that seek it in the Situation, and those that seek some external Standard. We will look at and critique examples of each of these before presenting the foundational ideas of biblical morality.

THE SELF

For most of human history, people have believed that morality was something larger than the individual - that it had its foundation in God, in the gods, or in society as a whole. In modern history, however, such is often no longer the case. Morality has become an individual matter, and the search for right and wrong begins and often ends inside oneself. Where do we find the roots of such teachings? While the individualism of the Renaissance and the Enlightenment contributed to this mindset, they never went so far as to argue that moral standards should vary from person to person. Only at the turn of the twentieth century do we find such teachings emerging.

EMOTIVISM

Emotivism is an ethical approach associated with the teachings of A.J. Ayer (1910-1989). One of the leading proponents of analytical philosophy (also known as Linguistic Analysis or Logical Positivism), Ayer was among those who, in the early twentieth century, gave up on the possibility of philosophy being able to answer the questions to which it had historically given its attention. Since absolute knowledge is impossible, philosophers who ask questions like "What is truth?", "What is the meaning of life?", and "What is virtuous behavior?" are wasting their time. Instead, the true task of the philosopher is to analyze human communication; the task of the philosopher is not to discover truth, but to discover how and in what way meaning can be communicated from one person to another. According to Ayer, a statement may only be considered meaningful communication if it is *falsifiable* - if it is in some way open to an empirical test. On this basis, he argued that moral assertions were not propositions at all, but mere expressions of emotion.[1] In other words, if I say, "Stealing is wrong," I am in effect doing nothing more than expressing my feelings about stealing: "Stealing - YCCH!" Those who say such things, of course, also by implication suggest that others should feel as they do about the given subject.

What are the consequences of such an approach to ethic? Obviously it would lead to a moral free-for-all where no standards for the larger society can possibly exist. Moral chaos is never good for any culture, and means that those who are in positions of power may easily consider themselves justified in imposing their views on others. But more subtle criticisms of Emotivism should also be noted.

First of all, it fails to account for moral uncertainty. If moral decisions constitute nothing more than an expression of my feelings, how can I ever feel that what I want to do is nevertheless wrong? Such ambivalence seems foreign to anyone who would reduce morality to feelings alone. Secondly, it removes from human vocabulary any significant use of the word *ought*. One who feels a certain way about a particular form of behavior may wish others shared his feelings, but has no basis for imposing that preference upon them and insisting that it is right to do so. In fact, one could only place confidence in such an approach to morality in a highly uniform society where most people feel the same way about important ethical issues, if then.

What does the Bible say about limiting morality to feelings? Scripture tells us that "The heart is deceitful above all things" (Jeremiah 17:9), and Solomon notes that "The way of a fool is right in his own eyes" (Proverbs 12:15) and "There is a way that seems right to a man, but its end is the way of death" (Proverbs 14:12). In other words, our emotions are simply not to be trusted as ultimate standards for right and wrong. Emotions, like every other aspect of human nature, are tainted by the Fall, and thus often driven by selfish desires or the pressures of the moment and subject to constant change. While a Christian's emotions should increasingly be shaped by the teaching of God's Word and the presence of the Holy Spirit, he can never trust his emotions as the basis for determining right or wrong without checking them against the Scriptures.

---

[1] Critics called this the "boo/hurrah" approach to ethical discourse.

Because emotions are so changeable and so much subject to the pressures of the moment, your students should be aware of the importance of formulating moral standards *before* facing the ethical dilemmas to which those standards apply. One who follows the popular maxim that "you can't really know what's right or wrong until you've been there" is setting himself up for moral disaster. Only the person who has established firm standards based on God's Word will be in a position to resist the peer pressure and panic often associated with difficult moral dilemmas.[2]

EXISTENTIALISM

Despite the fact that Logical Positivism has been an influential philosophy in the twentieth century, Emotivism has drawn relatively little attention. Such is not the case with our next example, however. Existentialism has influenced the moral thinking of modern Western society in countless ways. While many names can be associated with Existentialism, we will focus on Jean-Paul Sartre and Albert Camus, two French writers from the middle of the twentieth century.

Jean-Paul Sartre (1905-1980) was a philosopher, literary figure, and political activist. His exposition of Existentialism was predicated on the assumption that life is essentially meaningless. While all desire and search for meaning, most satisfy themselves with comfortable fictions such as religion that give them an illusion of meaning in a meaningless world. Only the courageous are willing to face the meaninglessness of life head-on and discard the illusions most create to give them comfort. These few live truly authentic lives by making hard decisions outside of the influence of others. They thus choose the hard path of freedom rather than the ease of bondage to illusion, defining themselves rather than allowing themselves to be defined by others. One of his most famous works, a play called *No Exit*, illustrates the bondage of depending on others for the evaluation of one's behavior. In the play, three people find themselves in Hell, which consists of a Second Empire drawing room. Conversation leads to the exposure of the sins that led to their destiny, but they all wonder what has become of the fire and brimstone of which they have heard so often. They finally conclude that the tortures of Hell consist of having themselves defined by the others with whom they are confined - as one of the characters famously says, "Hell is other people." Sartre, of course, did not believe in a literal Hell. Instead, his drawing room is a metaphor for human existence, in which we are forever condemned to be defined by the perceptions of others.

The solution to this dilemma is portrayed in one of the novels of Sartre's contemporary, Albert Camus (1913-1960). Born in Algeria to French parents, Camus struggled mightily with the ethical problems posed by his existentialist beliefs. In *The Stranger*, he presents Meursault,

---

[2] The protagonist in Charlotte Bronte's *Jane Eyre* captured this idea perfectly when she was struggling with Rochester's proposal that she enter into a bigamous marriage. "I will keep the law given by God; sanctioned by man. I will hold to the principles received by me when I was sane, and not mad - as I am now. Laws and principles are not for the times when there is no temptation: they are for such moments as this, when body and soul rise in mutiny against their rigour; stringent are they; inviolate they shall be. If at my individual convenience I might break them, what would be their worth? They have no worth - so I have always believed; and if I cannot believe it now, it is because I am insane - quite insane: my veins running with fire, and my heart beating faster than I count its throbs. Preconceived opinions, foregone determinations, are all I have at this hour to stand by: there I plant my foot."

a rootless man leading a meaningless life. One day he is walking on the beach and meets an Arab. For no particular reason, he pulls out a gun and shoots the man. He is arrested and brought to trial, is given a totally incompetent defense, and is condemned to death. While awaiting his execution, he argues with the judge, whose belief in moral standards is ridiculous to the prisoner. The book ends with the protagonist saying, "For all to be accomplished, for me to feel less lonely, all that remained to hope was that on the day of my execution there should be a huge crowd of spectators and that they should greet me with howls of execration." Why does this demonstrate the view of morality promoted by Existentialists? The "howls of execration" that Meursault anticipated would be a final affirmation of the authenticity of his life choices. After all, if everyone hated and despised him, he clearly had not made choices that were influenced by society. Some Existentialists even went so far as to argue that the only authentic decision a person can make in the light of the meaningless of life is to choose to end it.[3]

The impact of Existentialism on contemporary morals has been significant indeed. When I was in college in the late sixties and early seventies, Existentialism was all the rage on campus. My first reading assignment in English was Sartre's *Existentialism and Human Emotions*. But students were not simply reading Existentialist authors. By this time, other writers had begun to apply the seminal views of these men to issues like campus rebellion, the sexual revolution, and political activism. What these had in common was the rejection of all authority - a fundamental tenet of Existential philosophy. Thus authentic living came to mean sleeping around, staging sit-ins in campus administration buildings, and rioting against the war in Vietnam. This fundamental distrust of authority has never been purged from American society despite the fact that the campus radicals of the sixties are running the country today. Sadly, their moral philosophy has been translated into a rejection of all fixed moral standards and an emphasis on individual freedom that rejects restraints on much of what for most of American history was rightly considered immoral.

Aside from the problem of moral chaos that we have already seen in connection with Emotivism, how should a Christian respond to Existentialism? To begin with, we must recognize that, to some extent, Existentialists have a point. If, as they believe, God does not exist, then life *is* meaningless. And if life is meaningless, any attempt to impose standards of morality on others, either by persuasion or by law, is an unwarranted imposition on human freedom, and should be rejected. Though Existentialists draw understandable conclusions from false presuppositions, this does not mean that we cannot address those conclusions. One of the obvious problems with Existentialism is that one may not live it consistently. If one believes that allowing anyone else to define or influence you produces inauthentic living, why should an Existentialist write or teach? Is such a one not encouraging inauthentic choices on the part of others? How much of the rebellion of the sixties constituted little more than yielding to peer pressure? After all, why should rebellion be defined as acting like all the other rebels do? Sartre himself was a political activist, often demonstrating against continued French occupation of Algeria and in favor of independence for the colony. Is this not seeking to influence others?

-----

[3] One could only imagine the response of a university student to a professor who is promulgating such dogma when one can clearly see that he is still breathing.

Finally, of course, Existentialism is wrong, not because it arrives at wrong conclusions and cannot be lived consistently, but because its worldview is contrary to Scripture. God *does* exist, human life has meaning, and that meaning is defined by God, not by us. Existentialism, like all others godless philosophies, leads people to follow their own paths down the road to certain destruction. While human authorities may legitimately be questioned and should never be accepted uncritically, the authority within - that of the individual mind and heart - is certain to produce falsehood every bit as much as a life of conformity to human standards.

UTILITARIANISM

Another way in which Existentialists are right is that most people simply are not comfortable with moral chaos or a meaningless world. While the obvious implication of any self-oriented approach to ethics is total relativism, this is simply not a comfortable way to live. As any parent with young children will readily testify, human beings, whether they will admit to it or not, *like* rules. Thus, most of those who want to base moral decisions on something within opt for general principles that are broad enough to provide some kind of ethical mooring, but vague enough to allow for a wide range of individual differences. One example of this is a moral system known as Utilitarianism, which arose in recognizable form in the nineteenth century in England and has been popular among many people ever since. Two of the key thinkers in the development of Utilitarianism were Jeremy Bentham (1748-1832) and John Stuart Mill (1806-1873).

Jeremy Bentham was a British social reformer and political radical who argued in favor of separation of church and state, equal rights for women, legal acceptance of homosexuality, the outlawing of corporal punishment, even in the home, and advocating what today is known as the welfare state in opposition to *laissez-faire* capitalism. He believed that an ethical society could be constructed apart from any religious strictures by following one fundamental principle - "the greatest good for the greatest number." For Bentham, good and evil could be reduced to pleasure and pain, therefore what produced the greatest amount of pleasure and the least amount of pain for the greatest number of people was the greatest good. He attempted to construct a moral calculus based on fourteen measures of pleasure and twelve of pain. Many criticized his system, however, for implying that the torture of an individual would be good if it produced pleasure for many. He even extended his emphasis on the centrality of pleasure and pain to moral decision-making to arguing for animal rights on the basis that the ability to feel pain rather than the ability to reason distinguished a moral being.

One of his pupils, John Stuart Mill, also contributed significantly to utilitarian ethical theory. Mill had broad-ranging interests, and was influential in social reform, political science, and economics. He championed individual freedom as Bentham had done, but argued that government ought to protect minorities against the tyranny of the majority for the good of society at large. He, like Bentham, argued for the rights of women as well. In general, each individual should be permitted to do exactly as he pleases so long as it does no harm to others. His major refinement of Utilitarianism was to define the good in qualitative rather than quantitative terms. While Bentham had argued that all pleasures are equal, Mill believed that some pleasures are of more value than others. Cultured pleasures are more valuable than uncultured pleasures, thus the state should promote the opera rather than bear-baiting; intellectual pleasures are more valuable than sensual pleasures, so much so that university graduates should be given double votes in national elections.

Utilitarianism has influenced the thought and practice of many since its appearance in the nineteenth century. How many politicians today, for example, argue for their policies in terms of their impact on the common good? The Christian must recognize, however, that Utilitarianism has serious flaws. The first has to do with the question of defining the good that was such a central matter of concern to Bentham, Mill, and others. How can one make decisions based on the amount of pleasure and pain actions produce when different people experience the same things differently? What produces a great deal of pleasure for one person will not have the same impact on another (Mill's example of the opera, for instance, or modern rock concerts). Furthermore, some people, for strange reasons of their own, take pleasure in pain.[4] Ultimately, the definition of the good becomes so subjective that Utilitarianism differs little from the moral chaos it seeks to avoid.

The second problem has to do with the issue Mill raised, quite legitimately, against Bentham. If quantity of pleasure is the deciding factor, what is to prevent the abuse of the minority, or even the use of torture for popular entertainment.[5] As far as Mill's attempts to qualify pleasures is concerned, does not this ultimately boil down to a matter of opinion? Hitler frequently used utilitarian arguments to justify the Holocaust, for example.

The third problem stems from the Utilitarian's understanding of human nature. In simple terms, the ethical theory ignores human sin. Bentham and Mill both assumed that people basically want to live for others rather than themselves, to seek the good of others rather than their own. But Romans 3:12 tells us that "no one does good, not even one." The optimism about human nature demonstrated by Utilitarians is unrealistic, as one may clearly see by the great damage done by those in power who have sought to implement it.

The biggest problem with Utilitarianism from a biblical perspective, however, is that, in order to implement it effectively, man must be God - he must be omniscient. After all, who among us can predict the consequences of our actions? We may reliably guess a few short-term results, but, as in the famous Butterfly Effect,[6] large consequences arise over time from small decisions, and these are by their very nature unpredictable. Utilitarianism thus displays the height of arrogance in proposing that any person is able to judge the amount of pleasure and pain produced by his decisions, not only for himself, but for anyone who might be affected by them.

---

[4] We call them masochists, or sometimes body-builders - "No pain, no gain."

[5] The people of the Middle Ages found witch-burning and drawing and quartering fascinating, and the French peasants in the late eighteenth century flocked to witness executions on the guillotine.

[6] The Butterfly Effect derives its name from the notion that a butterfly flapping its wings in China could cause minute alterations in air flow that would eventually lead to a hurricane in the Americas. This was famously referenced in Michael Crichton's *Jurassic Park* to explain the reproduction of the dinosaurs in the park, and ultimately to criticize the hubris of scientists who think they can control nature.

We must note at this point that what has been said above is true for all results-oriented approaches to ethical decision-making. Any time one tries to justify a particular action by describing its results, he is showing the absence of the kind of humility required of us in James 4:13-16. Biblical morality is based on unchanging principles, not anticipated results. Scripture requires that we simply obey God and leave the results to Him. The importance of this cannot be emphasized enough. How many professing Christians, in their everyday decision-making, attempt to justify what they choose to do or not do by perceived results? We know from Scripture, as Asaph discovered in Psalm 73, that sometimes the wicked prosper and the righteous suffer. Wrong actions appear, at least in the short term, to produce good results, while doing right can lead to suffering, or even death, though God ultimately uses the suffering of His people for good - after all, as third-century Church Father Tertullian insisted, "the blood of the martyrs is the seed of the church."

INTUITIONISM

The next example on our list also seeks some undergirding principle that avoids the charge of moral chaos. This approach is Intuitionism, championed by British philosopher G.E. Moore (1873-1958). Moore, another exponent of analytical philosophy, argued that the good could not be defined, either by experience or by empirical testing. While one might describe the characteristics of the good, one could not prove thereby that the action was in fact good. As a result, the good can only be known through self-evident propositions that are not subject either to proof or disproof. These propositions will be understood by all ethically-informed and thoughtful people. No debate will be necessary, because all right-thinking people will arrive at the same conclusions. In simple terms, Intuitionism may be described as Jiminy Cricket ethics - "always let your conscience be your guide." Morality may not be discovered by reason, but only by moral intuition, which is essentially equivalent to the conscience.

How should a Christian respond to Intuitionism? First of all, note that Moore's assertion that everyone is born with a conscience is true. Romans 2:14-15 affirms that even those far from God have active consciences. The big problem with Intuitionism, as we have already seen with Utilitarianism, is that it ignores the reality of human sin. Paul tells us that consciences "accuse or even excuse" those who possess them. Sometimes, yes, a person's conscience, no matter his moral or religious upbringing, will accuse him of wrongdoing. But how often do people's consciences justify the wrong they wish to do, excusing rather than convicting of sin? Paul speaks in I Timothy 4:2 of those whose "consciences are seared" (NIV adds "as with a hot iron"). The image here is clear. When one burns his hand on the stove, the nerve endings are destroyed so that the person can no longer feel external stimuli. In the same way, one who ignores his conscience with sufficient frequency, or whose conscience justifies sinful behavior often enough, can no longer feel pangs of guilt.[7] The treatment of disputable matters in the Pauline epistles, which we will consider later in the chapter, provides a perfect example of the ability of the conscience to malfunction in the other direction - sometimes prejudice or upbringing cause people to feel guilty about behavior that is not wrong in the least.

---

[7] Note that this is also one of the reasons why leprosy, which destroys the nerves, making the sufferer unable to feel when his extremities are being injured, provides such an effective picture of sin in the Bible.

Thus the conscience, God-given though it may be, cannot ultimately be trusted for moral decision-making. Like the emotions or the reason, the prompting of the conscience must be checked against the teachings of Scripture, and only then may the conscience be trusted, though a Christian ought to experience an increasingly sanctified conscience as he develops spiritual maturity through the study of the Word and years of godly living. As we will see later in the chapter, however, violating the conscience is sin in itself (Romans 14:23), so we should never go against the prompting of conscience in a cavalier fashion. Realistically, though, we find far more often that our consciences justify wrong actions than that they condemn right ones.

PRAGMATISM

The final example of a self-oriented approach to ethical decision-making that we will consider is Pragmatism. This approach - doing whatever works, whatever produces the desired results - has been around for many centuries, most notoriously in the political theory of Niccolo Machiavelli (1469-1527). His classic work *The Prince* advised rulers of the Italian city-states during the Renaissance to do whatever necessary to keep themselves in power. He argued that, since a stable government benefits the people, any action on the part of the prince that keeps him in power will ultimately help those he rules, including lying, theft, assassination, and unjust executions. Machiavelli even said that, given the choice of being loved or feared, the prince should choose to be feared, since the actions that generate love sometimes embolden enemies who would overthrow him, while fear would keep revolutionary movements from emerging. Renaissance rulers such as Cesare Borgia and Henry VIII put Machiavelli's theories into practice, sometimes to great effect. The same approach in the hands of Otto von Bismarck of Prussia was called *realpolitik*, and displayed the same lack of values in favor of doing whatever was required in order to build the power of what eventually became the German Empire.

In modern times, Pragmatism as an ethical theory has been associated with the names of American thinkers William James (1842-1910) and John Dewey (1859-1952). Both expanded the application of Pragmatism far beyond the realm of political theory. William James grounded Pragmatism in his epistemology. He argued that truth should be defined as that which proves useful to the one who believes it. Truth, according to James, ought to be coherent - it should fit together - and also ought to correspond to our experience of the outside world. True beliefs are also those that have "cash value" - they function beneficially in the lives of those who hold to them. Coinciding with his emphasis on the functionality of belief as the best test of truth, James also argued strongly for free will in opposition to various forms of philosophical determinism. The different ways in which he applied his ideas on values, beliefs, and free will made him a pioneer in the fields of psychology and educational reform. His writings on religious experience were also very influential.

John Dewey, also influential in the fields of psychology and especially education, shared with James an emphasis on free will that led him to argue that democracy is the ideal form of government. The application of his democratic ideals to education led to the advocacy of the child-centered classroom, where the communication of knowledge takes a back seat to the fulfillment of the child's potential. Hands-on learning was the only kind of learning that worked, and any approach that mitigated against the fulfillment of the child was to be rejected. The applications of Dewey's approach to educational reform, much to his dismay, led to the decline of discipline in the classroom and the "dumbing down" of American education. One idea he did advocate, however, is the use of the classroom for the purpose of socialization. He insisted that education should be viewed as "a regulation of the process of coming to share in the social consciousness; and that the adjustment of individual activity on the basis of this social consciousness is the only sure method of social reconstruction." In other words, schools should be used to reprogram students into conformity with accepted societal norms. Anyone who is familiar with the heavy dose of social advocacy that characterizes the public school system of America today, and even more the environment on college and university campuses, will understand the extent of Dewey's influence.

The critique of Pragmatism follows the same lines as that of some of the theories we have already discussed. Like Utilitarianism, it is results-oriented, thus requiring a degree of knowledge that human beings simply don't possess. While claiming to promote democracy, it in reality advocates social conditioning that at times approaches brainwashing, while denying the need for the authority, control, and discipline that are essential in a sinful world. And what better critique of Pragmatism can be found than the writings of its best-known early advocate? Machiavelli's pragmatic approach to politics is morally bankrupt. For a system that insists that decisions be judged by their results, one can easily see the deplorable consequences that have come, both in the past and in the present, from those who have argued that one should do whatever works.[8] While practical considerations are never entirely out of place, the Christian should never make decisions solely on the basis of what he thinks might work.

THE SITUATION

While the spirit of this present age, including modernism with its flexible approach to morality and postmodernism with its flexible approach to truth, tends to favor the individualistic ethical theories discussed in the previous section, we should note that not all wish to make ethics purely subjective to the individual. Some today argue that morality is not ultimately dependent on the internal condition of the decision-maker, but rather on the external circumstances in which he finds himself. We must, they argue, look outside of ourselves rather than into our own minds and hearts when making moral decisions. Nonetheless, those who choose to ground morality in external circumstances continue to reject a fixed standard for making such decisions.

SITUATION ETHICS

Certainly the best-known example of this approach is Situation Ethics, a moral philosophy expounded by Joseph Fletcher (1905-1991), an American Episcopal priest, in his book *Situation Ethics: The New Morality* (1966). He went on later in life to advocate abortion, euthanasia, infanticide, human cloning, eugenics, and voluntary sterilization for population control. The basic argument in his book is that all laws have exceptions except the law of love - "love your neighbor

---

[8] To use another extreme example, the Holocaust *worked*, at least for a while, in helping Hitler to achieve his goal.

as yourself." Loving behavior will, sooner or later, require all other divine commandments and human laws to be violated, and such violations will be justifiable. Needless to say, Fletcher's work became immensely influential in the freewheeling sixties. After all, if breaking God's law or man's can be justified by love, surely lying to protect your best friend's feelings, violent demonstrations against the System in order to save lives, and premarital sex within a loving relationship cannot be wrong!

Fletcher defended his assertion that love may at times require the breaking of other laws by presenting a series of classic examples. He defended lying by citing a situation in Sir Walter Scott's *The Heart of Midlothian* in which a woman was called to testify at her sister's trial. The sister had been falsely accused of killing her child, and the only way the woman could save her was to lie. Real-life examples might include the dilemma of courageous rescuers who hid Jews from the Nazis during World War II and were forced to lie to preserve their lives from curious members of the Gestapo. One might also cite, of course, the famous case in Joshua 2:5 of Rahab, who lied to protect the Israelite spies from the authorities in Jericho.

Fletcher also defended the rightness of killing in certain situations. Not only did he note that even moral absolutists defended killing in cases such as war and capital punishment, but he also argued for certain personal choices. He spoke of a Christian woman in a Nazi concentration camp who had chosen to go to the gas chamber in the place of a young Jewish girl, arguing that suicide is killing, and in this case it was the loving thing to do. He also brings up examples of a naval commander in the Pacific who allowed survivors from a sunken Allied vessel to drown in order to avoid having his own ship sunk by the Japanese, and the classic case of those who chose to drop atomic bombs on Hiroshima and Nagasaki in order to save the millions of lives that might have been lost in an invasion of Japan. Or what of the person who cannot, in love, ignore the pleas of a man trapped in a burning car who begs to be put out of his misery?[9] Another example of killing justified by love is the "lifeboat problem," where an overcrowded lifeboat threatens to capsize, killing all aboard, unless the sailor in charge chooses to throw a few people overboard.[10]

Situation Ethics even covered adultery, much to the delight of the 1960s American college student population. Fletcher gave the example of a woman captured by the Soviets after the Second World War and placed in an internment camp. She received word that her husband had survived the war and had been united with her children, but the Soviet authorities refused to release her. The camp policy did allow, however, for pregnant women to be set free as liabilities to the work program. She found a cooperative guard who was willing to impregnate her, and soon was released and accepted into the bosom of her family, who rejoiced over her decision and accepted the child who was born of the adulterous relationship with great affection. And what about the female spy who is called upon to seduce an enemy officer in order to gain information that will save many lives?

---

[9] It's worth nothing that Fletcher was for a time president of the American Euthanasia Society.

[10] This last example has become notorious for its use in "values clarification" instruction in public schools, where the situation is expanded so that the characteristics of each passenger are described, and the student is required to choose who should be thrown overboard and defend his choice!

While one has little difficulty understanding the popularity of Situation Ethics in our modern world, the Christian must recognize the serious flaws, both logical and biblical, in Fletcher's system. This is doubly important because of the biblical framework within which he couches his arguments, which makes them much more seductive to the unaware Christian. Note the following:

- First of all, any time anyone argues that "there are absolutely no absolutes," he is contradicting himself. Fletcher attempts to avoid this by arguing that love is the only absolute, but that leads him to other problems.
- He fails to define love, but assumes that everyone knows what love is. Such an approach rapidly deteriorates into Emotivism or some other subjective morality we discussed earlier.
- Not only is his open approach to understanding love subjective, it is also rooted in human autonomy. The individual is the only one who is able to decide what is the loving thing in any given situation.
- In Scripture, love is defined in passages such as I Corinthians 13:4-7. We are not left to our own devices to discover what loving behavior looks like.
- Love does not contradict the law of God, nor does God contradict Himself. His law is perfect (Psalm 19:7), and He will never require us to break it in order to please Him.
- Fletcher's examples, even though they are taken from real life, are rigged in the way they are presented. In each case, only two alternatives are given - one that involves a monstrous outcome, and one that requires the loving violation of God's law. Real life is not like this. Decisions are far more complex, and God has promised that His children will never face a situation in which sin is inevitable (I Corinthians 10:13). Third alternatives do exist, and even if obedience leads to undesirable consequences, obedience is still the only right thing to do. What third alternatives might have existed in the examples Fletcher uses that would have allowed the decision-makers to keep God's law while avoiding the impending tragedies?

HIERARCHICALISM

The situational approach to morality is dangerous to the Christian, not only because of its prevalence in the surrounding society, but also because of the extent to which it has permeated the teachings of the evangelical church. This may be seen in *Ethics: Alternatives and Issues* (1971), written by well-known evangelical theologian Norman Geisler (b.1932), a defender of biblical inerrancy. Sadly, the hierarchical approach to ethics he advocated in his book, in its ultimate conclusions, differs little from that proposed by Fletcher, though the nature of the argument is different.

Geisler begins by noting that, because we are sinners in a sinful world, we sometimes find ourselves in situations where all our options are sinful ones. In such situations, we must choose the lesser of two evils - violate the lesser law in order to keep the greater one - and in so doing, no sin is committed. The obvious question this raises is how greater and lesser laws are to be ascertained. The author helpfully provides seven principles, guidelines that allow one to determine the greater law in each case. His seven principles, with brief explanations and proposed applications (his, not mine) are summarized below:

1. "Persons are more valuable than things." Persons are to be loved, while things are to be used. Persons are to be treated as ends, not means, because they are self-conscious, self-determining, and relational.

2. "Infinite Person is more valuable than finite persons," i.e., we ought to obey God rather than man. When conflicts between obeying God and obeying man arise, the choice for the Christian is obvious.

3. "A complete person is more valuable than an incomplete person." Sadly, he uses this one to justify certain forms of euthanasia.

4. "An actual person is more valuable than a potential person." Given the choice between mother and unborn baby, Geisler argues that abortion is justified.

5. "Potential persons are more valuable than actual things." Here limits are placed on abortion. It may be acceptable when the life of the mother is at stake, but is not justifiable for financial reasons.

6. "Many persons are more valuable than few persons." This sounds a lot like Utilitarianism, and would lead to the same conclusion in responding to the lifeboat problem, among others.

7. "Personal acts which promote personhood are better than those which do not."

How should a Christian respond to these arguments? Several things ought to be noted:

* As already indicated in response to Fletcher, God's law is perfect and never contradicts itself. God will never tell us that the right thing to do is to break His law.

* Scripture gives us no indication that some sins are greater than others. All sins equally separate a person from God, and no choice of sin can mitigate that hard truth.

* It is clearly inappropriate for an author to suggest that, though God's laws conflict, his principles can help us sort them out!

* Geisler's seven principles are not all demonstrably biblical. Some of them clearly are, but others seem designed specifically to provide easy answers to complex moral dilemmas.

* The conclusions Geisler draws about significant ethical issues line up with those drawn by Fletcher. This is not a good sign. Though it is illogical to argue that because someone who advocates a position promotes immorality, then that position must be wrong, one nonetheless ought to be suspicious of any evangelical scholar who winds up sharing common moral ground with the notorious purveyor of Situation Ethics.

The sad case of Norman Geisler should serve as a warning to Christian students. The man is a respected evangelical scholar, and has done much good work for the Kingdom of God. Yet, in this area at least, his approach is clearly unbiblical. If the Bereans found it necessary to check the Scriptures to confirm what they were being taught by the Apostle Paul (Acts 17:11), students today must not accept what they are taught uncritically, whether from the pulpit, in a Christian school classroom, or in a Christian college or university.

TRAGIC MORAL CHOICE

The last situational approach we will examine is similar to that of Geisler with a few key differences. I first encountered the idea of Tragic Moral Choice in the sidebar of an article in

Christianity Today many years ago, and have never been able to put a name to the theory, though evangelical theologian and apologist John Warwick Montgomery (b.1931) used it in a debate with Joseph Fletcher on ethics a number of years ago. The starting point for Tragic Moral Choice is the same as that for Hierarchicalism - that sinners in a sinful world will sometimes find themselves in situations where all alternatives are sinful. Like Geisler, advocates of this position argue for choosing the lesser of two evils, but, unlike supporters of Hierarchicalism, recognize that any violation of God's law is sin. Consequently, they advocate sinning purposefully and asking forgiveness afterward.[11]

What responses may be given to this teaching that have not already been given previously?

- First of all, while Geisler may hope to escape the implications of I Corinthians 10:13 by arguing that choosing the lesser sin *is* the way out that God provides, advocates of this position have no such facile response. They create a position where someone must *choose* deliberately to sin because there *is* no way of escape.
- They thus place God in the position of both prohibiting and requiring the same behavior.
- A critical response to Tragic Moral Choice is the teaching found in Hebrews 4:15 concerning the nature of Christ. If the Savior faced all temptations that we face, and if Tragic Moral Choice exists, He must have faced it, and therefore must have sinned, which blatantly contradicts the affirmation of the sinlessness of Christ found in this verse.

The fact that all three examples in this section have been taken from the teachings of professing Christians, two of whom are highly-reputable evangelical scholars, shows the extent to which the situational approach has seduced the church. Christians must be on their guard against any who would seek to solve the great moral issues of the day by arguing that God's laws simply are not sufficient to provide answers to those issues. In the same way that theistic evolutionists seek to reinterpret Scripture in a way that allows them to stand with the prevailing scientific conclusions of the non-Christian world, so the temptation is great for Christian moralists to seek in the Scriptures justifications for whatever the shifting moral landscape of the surrounding world chooses to advocate. We must instead rely on the unchanging Word of God - morality that is based on a standard that does not require circuitous justifications for what it clearly condemns.

THE STANDARD

For most of human history, morality has been based on standards. Sometimes these standards have been tribal and communicated by oral tradition. At other times, they have been formulated through written law codes. Most notably, moral standards have been incorporated into religious writings. The Bible is not the only book that fits into this category, of course. The Qur'an, along with the secondary writings of Islam such as the *Hadith* and the *Ijma*, provides such a standard for Muslims, as do the *Mishnah*, and especially the *Talmud*, for Orthodox Jews. We will not take time to examine or critique these sources of ethical behavior, but we will look at one

---

[11] Reputedly, Fletcher thrashed Montgomery over this response in the debate, and with considerable justification.

example of what one might think at first glance could not exist - an attempt to develop a fixed standard for ethical decision-making apart from divine revelation.

THE CATEGORICAL IMPERATIVE

Immanuel Kant (1724-1804) was a German philosopher and forerunner of Romanticism. He grew up in a Lutheran home under Pietist influences, and thus placed great value on ethical behavior, as did all Pietists. His work in epistemology, however, led him to the conclusion that we can have no absolute knowledge of reality outside of ourselves because our minds alter and categorize whatever is brought into them by our senses. Thus what we call *knowledge* can never correspond to what is really "out there," but instead is the result of our minds operating on our sensory perceptions. While this may seem on the surface to be somewhat reasonable, it has devastating conclusions for biblical morality. After all, God is "out there," and the Bible can be, at best, no more than the product of the minds of the authors operating on their encounters with that God. Thus the Bible cannot be said to be the Word of God in any absolute sense, but rather is the product of very human minds reflecting on ineffable encounters with the divine.

As one can clearly see, this undermines the Bible, not only as a source of absolute knowledge, but also as a source of absolute morality. Kant recognized this and feared the consequences. He knew that a society without a fixed standard of morality cannot long survive. The result of his concern for the good of society in this matter led him to formulate the Categorical Imperative. His formulation of this imperative goes as follows: "Act only according to that maxim whereby you can at the same time will that it should become a universal law." What does this mean? In simple terms, Kant asks people to consider, when making an ethical decision, what would happen if everyone were to make that same decision. If a logical contradiction results, then the behavior is clearly wrong. For example, murder is obviously wrong, because if everyone were to murder, murder would soon become impossible because there would be no one left to murder. Similarly, stealing is wrong because if everyone were to steal, the very idea of private property would disappear, so that stealing, which is dependent on the concept of ownership, would become impossible. The same is true with lying - if everyone were to lie, truth would lose all meaning, and without such a thing as truth, lying would become impossible; all too often we see the consequences of such thinking in the world around us.

Kant's approach fails on both the large and small scale, however. In the big picture of ethical decision-making, Kant's categorical imperatives would inevitably collide, as Fletcher has demonstrated. Man is incapable of constructing a perfect ethical system, and what seems to work for the basics of the moral law would inevitably collapse when faced with the complexities of real-life moral dilemmas.

Kant's system also fails on the level of the specific. Suppose I were to steal a pen from one of my students, but instead of asking whether stealing ought to become a universal law, I consider instead, "Suppose it were to become a universal law that, on the morning of December 3 at 9:15, every teacher named Robert Walton would steal a pen from every student named _____," no contradiction would arise. The Categorical Imperative could thus easily be used to justify almost any specific action by special pleading - defining the situation by focusing on its unique qualities. Besides, who, when facing a moral dilemma, would take the time to ask himself Kant's rather convoluted question?

BIBLICAL ETHICS

The system of ethics given to us in the Scriptures is clearly based on an unchanging standard. Yet, as indicated in the Introduction to this book, many question the extent to which Christians today should use the law of God as their standard for behavior. In this closing section of the opening chapter, we will consider in broad terms some of the foundational ideas associated with the law of God as the basis for Christian ethical decision-making.

THE PERMANENCE OF THE LAW

Too many Christians are more than willing to push the law of God to one side under the pretext that we now live in the Age of Grace, and the law is no longer binding on us. Consequently, the first issue we must address when considering the role of God's law in ethical decision-making is the extent to which that law is permanent. The response of Jesus in Matthew 5:17-18 appears to answer our basic question: "Do not think that I have come to abolish the Law or the Prophets; I have not come to abolish them but to fulfill them. For truly, I say to you, until heaven and earth pass away, not an iota, not a dot, will pass from the Law until all is accomplished." Given that heaven and earth have yet to pass away, our default position must be that the Law of God is intended to exercise a permanent role in the lives of His people. Others argue, of course, that some aspects of the Law have been "accomplished," and are therefore no longer applicable, and this will enter into our consideration of Jesus' teaching.

In dealing with this question, the divisions of the Old Testament law proposed by Thomas Aquinas in the Middle Ages, though not strictly in themselves biblical, can nonetheless be helpful, as the church has found in succeeding years. Aquinas argued that Old Testament law was of three kinds - moral, civil, and ceremonial, and that each had its function in the life of God's people, and the world in general. Basically, I would argue that, though all of God's law is permanent, different aspects of the law are permanent in different ways. Let's look at each kind of law.

- The moral law is exemplified by the Ten Commandments. This is law that is intended for all people at all times in all places, and has nothing to do with cultural differences or religious profession. God holds all people accountable for keeping this law (Romans 5:12-14), visiting death on those who break it even if they know nothing of its provisions. The Old Testament demonstrates this repeatedly when God brings judgment on pagan nations for violating His law, including the Canaanites, the Assyrians, and the Babylonians. Thus everyone is accountable to God's moral law, including contemporary American society. This issue will surface again when we discuss the questions of Christian involvement in the political and legal arenas and the appropriateness of "legislating morality" - a term frequently used to exclude biblical values from public discourse.
- The civil law is the law that served as the governing document of the Old Testament nation of Israel. This includes laws concerning property and personal conflicts, along with the

punishments to be meted out by the government for certain moral offenses. In short, it is the Constitution of the Israelite theocracy. These laws ceased to be binding when the theocracy fell in 586 BC - we will see later that the response of Jesus to the Pharisees concerning the woman taken in adultery in John 8:1-11 hinged on the status of the theocratic law. But if the civil law was intended for a theocracy and that theocracy no longer exists, in what sense is the civil law permanent? Some would argue that the intended permanence of the law requires the reestablishment of the theocracy. Jesus' rejection of any attempt to establish His kingdom by force, however, would mitigate against such an answer. Instead, we should see in the civil law examples of God's view of justice. While we may not observe a sabbatical year or practice gleaning, what principles of justice may be found in these practices? It is to these unchanging principles that we must look when seeking the meaning of the permanence of the civil law.

• The ceremonial law regulated the religious life of Israel. It included requirements for the priesthood, sacrifices, and religious festivals, among other things. If anything in Scripture is clear, it is that these things have been fulfilled in Christ and are no longer to be practiced; this is one of the main emphases of the book of Hebrews. How, then, could one possibly assert the permanence of the ceremonial law? I would argue that the ceremonial law is permanent in the sense that it remains as a useful teaching tool, a picture that points to Christ and His work on the cross. If the law was intended to be a "schoolmaster" to Israel, how much more can it serve that function when we, unlike they, have seen that toward which it points? While those who practiced the sacrifices and observed the feasts had little idea of their real significance, we today have the benefit of knowing the significance of all that magnificent symbolism, and in studying it, we are again struck by the glory of Christ's sacrifice for sin.

THE APPLICABILITY OF THE LAW

The perfection of God's law appears not only in its permanence and significance for all people at all times and all places, but also in the breadth of its applicability. In short, no Christian ever faces a decision that is not covered by the revelation God has given us in His Word. After all, the command to glorify God in all that we do, even simple acts like eating and drinking (I Corinthians 10:31), implies that every decision is an ethical decision because it involves choosing to honor God or to dishonor Him (though many of our decisions may be between two things that are equally honoring to God). Thus no decision we make is outside the scope of God's law.

This truth can be illustrated in a number of ways. First of all, James 2:10 says, "Whoever keeps the whole law but fails in one point has become accountable for all of it." In other words, if you break one law, you've broken them all. How can this be? In one sense, God's law is a single unit rather than a series of discrete requirements. Think of different kinds of windows you have seen. Some consist of a lattice of small panes separated by plastic, wooden or metal dividers. On the other hand, one sees picture windows consisting of a single large pane of glass. People often think of God's law as like the first window - if you throw a rock through one of the small panes, the others remain intact. On the contrary, God's law is much more like the picture window. It doesn't matter where the rock hits the window - the entire window is broken. One of the implications of this idea is that there are no greater or lesser sins (contra. Geisler). Any sin separates a man from God, no matter what that sin may be (though sins clearly differ in their *consequences*).

In my Doctrine of the Christian Life class at Westminster Seminary from which much of this course has been derived, Professor John Frame illustrated it this way. He argued that every sin broke every one of the Ten Commandments. The argument went something like this:

- Every sin violates the First Commandment because it involves putting myself and my own desires before God.
- Every sin violates the Second Commandment because it is an act of idolatry, for much the same reason.
- Every sin violates the Third Commandment because it insults the divine Name that God has placed on those who bear His image.
- Every sin violates the Fourth Commandment because it is an improper use of time; the Fourth Commandment tells us how we are to use *every* day, not just one day out of seven, to please God.
- Every sin violates the Fifth Commandment because it involves rebellion against God's authority and the authority of those who serve as His representatives on earth.
- Every sin violates the Sixth Commandment because it does violence to the image of God (see Jesus' application of the Sixth Commandment in the Sermon on the Mount).
- Every sin violates the Seventh Commandment because it is an act of spiritual adultery.
- Every sin violates the Eighth Commandment because it steals glory from God.
- Every sin violates the Ninth Commandment because it bears false witness to the truth.
- Every sin violates the Tenth Commandment because it involves coveting human autonomy and independence from God.

This may be a bit of a stretch (my students tend to think so), but it makes the point Dr. Frame was trying to communicate. No one should ever go through a study of the Ten Commandments and conclude, "I don't have to worry about this one - it is not a problem for me." The broad applicability of the moral law of God exists not only because the principles found in it relate to all of life, but also because it digs into the motives and intents of the heart rather than simply settling for an analysis of overt behavior.

Another way in which the applicability of God's law may be seen is to consider that the law serves, not as an exhaustive list of all possible behaviors in all possible circumstances, but as a summary of God's will for human behavior. In fact, the moral law found in the Decalogue is only one of many such summaries, as illustrated in the chart found at the top of the next page, which relates the simplest summary of God's Law through increasingly complex enumerations down to the foundation upon which all are built.

```
+---------------------------------------+
|          THE GOLDEN RULE              |
+-----------------------------------------+
|      TWO GREAT COMMANDMENTS             |
+-------------------------------------------+
|         TEN COMMANDMENTS                   |
+---------------------------------------------+
|     613 COMMANDS OF THE O.T. LAW            |
+-----------------------------------------------+
|    GOD'S REVELATION IN THE BIBLE              |
+-------------------------------------------------+
|       THE CHARACTER OF GOD                      |
+-------------------------------------------------+
```

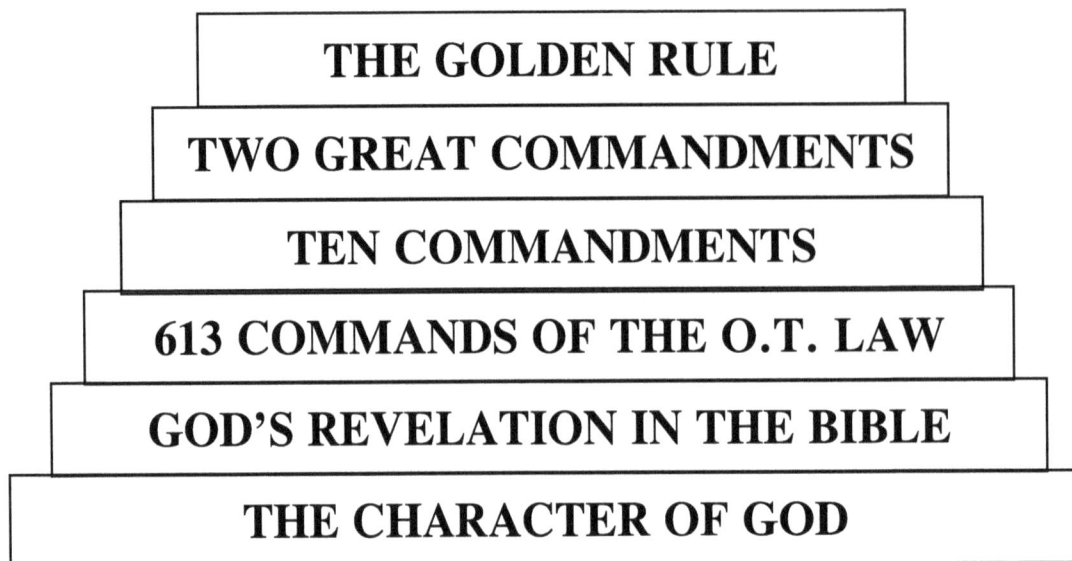

The simplest summary of God's will for human behavior is the Golden Rule. Matthew 7:12 says, "So whatever you wish that others would do to you, do also to them, for this is the Law and the Prophets." Jesus identifies His words as a summary of the whole law. But while these words are comprehensive, they are easily open to misunderstanding. If this is all we knew of God's will, what would keep us from imputing our own desires to others and acting accordingly? After all, some people have rather bizarre likes and dislikes. Those who claim to "live by the Golden Rule" rarely attempt to define what likes and dislikes are appropriate according to Scripture.

The second level of the pyramid, the two great commandments, takes a step in this direction. In Matthew 22:37-40, Jesus said, "You shall love the Lord your God with all your heart and with all your soul and with all your mind. This is the great and first commandment. And a second is like it: You shall love your neighbor as yourself. On these two commandments depend all the Law and the Prophets." This, too, is identified as a summary of the whole law, but extends our understanding of doing to others by insisting that this must be carried out within the context of love for God (we will look into these in more detail later in the chapter).

The third level of the pyramid is the Decalogue (Exodus 20:1-17). Many have noted that the Ten Commandments are divided into those that speak of love for God and those that address love for neighbor. This connection does not allow for Fletcher's dichotomy. Loving one's neighbor *means* respecting human authority and refraining from murder, adultery, stealing, lying, and coveting, thus one cannot use love as a justification for violating those commands that, according to God, *define* love.

The rabbis of the Intertestamental Period took the time to count the commandments found in the Old Testament and determined that there were 613 of them. These, too, are a summary of God's law for human behavior. How is this the case? Because they flesh out the applications of the moral law to specific situations of human and societal relationships and divine worship. One cannot easily read the Old Testament law and conclude that the prohibition against stealing in the

Eighth Commandment rules out governmental attempts to mandate assistance for the poor, for instance.

On a deeper level, the entire Bible is the summary of God's will for human behavior. In addition to laws, we find there a multitude of examples that illustrate the value of living a godly life. No one can study the lives of kings and patriarchs without coming away with the impression that obeying the law of God *matters*. The incarnation of the law into the personal experiences of real people demonstrates what it means in practice. The greatest example of this is the life of Christ Himself, who lived out the law of God perfectly.

We still have not reached the bottom level of the pyramid, however. Ultimately, we must recognize that the law of God is grounded in His character. When Jesus said in Matthew 5:48, "You therefore must be perfect, as your heavenly Father is perfect," He was not engaging in hyperbole. The law of God is an expression of who He is, and therefore law-keeping is in the end an exercise in godliness or Christlikeness. God did not simply make up a list of laws arbitrarily in order to make His creatures miserable and restrict their enjoyment of life. He knew that their only happiness was to be found in being like Him, and thus following the pattern of life for which He had created them.

God's law is thus as comprehensive as His revelation, as comprehensive as the example of Christ, as comprehensive as God's very character. No aspect of human life is outside the provisions of what He has revealed to us in the Scriptures, and we can safely and confidently look to what He has given us for "all we need for life and godliness."

WHAT ABOUT THE ADIAPHORA?

If God's revelation is comprehensive with regard to moral questions and gives us all we need to know, why then do people speak of issues that are morally indifferent? What about issues that Scripture does not address? What of the *adiaphora*? The term was originally used by the Stoics in ancient Greece and Rome, who argued that some questions were outside the scope of moral law, and thus needed no discussion when ethical questions arose. Some look at Paul's treatment of issues like eating meat offered to idols in I Corinthians 8 and Romans 14 and suggest that, for Christians as well, some matters are morally indifferent. As we will see, this is not really the case. While Paul does argue that each man should follow his own conscience in such matters and refrain from condemning others, the issues addressed are very much matters of ethical concern because of the attention Paul gives to the attitudes of the people involved. Furthermore, the passages we are about to examine tell us how such questions should be addressed, implying that there are right and wrong ways of doing so. Thus while the *practices* may be matters of moral indifference and can be carried out or refrained from to the glory of God, the attitudes of the heart that underlie those choices are anything but indifferent.

After reading I Corinthians 8 and Romans 14, several points should be noted:

- The issues with which Paul deals are those that tended to separate Jewish and Gentile members of the congregations in Corinth and Rome. With regard to meat offered to idols, pagan temples often received food from their worshipers. If the temple was particularly popular or prosperous, it would receive more food than the priests could possibly consume. They would often then offer it for sale in the marketplace, usually at cut-rate prices. Should Christians buy such meat? Some argued (as did Paul), that the meat ultimately came from God, and that since idols didn't exist in any case, no harm was done, and Christians could freely partake. Others, however, were reluctant to touch anything that had been connected in any way with idolatry. Perhaps Gentile Christians' experience of pagan worship was too recent, and they could not in good conscience touch the stuff, or perhaps Jewish members of the congregation were reluctant to eat food that clearly would violate their dietary laws because the meat had not been prepared in kosher fashion. As far as considering days holy, the problem here was the continued observation of Jewish feasts. Should this be done by those who had become Christians or not?

- This enables us to categorize the kinds of questions that are covered by the exhortations in these chapters. We are not dealing with behavior here that is in itself sinful (I Corinthians 8:4-6) - *there was nothing wrong with the meat!* One thus cannot apply Christian liberty, with its inevitable reference to Matthew 7:1 ("Judge not, that you be not judged"), to issues like premarital sex, which is never a matter of individual conscience. While Christians may differ even with regard to such an obvious question, this does not mean that this behavior ought to be tolerated in the spirit of mutual love and acceptance.

- Paul identifies two kinds of Christians in I Corinthians 8 - the *weak* and the *strong*. Contrary to the legalism that dominated so much of twentieth-century American Fundamentalism, the strong are those who can engage in the practice with no qualms of conscience, while the weak are those whose consciences do not allow them to do so. Counter-intuitively, then, the weak are more strict in their view of the issue in question than are the strong.

- What is a stumblingblock? In these chapters, it is something that causes someone else to sin. Again, American Fundamentalism has tended to misunderstand this concept. Instead of viewing it as something that causes someone else to sin, it has more often been understood as something that causes someone else to gasp! The cause of this misunderstanding was the translation of the relevant word in the KJV as *offend*, which in the seventeenth century *did* mean to cause someone to sin. Today, however, it means something quite different, and this has often led to the tyranny of the weak, where the person with the most sensitive conscience gets to dictate the behavior of everyone else because it would be wrong for them to offend the person in question.

- In dealing with the issues and with one another, sin is found on both sides. The weak are wrong in their assessment of the practice while the strong are right, but the real problem lies in their attitudes toward one another (I Corinthians 8:9-13). In simple terms, the weak condemn the strong because of what their consciences allow ("How can anyone who claims to be a Christian do *that*? You're probably not a real Christian at all!"), while the strong ridicule the weak because their consciences are hyperactive ("Come on, what's the matter with you? Try a little of this pork! Doesn't it smell *good*?").

- What, then, is to be done? What does it mean to love your neighbor as yourself when such potentially church-splitting disputes arise? For one thing, the condemnation and ridicule must stop. Each person must stand before God on the basis of his decision, and others should respect that.

- Secondly, the strong should be patient with the weak and not attempt to coerce them into violating their consciences (this is what a stumblingblock is, not simply doing privately what other people think is wrong - see I Corinthians 9:19-23), while the weak should be open to learning from the strong rather than condemning them and feeling spiritually superior. After all, spiritual pride appears to be a problem on both sides.
- Thirdly, both sides should call a moratorium on the argument. Romans 14:22 promotes the virtue of keeping quiet and minding one's own business. If more people followed this instruction, fewer church splits would occur.
- Fourthly, the weak should never be encouraged to violate their consciences, since it is a sin to do what you believe to be wrong, even if you are wrong in thinking so (Romans 14:23).[12]
- Fifthly, we ought to recognize that the categories of strong and weak brothers are not ways of labeling Christians in general. The truth is that most of us are "strong brothers" on some issues and "weak brothers" on others, and therefore need to heed the warnings that Paul gave to both groups.

We thus find in Scripture principles for dealing with matters where the behavior in question is not sinful in itself, but where Christians disagree. These are moral questions because they are heart issues, dealing with people's desire to glorify God with their choices and encourage one another by showing love rather than a judgmental spirit. What issues in the church today fit into this category? Perhaps musical styles and dancing in worship would be appropriate contemporary examples of issues to which the principles given by Paul in these chapters should be applied.

THE TWO GREAT COMMANDMENTS

Before moving on to the main body of the book, which deals with a survey of the Ten Commandments and their application to contemporary issues, we need to spend a few pages considering the significance of the two great commandments cited by Jesus in Matthew 22:37-40. Here Jesus tells the Pharisees that the Law and the Prophets may be summed up in two simple statements - love God and love your neighbor. What lessons should we draw from this summary before moving on to the more detailed summary found in the Decalogue?

First of all, we need to revisit the definition of love. We saw that Joseph Fletcher missed the point here, allowing love to be defined by the individual, opening it to the usual mushy thinking of contemporary culture. We should note, however, that the Bible allows no such approach. It is of value to note that the world of the New Testament had its own form of mushy thinking on the subject. The Greek language that linked together the vast Roman Empire and in which the New Testament was written had three words for love:

---

[12] Students typically have a bit of trouble wading through this one. Remember that the key issues here are *heart* issues. If one acts with a wrong motive - "I believe in my heart that this is wrong, but I'm going to do it anyway to shut those strong brothers up" - the sin is not in the action, but in the attitude of heart that puts pleasing men before pleasing God.

- *Eros*, from which we get our word *erotic*, referred to physical and romantic love - this is the most common use of the term today in a relational context, but the word is found nowhere in the New Testament and is clearly not what Jesus had in mind.
- *Phileo*, from which we get the name Philadelphia, the City of Brotherly Love. This was the love of friendship, the mutual regard that bound relatives and close companions together. This term is used in Scripture, most notably in the exchange that occurs between Jesus and Peter in John 21:15-17, where Peter is afraid to claim unconditional love for Jesus after his betrayal, and instead affirms that he is Christ's friend. When Jesus questions even that in verse 17, Peter breaks down and Jesus is able to lift him up. This, however, is also not the word used in the two great commandments.
- *Agape*, the word used in the passage before us, refers to unconditional love, the love of Romans 5:8, the love of Christ on the cross, the love of God for sinners. This is also the word used in I Corinthians 13. Thus love in Scripture is not a feeling, but an action - to see a person from God's perspective and to translate that insight into action on his behalf. If this were not so, it could not be commanded, for who can command a feeling?[13]

Thus biblical love is volitional, active, and possible only by the grace of God. We can only love Him because He first loved us, and we are only able to love one another because of the life-changing power of the Holy Spirit within. We must therefore conclude that the kind of love demanded by the two great commandments is a love that is possible only to believers. Others may act in loving ways toward their neighbors, but if the motive is not to glorify God, then what is being practiced is not *agape*.

We must next consider the commandment to love God. Why is this the first and greatest commandment? Note the following:

- We are to love God because of who God is. He is deserving of all worship and praise, and to do anything other than to love Him would be a betrayal of everything we are as His creatures. After all, "The chief end of man is to glorify God and to enjoy Him forever." Love for God is the only acceptable motive for obeying Him. If you do not love God, this book will have little meaning to you, because the desire to please God is presupposed in every issue discussed in it.
- Secondly, loving God is to involve our whole being - our "heart, soul, and mind." Love for God requires total commitment, with nothing held back. One who loves God does not confine Him to one area of life in order to live the rest as he pleases.[14]
- Thirdly, this implies that ethical problems are not at their foundation matters of education or knowledge, but of relationship to God; all moral questions thus have spiritual roots.

---

[13] This should not be construed to deny the fact that God has a heart of compassion for His people. Human emotion is part of what it means to be in the image of God, and thus love should never be cold and mechanical.

[14] Robert Boyd Munger wrote a famous pamphlet called *My Heart, Christ's Home* in which he imagines his heart as a house with many rooms for many purposes. When Christ invites Himself for a visit, the host gladly shows Him some of the rooms, but tries to avoid others. The Savior not only insists on seeing every room, but finally moves in; by the time the story is over, the narrator realizes that the home is not his, but belongs to Christ.

- Finally, the love of God provides the essential foundation for the love of man, both in motive and ability. One who does not love God can never truly love his neighbor, both because he at root wants to serve himself, and because only one with a transformed heart is able to love another. Love is thus the product of transforming grace, and cannot be exercised in a biblical fashion without it.

When we consider the second great commandment, "love your neighbor as yourself," we must note first of all that many people read this passage and find three commandments rather than two. After all, they argue, the commandment to love others as one loves oneself implies the need to love oneself. Such thinking has drawn many Christians into the self-fulfillment and self-esteem bypaths so prevalent in contemporary society. The argument states that only those who love themselves can be free to love others, so we must devote attention to loving ourselves and teaching others to do so as well. How should one respond to such an argument?

First of all, we should note that self-love in Scripture is never commanded, but instead assumed. Ephesians 5:29, in talking about the need for husbands to love their wives, notes that no one hates himself, but cherishes and nourishes himself. What, then, are we to say of those who are chronically depressed, have bad self-images, or have "inferiority complexes"?[15] Do not such people need to work on their self-love? In fact, they do not lack self-love at all. Instead, what they experience is a self-love every bit as perverted as that of the braggart or egomaniac. Focusing on one's misery is no less self-centered than focusing on one's achievements or skills. Both suffer from the sin of pride and both are in need of the grace of God to find deliverance from a distorted view of themselves. As John Piper put it, what we need is "not to think less of ourselves, but to think of ourselves less."

A biblical view of self thus does not involve giving undue attention to the ways in which we are "fearfully and wonderfully made." Too many individuals today, children and adults alike, are constantly told how wonderful they are in the hope that such affirmations will lead to more positive behavior and better academic performance. What those who do such things fail to realize is that a proper view of self is not the cause of behavior that reaches out to others, but the result of it - they put the cart before the horse. Only those who are forgetful of self in order to reach out to others can know the satisfaction that comes from a life of ministry, of doing what God has put us in this world to do. Note that a proper attitude toward self is also a matter of faith - God is not finished with us yet (Philippians 1:6), and He has promised to complete what He has started. We must see ourselves from God's perspective and act accordingly.

Furthermore, negative attitudes toward ourselves often come from comparison. Someone who tends toward feelings of superiority can always find evidence to support his conceit by concentrating on those who are inferior to him in the qualities he prizes. Similarly, the person who is prone to feelings of inferiority can always find cause for discouragement by looking at all the ways in which others are better. Rather than comparison, however, we should seek in Christ

---

[15] Often those who have been abused express self-hatred in destructive ways such as anorexia, bulimia, or cutting. Only the healing power of God's grace can restore a proper view of self to those who have gone through such horrifying experiences.

a spirit of contentment with the unique gifts and ministries He has given to each one (see I Corinthians 12).

What, then, about love for others? We are to act toward others in a godly way independent of our feelings for them. In fact, such loving actions will often be used by God to transform negative attitudes - if we act toward someone in a loving way, we may soon find ourselves developing loving feelings we never had before. If we are to view ourselves from God's perspective and act accordingly, we must then do the same in relationship to others. We also need to pray that God would change negative feelings we may have about others, which may themselves be sinful and in need of correction.

But toward whom is this love to be directed? A lawyer asked Jesus this very question in Luke 10:29. The answer may be obvious to us, but it was not what the lawyer expected. Jesus responded with the parable of the Good Samaritan, in which love is shown to someone who, in normal circumstances, would have been the man's worst enemy. We are thus to love all people, independent of the personal differences and prejudices that divide us so easily.

But how can this be? Does not love require a commitment of time and effort? How can we possibly hope to love *everyone*? The answer to this question rests in an understanding of the nature of the relationships in which we are all involved. Every person is involved in relationships on many levels, from the most intimate - spouses, parents and children - through friendships, casual acquaintances, brief encounters, to the billions of people in this world we will never meet at all. How can we possibly love all these people? Clearly, loving one's neighbor is going to mean different things in the context of these different relationships. For example, one cannot and ought not love one's next-door neighbor in the same way one loves one's spouse; that would be immoral. Yet on the levels on which each of our many and varied relationships exist, we can love our neighbors in a godly way, whether by taking time and listening, surprising friends with special remembrances, helping someone in the hallway who has dropped his or her books, letting a car into line in congested traffic, or giving to and praying for the work of missions in foreign lands. All of these are manifestations of seeing others as God sees them and acting accordingly, thus loving our neighbors as ourselves. We must always remember, however, that the most intimate relationships we have involve sharing what is most important about ourselves and our lives, and thus Christians should only seek such relationships with those who share their most fundamental values and desires.

2

THE CHRISTIAN AND GOD'S BEING

Exodus 20:3 - "You shall have no other gods before me."

After God brought the Israelites out of Egypt, through the Red Sea, and to the foot of Mount Sinai, He made a covenant with them. The form taken by that covenant, as pointed out by Meredith Kline in his groundbreaking work on the subject, is similar to the standard form of treaties between nations in the second millennium BC. Such treaties always began by calling the gods of the participating peoples to witness the agreement (in this case not necessary because God Himself initiates the treaty) and summarizing the history of the relationships between the two nations (Exodus 20:2). Next came the covenant stipulations - the Decalogue in this case, along with the enumerated civil laws that followed.

The first stipulation of the covenant between God and His people is one of exclusive loyalty - the vassal may serve only one lord. Sometimes the translation of this verse causes some confusion. When we hear the words, "You shall have no other gods before me," it is easy to think, as in contemporary English usage, that the commandment insists that Yahweh be given priority over all other gods. It means no such thing, of course. Other gods are not to be permitted or even considered. This becomes clear when one understands that the phrase translated "before me" in English literally means in Hebrew "before my face," i.e., "in my presence."

And what did the Israelites understand by the presence of God? In one sense, the Tabernacle they were about to build was intended to house the presence of God in the Holy of Holies, and this religious application of the commandment is a legitimate one. God would not tolerate other gods in His sanctuary, as Manasseh of Judah discovered (II Kings 21:4-7).[16]

Yet the Jewish people were not so parochial as to believe that their God was localized, restricted to a cubical room in a sanctuary they had built with their own hands (I Kings 8:27). They knew perfectly well that Yahweh is omnipresent. Therefore the command that forbid any gods in His presence banished them altogether from the created universe. For us, as for Israel, there is no room for other gods of any kind. If the Lord is God, He alone is to be worshiped.

---

[16] Other examples occurred during the Intertestamental Period, when Antiochus Epiphanes sacrificed a pig on the altar in the Temple and set up an image of Zeus bearing his face in the Holy of Holies, which caused the outbreak of the Maccabean Revolt, and in the first century, when the Roman emperor Caligula ordered the construction of a great statue of himself to be erected in the Holy of Holies; he was assassinated before the statue could be brought ashore in Judea, and it was dropped into the bottom of the Mediterranean.

Such a demand for exclusivity impinges on any desire we might have to worship lesser things, whether they be possessions, people, or our own ideas and desires. As noted in the introductory chapter, any sin is in a sense false worship, and violates the First Commandment.

One other idea needs to be considered before we move on to specific applications of the First Commandment, and that is the biblical teaching concerning the jealousy of God. Though the issue is also raised in connection with the Second Commandment (Exodus 20:5), we would do well to consider it here. God is many times in Scripture described as a jealous God (Exodus 34:4; Deuteronomy 4:24; 5:9; 6:15; 32:16,21; I Kings 14:22; Psalm 78:58). How are we to understand these passages when the Bible so clearly condemns human jealousy (Proverbs 6:34; Song of Solomon 8:6)? Is something that is sin for man acceptable when God practices it?

We should note first of all that not all human jealousy is wrong (Numbers 5:11-31; II Corinthians 11:2). Like anger, jealousy can be righteous or sinful. What makes the difference? If we understand righteous jealousy to be a negative response to the destruction of a rightly exclusive relationship, the matter becomes clearer. If a man becomes jealous of his wife because of unfounded rumor or innuendo, as did Othello in Shakespeare's play, his jealousy is sinful because his rightly exclusive relationship with his wife was not really being threatened. On the other hand, the situation of the unfaithful wife in Numbers 5 elicits righteous jealousy because the exclusive bond has been broken. Similarly, jealousy is only legitimate when the relationship in question is truly exclusive. A woman may rightly become jealous if she finds her husband in bed with someone else, but a high school boy ought not fly into a rage if his girlfriend talks with another guy at her locker.

Note that the jealousy of God passes both these tests. It is righteous because He legitimately may claim an exclusive relationship with all people by right of creation and with His chosen people by right of redemption.[17] Furthermore, worship of other gods is a genuine violation of that relationship, as Paul's response to the Corinthians being seduced by another gospel indicates. We find, then, that the focus of the First Commandment is on the exclusive nature of the relationship between the only true God and His people. What are some of the contemporary applications of this commandment that we should consider?

THE OCCULT

The first application of the First Commandment we will examine involves occult practices. We begin here because this is perhaps the earliest documented form of idolatry. What, then, is the occult? While students often confuse the term with *cult*, which is any form of worship for a sociologist and a minor offshoot of a major religion unrecognized by the mainstream for a student of religions,[18] the term *occult*, which comes from a root meaning *to hide or conceal*, refers to

---

[17] Note, however, that all biblical references to the jealousy of God are in relationship to His people.

[18] While Christians tend to think of Jehovah's Witnesses and Mormons when they hear the term, all religions have cultic offshoots - Baha'i for Islam, Hare Krishna for Hinduism, etc.

seeking after spiritual mysteries or trafficking with spiritual beings or forces. For the Christian, such practices are always condemned.

OCCULT PRACTICES

We'll begin this topic by surveying some of the practices often considered occult. Considerable variety exists, so this sampling will not in any sense be exhaustive, but should allow the student to get an idea of the variety of phenomena in which practitioners of the occult are engaged.

ASTROLOGY

Perhaps the oldest form of occult practice is astrology. Evidence of the practice of astrology goes back to the beginnings of recorded history. Some suggest that the Tower of Babel in Genesis 11 was an astrological temple ("with its top the heavens" is a possible translation of Genesis 11:4), since archaeologists have found that ancient ziggurats, of which the Tower of Babel is an example, had astronomical observatories decorated with symbols of the gods of the zodiac on the top level. While people do not often place astrology in the same category as some of the more overt forms of contact with the spirit world, it does involve the belief that the heavenly bodies exercise mysterious powers over human life and destiny.

While in the early centuries of human history no clear distinction was made between astronomy and astrology, today astrologists, despite their pseudo-scientific pretensions, continue to make predictions and dispense advice based on the belief that the stars influence the destinies of human beings. Such beliefs have no scientific validity, of course, despite the fact that the cycles of the moon influence tides and certain periodic forms of human behavior. The whole idea on which horoscopes are based - that of the constellations of the zodiac - assumes that a constellation is a scientifically meaningful entity, which of course it is not, because constellations only exist from the perspective of earthly observers; the stars in Virgo, for example, have no relationship to one another in reality, and thus cannot act in concert to influence anything.

Astrology was common in Bible times (e.g., eight references to astrologers among the wise men of Babylon in the first five chapters of Daniel; even the magi of Matthew 2:1-12 were probably astrologers), and the practice is clearly condemned by God (Deuteronomy 4:19; Isaiah 47:13-14). Why does God condemn it? First of all, it was closely associated with the worship of false gods. In every society in the ancient world, astrology was not only practiced, but the heavenly bodies were identified as gods; this was true in China and Egypt as well as with the Greeks and Romans in the Classical Age. Furthermore, it was almost always associated with other occult practices that were carried out to placate the gods about whom astrology gave information. Today, astrology continues to be wicked because it turns people's faith to something other than God. Those who believe that their personalities and destinies are shaped by the mysterious powers of the stars are denying the sovereignty of God and allowing themselves to make decisions based on an illusion and a lie. Despite the scientific absurdity of astrology, however, people in our supposedly scientific age continue to be drawn to it, both because the overwhelming secularism of the age has left a spiritual vacuum that must be filled with something and because the predictions of horoscopes tend to become self-fulfilling prophecies; someone who has once seen a horoscope "come true" is much more likely to believe them in the future, and, at least subconsciously, to act accordingly.

DEMON POSSESSION

In the Preface to *The Screwtape Letters*, C.S. Lewis said, "There are two equal and opposite errors into which our race can fall about the devils. One is to disbelieve in their existence. The other is to believe, and to feel an excessive and unhealthy interest in them. They themselves are equally pleased by both errors, and hail the materialist and the magician with the same delight." Both tendencies are present in our postmodern age. While most people's exposure to demon possession consists largely of its portrayal in the popular media for entertainment purposes, the projectile vomiting of *The Exorcist* often hardens the hearts of observers to the realities of the evil supernatural realm. Part of the power of the social criticism contained in a play like Arthur Miller's *The Crucible* is the implication that, of course, we all realize that demons don't exist.

From a biblical standpoint, however, nothing could be clearer than the reality of demons and their ability to possess the bodies of living beings. Demons are not the souls of the wicked dead, nor are they Hell's appointed torturers (as Dante portrays them in the *Inferno*), but are the angels who joined in Satan's rebellion against God and with him were cast out of heaven (Matthew 25:41; Jude 6). Though some are confined in Hell, others roam the earth and are able to possess people and animals, as the Gospels often bear witness.

While the Gadarene demoniac in Mark 5:1-20 displays the stereotypical symptoms associated with demon possession in the public mind - supernatural strength, uncontrollable and violent behavior, strange cries - we should note that demon possession in the New Testament involves a great variety of manifestations, including the inability to speak (Matthew 9:32-33), blindness (Matthew 12:22), epileptic seizures (Matthew 17:14-21), and the ability to foretell the future (Acts 16:16). Note the significance of these descriptions:

- Demon possession is not always evident to an outside observer. The Gadarene demoniac was clearly demon-possessed, but someone who is epileptic, deaf, mute, or blind may not necessarily be.
- Satan's followers thus often counterfeit conditions with physical causes in order to gain control of people.
- This has two opposing consequences, as implied in the quotation from C.S. Lewis above. For some, this becomes an easy excuse to deny the existence of demons and seek naturalistic causes for everything, while others look for demons under every rock and convince themselves that anything bad in a person's life is traceable to demonic activity.
- The fact that demon possession was seemingly more easily recognized in the first century than it is today is no great surprise. People then believed in demons and were accustomed to their activity. In our naturalistic age, the default explanation is always to seek physiological or psychological causes for aberrant behavior.

- Some wonder why demon possession seems to have occurred much more frequently in Bible times than it does today, and in primitive cultures more often than in "advanced" ones. While I would argue that this is simply not the case - the problem is our inability to identify it for what it is - some suggest that demons were particularly active during Jesus' earthly ministry in order to mount a frontal assault on God's plan of salvation. One also might make the case that demons are openly worshiped in primitive cultures, and thus are active in much more open ways.
- Nothing is clearer in the passages in Scripture dealing with demons than that God's power over demons is absolute. When Christ or His disciples cast them out, they have no choice but to go, and they even come to Him begging to be sent to an alternative destination (Mark 5:12).

LEVITATION AND TELEKINESIS

The ability to move something with one's mind is usually associated with magicians and sleight-of-hand artists, but such phenomena can also be associated with occult powers, such as may be manifested at a seance. The confusion here can be a means of persuasion for Satan. How many magicians, fascinated with the powers they pretend to have over the natural world, are drawn into the occult, seeking in reality what they have heretofore produced only as an illusion? Even Harry Houdini, perhaps American history's most famous magician and a noted debunker of spiritist claims, became late in life so fascinated with the possibility of genuine contact with the dead that he arranged for his wife, Bess, to conduct seances on Halloween night for the ten years after he died in an attempt to contact him (those seances have been continued by magicians to the present day). Recent movies such as *The Prestige* and *The Illusionist* have also portrayed the close links between sleight-of-hand and occult practices.

DREAMS AND VISIONS

Many occult practitioners have claimed to receive secret knowledge by means of dreams and visions. This is nothing new - Scripture often speaks of those who foretell the future through dreams. Of course, in the Bible, God Himself sometimes communicates this way, as in the cases of Joseph and those whose dreams he interpreted, Daniel's interpretation of Nebuchadnezzar's dream and Belshazzar's vision, and Joseph's dream in which God told him to take Mary and Jesus into Egypt. Because God has at times utilized this medium, however, the question immediately arises, "How can one tell a dream that speaks truth from one that doesn't?"

Scripture gives two criteria. In Deuteronomy 13:1-5, the central test is the source of the revelation - Does the seer claim to speak the message of God? - and thus, by implication, the extent to which it conforms to what God has already said. One who speaks in the name of another god, *even if his prediction comes to pass*, is not only to be ignored, but is to be executed. Many occult practitioners would no longer be in business had they lived under such a provision.

The second criterion is found in Deuteronomy 18:18-22. Here the prophet "presumes to speak a word" in God's name, and thus passes the first test. But the second test is much more stringent: the prophecy must come to pass. Even professional psychic Jeane Dixon, who claimed her visions came from God and became famous for allegedly predicting the assassination of John F. Kennedy, made many wrong predictions, including the onset of World War III in 1958. Despite the pride she took in the high percentage of accurate predictions she claimed, she did not "bat 1.000," nor has any other dreamer of dreams other than those inspired by God.[19] While prophecies concerning the distant future obviously cannot be put to such a test when they are made, most seers are sufficiently arrogant that they can't resist making claims about their own time. No Christian should be deceived by such charlatans.[20]

While many purveyors of dreams and visions are frauds looking to enrich themselves, many others traffic in the occult. What has Satan to gain from such practices, and why do so many find them enticing? Note the following:

- Secret knowledge unavailable to others appeals to human pride, as does the thought that the future can be known, anticipated, and thus to some extent manipulated.
- Satan lures people to their destruction through false prophecies (see I Kings 22:6, where the words of false prophets led to the death of Ahab in battle). Often these prophecies are couched in such ambiguous terms that people interpret them according to their own desires (e.g., the prophecies of Nostradamus), again leading to destruction.[21]
- What of religious figures who claim visions, from Muhammad to Joseph Smith, the founder of the Mormons, Ellen G. White, the founder of Seventh Day Adventism, and many others? Scripture leaves us only a few alternatives: the recipient of such visions is right in claiming them to be from God (clearly not possible in the cases mentioned because they contradict previous revelation), he or she is demon-possessed, the person is mentally unstable (Mary Baker Eddy of Christian Science fame probably fits in here), is self-deceived, or is seeking to deceive others (Smith and Charles Taze Russell, the founder of the Jehovah's Witnesses, are best viewed in this light).
- While God certainly has the ability to communicate through dreams and visions today, any such claims must be carefully and humbly subjected to the biblical tests and compared to the clear teachings of Scripture.

---

[19] In February 2011, Romania, the home of Bram Stoker's Dracula and a land teeming with superstition and the occult, passed a law threatening fines or imprisonment to seers and fortune-tellers whose predictions didn't come true. The witches, needless to say, were up in arms over the legislation.

[20] Harold Camping's predictions of the Second Coming of Christ and the end of the world in 1993 and again in 2011 clearly mark him as a false prophet to whom no Christian should pay heed.

[21] One famous example of this in literature is in Act IV of William Shakespeare's *Macbeth*, where the witches assure Macbeth that "none of woman born can harm" him, and that "Macbeth shall never vanquished be till Birnam Wood to high Dunsinane Hill shall come against him." Sadly for him, "Macduff was from his mother's womb untimely ripped" and branches from Birnam Wood were cut down by the invading army as it prepared to launch an attack on Macbeth's castle at Dunsinane. His assurance of his own impregnability thus led to his downfall.

AUTOMATIC WRITING

This phenomenon involves a person writing something down while under the control of some spiritual power, so that the person has no knowledge of what he or she is writing. Note that the Ouija board, the use of which involves calling on the "spirit of the board" to answer a question or communicate a message, fits into this category, and is thus not an innocent party game that preteen girls play at sleepovers.

This practice was the source of my only direct contact with the realm of demonic activity. During my first year of teaching, I was going over this section of the course with my Ethics class. While talking about people who have dreams and visions or hear voices, a quiet girl in the front row said, loudly enough for only me to hear, "But they're nice to me." Needless to say, this necessitated further examination, and when I spoke to her after class, she poured out a story of bizarre occurrences in her room at night - things moving around the room, strange voices - that had begun after she and some of her friends had played with a Ouija board at a sleepover in her room. She was clearly frightened, but was afraid to tell anyone except me (for reasons I will never understand). As the year passed, she reported increasingly strange occurrences. One day she seemed particularly upset, and showed me a piece of paper with something she had written the night before, but which she didn't understand. The explanation was a relatively simple one - the writing was in French, of which she, a Spanish student, understood not a word. We went to the library, pulled out a French dictionary, and translated the writing, which turned out to be a vulgar and disgusting poem about blood and death.

Attempts to bring in her parents, her pastor, and the school guidance counselor availed little, because she refused to tell them what was happening. The next semester, she began to turn in odd essays for my Christian Perspective class. As she analyzed the excerpt of which the assignment consisted, she wrote in her usual style and with her usual vocabulary. Every once in a while, however, a sentence was inserted in the middle of a paragraph, vulgar and blasphemous, using words she would not think of using. When I showed these sentences to her, she denied having written them. The worst manifestation was one I directly witnessed. She was visiting my wife and I and suddenly began speaking threats and blasphemies in a deep voice that was clearly not her own. Rapid and fervent prayer quieted the demon, but she refused to turn her life over to Christ, insisting that the demon told her it would kill her if she attempted to do so. I lost touch with her after she went to college, but several years later I heard she had been killed in a plane crash, to my knowledge never having been delivered from the demons that plagued her.

I tell this story to my students every year. The purpose for doing so is so that they will take the occult seriously rather than viewing it in terms of popular entertainment or to satisfy curiosity. Demons are real; fooling around with the occult is dangerous and can be deadly.

CONTACT WITH THE DEAD

Mediums have conducted seances in an attempt to contact the dead ever since Bible times, and such practices were clearly condemned in Scripture (Deuteronomy 18:10; II Chronicles 33:6). Most practitioners of this art are simply frauds, as Houdini proved by duplicating their supposedly supernatural manifestations for the public.[22] Not all seances are frauds, however. In some cases, an occult practitioner uses a demonic spirit, who impersonates the dead person who is supposed to be "called up," either verbally or visually (we know from Scripture that even those who traffic with demons cannot really call up the dead because those who die go either to heaven or hell, and cannot leave either place without special divine intervention - see Luke 16:26). We should not be surprised when such "manifestations" give a rosy view of the afterlife that implies universal salvation - this is a fraud that Satan dearly loves to promote.

But what of the only example of a seance in Scripture? Did not the witch of Endor call up Samuel from the grave in I Samuel 28? This clearly was not a demonic manifestation; not only did Saul recognize Samuel, but the prophet also spoke the word of God to the doomed king of Israel. I would suggest, however, that this example cannot be used to argue that mediums can actually communicate with the dead because of the response of the medium herself. She certainly was expecting something other than what happened when she tried to call up Samuel. When the prophet actually appeared instead of the "familiar spirit" to which she was accustomed, she was frightened out of her mind and accused Saul of deceiving her. We must conclude, then, that God allowed Samuel to deliver this message to Saul in the same way that God made an exception at the Transfiguration, where Moses and Elijah appeared on the mountain with Jesus (Matthew 17:3).

GHOSTS

In popular culture, ghosts are thought to be the spirits of the dead who wander the earth or haunt specific locales. As noted above, however, spirits of the dead do not continue to roam the earth - the picture of Jacob Marley floating through the night sky bound by the chains he had forged on earth in Dickens' *A Christmas Carol* simply does not happen.

What are we to make of all the eyewitness accounts of ghosts with which human history is littered? Could they all be frauds, wishful thinking, or psychological manifestations? This is certainly possible. But we should also recognize one other possibility. We know that demons are fallen angels, and we know that angels, though they are non-material beings (Hebrews 1:14), have the ability to manifest themselves in visible form. Why might not demons retain that same capacity? Satan may well gain from such a practice, not only by the unhealthy curiosity it generates, but also because of the interest it creates in a warped view of life after death.

THE CHRISTIAN AND THE OCCULT

How, then, is the Christian supposed to respond to all of this? Several points should be noted:

- The Christian must never forget the sovereignty of God over the forces of evil. Satan is a fearful enemy (I Peter 5:8), but he is a defeated enemy (I John 4:4).

---

[22] Even Margaret Fox, who with her two sisters founded the Spiritualist movement in America, confessed before her death that the "rappings" that made them famous and led to them being hired by P.T. Barnum for his traveling circus were produced by cracking the bones of their toes!

- Occult practice is strictly forbidden in Scripture (Leviticus 19:31; 20:6, 27; Deuteronomy 18:9-14 and many other passages). Curiosity is no excuse, and can lead to dangerous consequences.
- What of research, or becoming knowledgeable about the occult in order to combat it or deliver those who are entrapped? This is clearly permissible, but great caution must be exercised (Jude 22-23), because research easily becomes fascination, leading to sticking one's toe into the quicksand that will inexorably lead to destruction.
- Should a Christian fear demon possession? No, since Satan can never conquer and expel the Holy Spirit, who dwells in believers. But Christians must be aware that Satan's temptations can be very severe, as Christ was tempted in the wilderness (Matthew 4:1-11) and as Peter was "sifted" prior to Christ's crucifixion (Luke 22:31-32).

SECULAR ORGANIZATIONS

The second topic we will take up under the First Commandment is the issue of participation in secular organizations. If the Christian is to avoid the worship of other gods and always put God first in everything, should he ever belong to an organization that does not share these values? Can he contribute to the goals of a business, school, sports team, or social club that has no interest in glorifying God?

This is one of the questions we will encounter in this book for which both extremes may be easily dismissed. In the Bible, some of God's people involved themselves in key ways in godless organizations, most notably Joseph, Daniel, and Esther in their participation in pagan governments. Jesus also had no objection to associating with sinners (Matthew 9:9-12; 11:19), so the isolationist stance is clearly eliminated. God did not call us to live the spiritual life by entering into a monastery and separating ourselves from the world. Nor is restricting ourselves only to Christian organizations practical. We may focus our activities on our church, send our children to Christian schools, and even work for a Christian company, but we cannot be flavorful salt and illuminating light if this entirely defines who we are.

On the other hand, *some* organizations are clearly out of bounds for the Christian. In the same way that one should not involve oneself in the occult in order to deliver others from it, so blatantly immoral organizations - houses of prostitution, abortion clinics, organized crime (the list could go on for some time) - cannot be open to Christian involvement.

This then leaves us with a question of line-drawing, which is always difficult. If one cannot blithely excuse oneself from any secular contacts, and yet must eliminate openly sinful organizations, how should a person decide which secular organizations to join? Students who are looking forward to college and/or the working world very soon must learn to think through this issue clearly and biblically. Scripture, of course, does not provide us with a checklist to apply to such decisions. I would suggest that someone facing a decision of this kind ought to ask several important questions in order to assist him in making a God-honoring choice.

- What is the underlying philosophy and what are the major goals of the organization? These days, everyone has a mission statement. You should get to know it. Though no secular organization will have a mission that promotes godly ends, one must determine if the underlying philosophy is compatible with Christian values. For example, a neighborhood group that attempts to reach out to at-risk young people or a business that stresses honesty and integrity may well be places in which a Christian can serve the Lord.

- To what extent does the organization adhere to its stated purposes? This question cuts two ways. On the one hand, some organizations talk a good game but don't practice what they preach. Secular universities, for example, may have a lot to say about tolerance and acceptance, but are in reality highly intolerant of Christian speech and activity. Alternatively, some groups allow a great deal of flexibility of opinion and practice, so that Christians who dissent from prevailing thought are free to speak their minds and present their ideas.

- What about the matter of influence? Is a Christian free to speak about and live out his faith, bearing witness to others, or will he be stifled and discriminated against? Does the potential exist for a Christian to help shape the direction of the organization for good, or does the greater danger exist that the Christian will be influenced negatively by his environment?

- Will involvement in the organization be a stumblingblock to others, causing someone else to sin?

- Even if all these questions can be answered in a way that gives a green light to involvement, one other important issue must be addressed, and that is the question of whether involvement will prevent the Christian from giving his time to something of greater importance. After all, we all must apportion a finite number of hours in the day. A perfectly beneficial association may still be wrong if it takes away from family time or prevents full involvement in the church, for instance. The question of drawing lines of this sort requires not only distinguishing good from evil, but also setting priorities that distinguish what is good from what is best.

APOSTATE CHURCHES

Another twist on the issue of choosing which organizations with which to involve oneself appears when the organization in question professes to be Christian, but no longer lives up to that profession. The history of the Christian Church is littered with apostasy - churches that have borne a strong witness to the surrounding world, but have through gradual compromises turned away from that profession and denied the central doctrines of Christianity, becoming ultimately indistinguishable from the world. We should also note that the same pattern is observable among schools founded by Christians. Most of the institutions of higher learning in the United States began as Christian schools, but most are today far from their original purposes, though some still claim to be Christian. How should a Christian respond to a "Christian" organization, whether school or church, that is Christian no longer? Such organizations rarely force one to sin (though exceptions can easily be cited), so other considerations must be raised.

THE MARKS OF THE CHURCH

The Protestant Reformers struggled mightily with this issue when considering whether and when they should separate themselves from the Catholic Church. Their study of the Bible led them to conclude that a true church was characterized by three marks:

- The true preaching of the Word - No church that preaches anything other than the Gospel of Jesus Christ may legitimately call itself a church. Sound doctrine is a must.
- The right administration of the sacraments - Jesus commanded His followers to observe the ordinances of baptism and the Lord's Supper until His return. Though churches may differ on the details of these observances, no true church will be without them.
- The biblical administration of church discipline - This means far more than excommunication. Biblical church discipline requires faithful adherence to and practice of the instructions Jesus gave in Matthew 18:15-20. In other words, a true church will practice mutual accountability, making sure that those who sin are humbly corrected (Galatians 6:1) and conflicts are resolved rather than being allowed to fester and divide.

One should note that, in the history of the church, the path to apostasy usually begins with the neglect of church discipline. If sin is ignored, soon tolerance of sinful choices becomes a matter of principle, and before too long doctrinal aberration is also tolerated. The last to go is almost always the sacraments - churches today that have been spiritually dead for centuries still administer the sacraments, though they believe little of what they symbolize.

And what of a sound church in an apostate denomination? Quite a few evangelical churches hang on today in denominations that, by their altered doctrinal statements and advocacy of unbiblical practices and lifestyles inside the church and without, have disqualified themselves as Christ-honoring institutions. When should such a church separate itself from a denomination that no longer promotes the truth? When key leaders deny fundamental teachings of Scripture, or promote the ordination of those who do so? When the denomination not only permits, but requires, unbiblical practices such as the ordination of women?[23] When the denomination ordains practicing homosexuals, or even makes them bishops?[24] This is not an easy question, and has been decided by many congregations by focusing on the question, "Does membership in the denomination cause us as a congregation to sin or to promote sin in others?"

Why is this question important for high school students? Simply because many of them, for the first time, will soon be facing the task of deciding for themselves which church to attend. So far, most have simply gone to the church chosen by their parents, but as they go off to college, most will have to make such decisions on their own. It is important that they ask themselves the right questions. It is far too easy to choose a church because it has an active youth group or young

---

[23] This was the issue that drove the renowned Tenth Presbyterian Church in Philadelphia out of the United Presbyterian denomination years after the doctrinal statement had been watered down.

[24] Many evangelical Episcopal congregations are leaving the Episcopal Church over this issue today.

adult ministry, or because the music is loud and lively. Students must understand what about a church is really important, and learn to look for these things and make them a priority in their own decision-making.

Finally, students who are soon to be on their own need to be encouraged to get involved in a good church, period. Too many who go off to college get so involved in campus life that church falls by the wayside. In doing this, they are neither honoring God nor showing concern for their own spiritual health. Furthermore, Christian campus ministries, though valuable as support structures, are no substitute for involvement in a good church. Those who go off to college and make no provision for their spiritual health will soon starve and fall by the wayside like the drought-stricken and weed-choked plants in Jesus' parable (Matthew 13:20-22).

3

THE CHRISTIAN AND GOD'S WORSHIP

Exodus 20:4-6 - "You shall not make for yourself a carved image, or any likeness of anything that is in heaven above, or that is in the earth beneath, or that is in the water under the earth. You shall not bow down to them or serve them, for I the Lord your God am a jealous God, visiting the iniquity of the fathers on the children to the third and the fourth generation of those who hate me, but showing steadfast love to thousands of those who love me and keep my commandments."

The first question we encounter as we examine the Second Commandment is, "Why is it in the Decalogue at all?" After all, the First Commandment forbids the worship of other gods, so isn't the prohibition of idols redundant at best? The important thing to note here is that the Second Commandment goes beyond the First because it does more than prohibit the worship of false gods; it also forbids false worship of the true God (cf. Deuteronomy 4:15-19). The use of images is not restricted to pagan deities - God also does not permit the use of man-made images by those who are worshiping Him. An obvious example of this is the Golden Calf in Exodus 32:1-6. Note that the calf was not a representation of an Egyptian deity, but of the God "who brought you up out of the land of Egypt." The golden calves installed by Jeroboam at Bethel and Dan served the same function (I Kings 12:28). God's disapproval in both cases quickly became obvious. The Golden Calf made by Aaron was ground to powder and the people were forced to drink it; when no repentance was forthcoming, the Levites were unleashed with swords in the camp and three thousand people were killed. As far as Jeroboam's calves were concerned, they became the benchmark against which all the idolatry that followed in the Northern Kingdom was measured - almost every king was said to have "made the people sin after the manner of Jeroboam the son of Nebat."

If, as indicated, the Second Commandment speaks about *how* we are to worship while the First Commandment addresses *whom* we are to worship, we next must consider why images of God are prohibited. After all, as long as God is receiving the worship of men, why should He concern himself with the manner in which this worship is being carried out? Note the following:

- God has already created in man an image of Himself (Genesis 1:26), and that image is not to be worshiped (Acts 12:22-23; 14:14-15).
- It would therefore be debasing to worship any of God's lesser creatures (Romans 1:22-23).
- It is both blasphemous and absurd for man to worship the labor of his own hands (Isaiah 44:9-20 is a classic example of biblical irony and sarcasm as the prophet mocks idolatry).
- Any visible representation of God is by its very nature a distortion.

Finally, we must recognize that manmade mental images are every bit as much distortions of God's nature as physical ones. How often have you heard someone say, "The God I believe in would never send anyone to Hell," or, "I picture God as a loving Father who accepts everyone"? Are these not manmade images every bit as much as the statue of wood or stone to which the most primitive of pagans may bow down? Thus our mental images of God must come from Him, not from ourselves. The Word of God alone can tell us who God is, and to formulate our own pictures of Him is to distort the truth of His glorious being.

This extends, as we shall see, to all the ways in which we worship God. We are not free to worship Him in any way we please. The Israelites were told not to add anything to the forms of worship prescribed for them by God (Deuteronomy 12:29-32; Isaiah 29:13), and the New Testament affirms that worshiping God in humanly-devised ways is to be avoided (Matthew 15:7-9; Colossians 2:20-23). Because God cares *how* we worship Him, it is incumbent upon us to understand what kind of worship He requires.

One further point should be noted in passing. The arrangement of the Ten Commandments used by the Roman Catholic Church is somewhat different from that to which we are accustomed as Protestants. Catholics number the commandments so that the first two are combined into one and the Tenth Commandment is divided into two. This has interesting implications for understanding how Catholics approach worship. By including the prohibition of images under the prohibition of false gods, the Catholic Church is able to justify its extensive use of images in worship. They see in the Decalogue no prohibition against images of the true God.

ART

Before we consider matters of worship, however, we must first address the question of art in general. The Second Commandment begins by prohibiting the making of images of anything in the created universe. Is this prohibition absolute, or is it intended to prohibit the making of such images only for the purpose of worship? In other words, is verse 4 a prohibition in its own right to which verse 5 adds emphasis, or does verse 5 describe the context within which the prohibition of verse 4 is to be understood? We can only answer this question by looking at the examples found in Scripture itself. If we look at the Tabernacle and the Temple, we find ornate structures decorated with images of created things, including cherubim (Exodus 26:31; 37:7-9; I Kings 6:23-28), flowers (Exodus 37:17-19; I Kings 6:18), pomegranates (I Kings 7:18), and oxen (I Kings 7:25). These had been incorporated into God's instructions for the place in which He was to dwell, and He specifically commanded that skilled artists should be commissioned to do the work (Exodus 31:1-11). Clearly, then, to God artwork is an appropriate human endeavor.

What, then, is the proper function of art in God's world? For one thing, it serves as a means of expressing the divine image. God is a Creator, and part of making man in His image is that He has made man with the capacity to create as well. We are thus reflecting who God has made us to be when we engage in the production of art. But art is not only intended as an expression of God's image. It is also a way in which man can exercise his dominion over the world that God has made. By portraying the beauty of God's created universe, man gives glory to the God who made it and him. This in itself can be a form of worship, as we see in the case of Bezalel and Oholiab.

But in order for art to honor the God who endowed man with creative powers, it must be both true and honest. It must be true in the sense that it portrays truth about what the world is, who the artist is, and by doing this speaks truth about who God is. Thus a non-Christian can still, by God's common grace, speak truth about the world and about himself, though too often the unbeliever sees the consequences of sin without portraying anything of God's redemptive grace. As far as honesty is concerned, honest art is art that speaks from the heart of the artist. It may portray something ugly or even terrifying, but it does not shrink from the realities of the world and the inner life of man.

IMAGES IN THE CHURCH

We now move on to the question of the use of images in the church. We have already seen that images *per se* are not prohibited, and that in the Scriptures these were incorporated into the place of worship by God's specific instruction. What, then, is the proper place of images in Christian worship? We will break our consideration down into three uses of images - veneration, decoration, and education.

VENERATION OF IMAGES

In the early Middle Ages, a question arose over the use of images in the worship of the church. Churches in the West used both paintings and statues in their places of worship, but those in the East shunned statues as violations of the Second Commandment but made extensive use of pictures called *icons* (after all, the commandment forbid *carved* images, not painted ones). These icons were believed to be not only portrayals of Christ and the saints, but were also seen as windows into the spiritual world. Thus the worshipers kissed them, prayed to them, and placed fruit and flowers before them as offerings. The controversy over such practices, known to history as the Iconoclastic Controversy (iconoclasts are icon-smashers), began with the invasion of the Byzantine Empire by the Muslims. The Muslims were winning battle after battle, rapidly annexing Byzantine territory. This raised an important question: Why is God allowing this to happen? Why are His holy people being conquered by godless infidels? A cursory examination of the Old Testament made it clear to many that God only allows such things to happen when His people have fallen into sin. What, then, could be the heinous sin that had brought the Islamic hordes down upon their heads? For some, the answer was obvious - idolatry. The way in which icons were being venerated was an offense to God and the cause of His judgment, especially since the Muslims rejected images of God or Muhammad completely. Those who took this position were the Iconoclasts - they favored, first moving icons higher on the walls so that people could no longer kiss them, and finally whitewashing over them or destroying them altogether.

This stance was very unpopular. Worshipers were lost without anything tangible on which to fix their devotion. Western (Catholic) theologians ridiculed the strictures of the Iconoclasts, pointing out the acceptance of their own statuary by the Pope. Their cause was assisted by Eastern theologian John of Damascus, a former monk who had retired from the monastery and become an advisor to the Caliph of Baghdad, who defended icons on a number of grounds. He argued first that veneration is not worship - one who venerates icons does not worship the picture, but what the picture represents. John also noted that images were used in the worship of the Old Testament (such as the bronze serpent and the cherubim over the mercy seat on the ark of the covenant), and that the destruction of images would deny the Incarnation, since it would imply that Christ had not had a physical body capable of being pictorially represented. He even argued that ascribing healing powers to icons was not unscriptural, since the book of Acts speaks of people being healed by Peter's shadow (Acts 5:15) and Paul's handkerchief (Acts 19:11-12). Inanimate things may thus be instruments for the transmission of the power of those they represent. Ultimately, the advocates of icons won the day. The Iconoclasts fell from power, icons were restored to the walls of Byzantine churches and the homes of the people, and even today continue to play a major role in the worship of the Eastern Orthodox Church.[25] What are we to make of all of this? Are these arguments valid? Note the following:

- It seems fairly obvious that this practice is precisely what the Second Commandment is forbidding. How do icons and statues of Mary and Jesus differ from the Golden Calf made by Aaron in the wilderness?
- God is pointedly said to be *unseen* (Romans 8:24; II Corinthians 4:16-18; Hebrews 11:1), so any visible representation of Him is a lie.
- God appeared in human form in Christ, but we really have no idea what He looked like (other than like a typical first-century Galilean Jew), and so any pictures of Him are bound to be misrepresentations (more on this below). The Incarnation does not stand our fall on our ability to place before people visible representations of Christ. He is the incarnate Word, and the Word is the only sufficient representation of Him.
- Saints, who are often the subjects of holy icons and statues, are not to be worshiped in any way, whether in visual form or not. Veneration of saints is in itself idolatry, and images that foster such a practice partake of that sin.
- The distinction between worship and veneration is technical at best, and fails completely in practice. When worshipers are kissing icons, carrying relics of the saints in holy processions, praying to statues, and making pilgrimages to images that supposedly bleed and cry, one cannot credibly argue that what is going on is not worship.
- The bronze serpent cited by John of Damascus was actually destroyed in the reign of Hezekiah because the people had begun making offerings to it (II Kings 18:4).

DECORATION WITH IMAGES

What if the images are not being worshiped, but are simply used to decorate the place of worship or private homes? What about stained-glass windows, pictures of Jesus in the church vestibule or on the wall of your bedroom, or even the cross on your necklace? Again, a few comments might be helpful.

---

[25] When I taught a course in Sofia, Bulgaria in 1998, the lawn in front of the central cathedral in the capital city was filled with tables at which monks were selling icons to tourists and the local populace.

- Clearly the examples of the Tabernacle and Temple give warrant for the decorative use of images. But does this mean that all decorative images are acceptable?

- Visual symbolism is also found in the New Testament in the ordinances of the church. Christ commanded baptism and the Lord's Supper as pictorial representations of Gospel truth.

- Images of God are *not* acceptable. For all of the reasons discussed above, the unseen God is not to be represented. With regard to the incarnate Son, we will consider that issue in more detail in the third section under this topic.

- Because of the ease with which people tend to venerate the place of worship itself, the danger always exists of decorative images becoming objects of veneration ("Don't you desecrate the Communion table by standing on it to change that light bulb in the ceiling!").

EDUCATION WITH IMAGES

For many Protestants, particularly those of the Reformed persuasion, the issue of the use of images for educational purposes has been a matter of considerable controversy. The educational use of images goes back at least as far as the Middle Ages, with Bible stories carved into the walls of Gothic cathedrals (along with gargoyles, of course) and processions on feast days including miracle, mystery and morality plays in which stories from the Bible were acted out. Many justified these practices by noting that an illiterate populace required visual forms of instruction. A similar argument is often heard today to justify the use of visual aids in the instruction of children (flannelgraph, illustrated take-home Sunday School papers, and videos of Bible stories) or those in preliterate cultures. Are such uses of images appropriate? Note the following:

- Again, the question of accuracy must be considered. Since we know little of what biblical characters looked like, are we creating false impressions in children by attempting to picture them? In a sense, this is not terribly important because it really matters little what Peter and David looked like, but visual images do create lasting impressions in impressionable minds.

- Many argue that, because children are not able to think abstractly, concrete images are essential in order for them to learn. Note that this argument cuts two ways. While children unquestionably learn better with visual stimuli, they are also unable to distinguish between symbol and reality.[26]

What of pictures of Jesus? He came in human form, and if cameras had existed in those days, someone could have taken and preserved a picture of Him. So why not use pictures today to teach people about the incarnate Son of God?

---

[26] One time my wife, very conscientious about not wanting to mislead young children in her class by her choice of visuals, used little Fisher-Price people to tell her Sunday School lesson; surely not even a child could mistake these for what people really looked like. She told a story from the life of Moses and the children seemed to enjoy and understand it. The next week, she tried again, this time with a story from the life of Elijah. She pulled out her box of Fisher-Price figures and began to tell the story: "Now, children, this is Elijah . . . " She was quickly interrupted with cries of protest - "But that's not Elijah; that's Moses!"

- Part of the problem here has to do with the paradox of the humanity and deity of Christ. God is not to be portrayed in visible form, yet Jesus was also fully man, and no such prohibition exists in regard to human beings. Note, however, that the issue of distortion remains, and is particularly important here.

- How many people's perceptions of Jesus have been formed by the famous paintings of Werner Sallman, in which Jesus appears with long, fair hair and a look that suggests He would not hurt a fly? Artists try to invest in Jesus what they value about His character. Can we argue that these do not deceive, and that the deceptions don't influence the thoughts of many?

- How often in recent years have many felt the necessity of picturing Jesus with secondary racial characteristics that match their own? After centuries of European Jesuses, we now have black Jesuses, Asian Jesuses, and Hispanic Jesuses. All of these subtly or not so subtly convey the idea that if Jesus is not like me, I cannot identify with Him. While the Incarnation did involve Jesus becoming like us, the important thing is not that we identify with Him, but that He identified with us, and this has nothing to do with external physical characteristics. Such portrayals focus attention on the wrong aspects of the Incarnation, and teach people that what makes Jesus worthy of our attention is how He *looked*.

- Movie portrayals are even worse in this regard. Here we have living, breathing actors attempting to portray the Son of God. This simply cannot be done in any way that even approximates the truth of who He is. Such visual representations, as is the case with paintings and drawings, tell us much more about the artist or director than they do about Jesus Himself.[27]

PURITY OF WORSHIP

If, as we already saw in the introduction to the chapter, the Second Commandment implies that God is only to be worshiped in the ways that He has commanded, exactly how much freedom do we have in how to approach Him? This was a particularly pressing question during the Protestant Reformation, largely because the medieval Catholic Church had incorporated so many unbiblical traditions into its worship that biblical worship was being buried under "smells and bells." What, the Reformers asked, was the kind of worship that truly pleased God?

THE REGULATIVE PRINCIPLE

Unfortunately, the Reformers were unable to agree on the answer to the question. When Martin Luther was in hiding after his death sentence at the Diet of Worms in 1521, the Reformation in Wittenberg was taken over by certain radical theologians who wanted to overturn the entirety of Roman Catholicism. They, like the Iconoclasts in the Byzantine Empire, went around smashing stained glass windows, "liberating" convents and monasteries, and giving relics a Christian burial, often with little attempt to avoid violence in the process. Luther, when he

---

[27] Even something as technically excellent as Mel Gibson's *The Passion of the Christ* overwhelms one with images of physical tortures, and in the process misses the heart of the Gospel, which is the spiritual suffering of Christ as He bore the wrath of God for His people.

heard about these things, quickly emerged from the Wartburg Castle and regained control of events. He concluded that the main focus of the Reformation ought to be biblical doctrine and preaching, and that the trappings of worship were secondary to the main issues. His approach was to argue that, while anything condemned in Scripture should of course be discarded and anything required in Scripture should be practiced, those things that the Bible doesn't mention - vestments, candles, chants, etc. - could without harm be retained. In other words, whatever is not forbidden in Scripture is permissible in worship.

The Swiss Reformers, most notably Ulrich Zwingli and John Calvin, disagreed. On the basis of passages like Deuteronomy 12:29-32 and Jesus' condemnation of the Pharisees' reliance on man-made traditions, they rejected any component of worship that was not specifically commanded in Scripture. The transitions from Catholicism to Reformed Christianity in Zurich and Geneva were generally peaceful, but the changes were significant. Not only were the places of worship shorn of all ornamentation and the worship itself streamlined to include only elements found in the Bible, but instrumental music was replaced by a capella congregational singing (the New Testament never mentions instruments). One of the consequences of this disagreement is that the Lutheran Church from its beginning remained closer to Catholicism than the churches that derive from the Reformed tradition, such as Presbyterians and Baptists. Such differences continue to be visible in the congregations within the two traditions today.

What are we to think about this dispute? When worshiping God, should anything not forbidden in Scripture be permitted, or should anything not commanded in Scripture be forbidden? We must first ask ourselves what Scripture actually commands in the worship of God. Note the following:

- The commands given in the Old Testament are excruciatingly detailed and explicit; much of the Pentateuch is occupied with instructions for worship. Thus when God told His people not to add anything to or take anything away from the prescribed forms of worship, they knew exactly what He meant. Even then, if we compare the Temple built by Solomon to the Tabernacle in the wilderness, we see a few differences, and not only in matters of scale (the basin in which the priests were to wash mounted on the backs of twelve bronze oxen?).

- There were at least two good reasons for God to prohibit strictly any alteration of the pattern He had revealed. First of all, the concern with idolatry was a very real one, as the Deuteronomy 12 passage makes obvious. God knew that if His people started getting creative with their worship they wouldn't be creative at all, but instead would copy the worship practices of the idolaters by whom they were surrounded.

- Secondly, we know from the New Testament, and especially from the book of Hebrews, that the particulars of the worship environment and practices were loaded with symbolism intended to point the people toward the work of the coming Messiah. Any change in the details of the worship environment or the worship itself would rob it of its teaching value and present a false picture of the redemptive work of Christ.

- The New Testament, on the other hand, gives virtually no details about how worship is to be carried out. No worship environment is specified - Christians are to worship "in spirit and in truth" wherever they are, whether in the Temple or in private homes. Practices to be carried out in worship, many borrowed from the Jewish synagogue, included preaching the Word (Acts 5:42), singing (Ephesians 5:19), reading the Scriptures (Luke 4:16-19), taking an offering (I Corinthians 16:1-2), prayer (Acts 12:12), baptism (Matthew 28:19-20), and Communion (I Corinthians 11:23-26). Even these are often seen only by example rather than by command. How, where, and when these are to be done is not revealed.

- The paucity of detail in the New Testament has its reasons, as well. New Testament worship is in many ways backward-looking - the focal point of human history has already come. We no longer need detailed pictures to focus our minds on that as-yet-unknown future event that will change everything. Thus we find liberty in the ways worship is offered to God; detailed restrictions are no longer necessary. The only way New Testament worship looks forward is that it anticipates the Second Coming - "As often as you eat this bread and drink the cup, you proclaim the Lord's death until he comes."

What, then, does the Regulative Principle (the name given to Calvin's position) mean for Christians today, if anything? Certainly we still need to care about worshiping God in ways that please Him rather than ways that please ourselves. Perhaps the best way to approach the question is to recognize that, while God has told us in general terms *what* we ought to be doing in worship as New Testament believers, He has not told us *how* to do it. We must preach - we are not free to eliminate preaching in favor of dramatic presentations or movies, for instance, but we are not told when, how often, or how long (at least not unless one considers Paul's sermon at Troas in Acts 20:7 normative!). We are told to pray, but postures may vary. We are told to sing, but are given little information about the nature of the songs or the music (but see below). In short, I would suggest that we must do the things the New Testament prescribes by command and example, and are not free to invent our own ways of worshiping God, but that we have great liberty in the ways in which these basic acts of worship are carried out. Furthermore, Christians should not criticize or condemn one another over differences in the way such acts of worship are offered up to God (see discussion of the adiaphora in Chapter 1).

EXCLUSIVE PSALMODY

One rather extreme example of the application of the Regulative Principle is found in the practice of exclusive psalmody that is found in some Reformed churches. These churches believe that worshiping God only as He has commanded implies that we must only offer up to Him in worship the words that He has revealed. In other words, singing should only include inspired lyrics, i.e., the Psalms. Worshiping God with words of our own composition is tantamount to presenting our offerings on an altar of hewn stones (Exodus 20:25). Exclusive psalmodists also shun instrumental music, as did the Swiss Reformers, because instruments are not mentioned in the New Testament. How are we to respond to this?

- Song is a form of teaching (Colossians 3:16), and thus, like preaching, is not restricted to the recitation of Scripture.
- Worship in the New Testament was not restricted to psalms (Ephesians 5:19).
- Those who practice exclusive psalmody use metrical translations that in most cases are loose paraphrases of the Psalms. Do these qualify as offering God's words back to Him?

- What about the fact that the Psalms sometimes designate tunes to which they are to be sung (e.g., Psalms 22, 45)?
- How can one claim to practice New Testament worship without focusing on Christ? Those who sing psalms speak of Christ only in those psalms containing Messianic prophecies.
- The New Testament contains what are probably songs of worship used in the first-century church, such as Philippians 2:5-11, which is in poetic form.

CHRISTIAN HOLIDAYS

Another aspect of the whole question of worshiping God as He desires to be worshiped concerns Christian holidays. Important holidays on which we recognize central redemptive events in the life of Christ are, after all, not commanded in Scripture. In fact, those who adhered closely to the Regulative Principle rejected holidays like Christmas and Easter. In Puritan New England, taking off work to celebrate the "pagan holiday" of Christmas was an offense punishable by time in the stocks. Today, groups like Jehovah's Witnesses refuse to celebrate not only Christmas and Easter, but birthdays as well. Before considering appropriate conclusions, we ought to spend a little time examining where these holidays came from; this will, if nothing else, help us to understand better why some devout Christians over the years have found them objectionable.

EASTER

The oldest annual festival of the church is Easter, which we know was observed by the middle of the second century, and probably much earlier. The church originally commemorated the resurrection of Christ by changing the day of worship from Saturday, the Jewish Sabbath, to Sunday, although many of the early Jewish Christian congregations continued to observe both days. As the church became predominantly Gentile, Sunday worship became the rule, and Constantine, the first Christian emperor, made Sunday an official holiday shortly after his accession to power. The annual celebration of the resurrection first comes to our attention because of a dispute concerning its date. Apparently the churches in Asia Minor celebrated Easter on the fourteenth day of the Jewish month Nisan, the beginning of the Jewish Passover, no matter what day of the week this happened to be, and claimed that such a practice had been initiated by the apostle John. The churches in the rest of the empire celebrated Easter on the following Sunday, insisting that Jesus had risen on a Sunday, and therefore Easter should be observed on a Sunday. The two observances survived side by side until 190, when Victor, the bishop of Rome, tried to assert his authority and force the churches of Asia Minor to do things his way. This dispute, known as the Quartodeciman Controversy (from the Latin word for "fourteen"), was the first instance in which the bishop of Rome tried to exercise authority over other churches. Though his position eventually became that of the church at large (Easter is now celebrated on the first Sunday after the first full moon after the vernal equinox), he was strongly rebuffed for his efforts to throw his weight around.

Easter early became the time of year in which people were baptized into the church, since baptism symbolizes the death and resurrection of Christ. It was preceded by a period of intense instruction, and often by fasting. The whole congregation would generally join the catechumens in their fast to demonstrate the unity of the people of God. This fast would typically last during the forty hours between Christ's death on Friday and His resurrection on Sunday morning. Gradually this practice of pre-baptismal fasting developed into the observance of Lent - a forty-day partial fast in place of a forty-hour complete one, now often associated with the forty days Christ fasted in the wilderness before being tempted by Satan. Other practices and symbols associated with Easter came to the church by way of the barbarian tribes that were converted to Christianity. They brought with them fertility symbols such as eggs and rabbits that were quickly adapted to the Christian festival as signs of new life in Christ.

CHRISTMAS

The celebration of the birth of Christ was a later development. No one in the early church ever claimed to know when Christ was born, which made it a little difficult to celebrate the event. In fact, we don't even know the *year* of Jesus' birth.[28] In any case, accuracy was eventually overcome by more pressing issues, and the church gradually began to celebrate Jesus' birth. After the conversion of Constantine, hordes of people had flocked into the church because it suddenly became the popular thing to do. These new converts understood little of the faith, and like the later barbarians, continued many of their pagan practices. Among these was the Saturnalia, the birthday of the Immortal Sun - a celebration of the winter solstice. To keep these semi-pagans from partying in the streets, the church set up something constructive to compete with the general party atmosphere, much as some churches today plan "harvest festivals" or Reformation Day parties for their children and young people on October 31. It was for this reason that the date of December 25, which also happened to be the birthday of the god of the popular Mithra cult, was chosen. As with Easter, the celebration gradually became encumbered with all sorts of pagan elements, including the giving of gifts, borrowed from the Saturnalia but justified by the gifts of the wise men.

HALLOWEEN

The situation with Halloween is quite different. The name of the observance is a contraction of "All Hallows' Eve" - the night before All Saints' Day. As the concept of sainthood grew in the Catholic Church and days were set aside to honor different saints, the Church soon ran out of days in the year. In order to avoid leaving anyone out and thus missing the blessing associated with honoring him or her, the Church decided to designate a day on which all saints were to be honored; the date chosen was November 1. During the superstitious Middle Ages, it was thought that Satan and his minions were particularly active on the night before such a holy celebration, so special precautions needed to be taken to scare them away (thus jack-o-lanterns). Like Easter and Christmas, pagan accretions soon followed. Fall harvest festival rites associated with pagan groups like the Druids were soon incorporated into the observance, giving it the occult flavor it continues to have today.

---

[28] The present calendar was devised by Dionysius Exiguus in the early Middle Ages. The information available to him was inadequate. According to the best guess by scholars today, Jesus was born in 6 BC; we know that Herod the great died in 4 BC, and his instructions concerning the slaughter of the babies of Bethlehem add two years to that date.

We again are faced with the basic question, "How should we respond to these things?" Note the following:

- Celebrating holidays that are not commanded in Scripture is not in itself sinful. In John 10:22, we are told that Jesus came to Jerusalem for the Feast of Dedication, and was in the Temple. This feast, today known as Hanukkah, originated in the Intertestamental Period, and was not commanded by God. Yet Jesus apparently had no problem celebrating it. Thus we must conclude that festivals like Easter and Christmas may not be rejected out of hand on the basis of the Regulative Principle as the Puritans did.

- The issue of the origins of Easter, and particularly Christmas, along with their later pagan accretions, needs to be considered. Should we give gifts at Christmas and stage Easter egg hunts at Easter if these practices have their roots in paganism? Many suggest that the focus of our attention should be not so much on the origins of these things as on their meaning now. Certainly one can give God heartfelt worship for the birth, death, and resurrection of His Son without getting all caught up in the materialistic trappings of the seasons. And make no mistake, the pagan accretions of today have much more to do with materialism than they do with the fertility observances of ancient barbarian tribesmen. Charles Dickens may have concluded that Ebenezer Scrooge "knew how to keep Christmas well, if any man alive possessed the knowledge," but his Christmas was a celebration of family camaraderie and material blessing from which Christ was mostly absent. Our greatest temptation is to do the same.

- Halloween is a completely different story. For the Bible-believing Christian, there is no such thing as "keeping Halloween well." The tradition of veneration of saints from which it sprang and the occult trappings that are so central to the celebration even today make it difficult to argue for any participation on the part of the believer. For those who think it "innocent fun," remember what we noted earlier concerning the dangers of being drawn gradually and imperceptibly into the realm of the occult.

- In conclusion, what Paul says when dealing with indifferent matters in Romans 14:5-13, which to him includes observance of special days, should guide our thinking and practice. Our own choices should be made "unto the Lord" rather than according to the culture or our own ideas of fun, and we should deal in love with those believers who, out of a sincere desire to please God, make different choices.

CULTURAL ACCOMMODATION

The final question under the Second Commandment that we will consider is the extent to which culture should influence worship practices. This has been a significant problem, particularly as Christianity has spread among unbelieving cultures. To what extent should the religious and cultural practices of the Western European barbarians have been incorporated into their worship of Christ? Roman Catholicism, in the missionary work the Church did during the Age of Exploration, practiced levels of cultural accommodation with which most of us would be uncomfortable. In India, one missionary forged a Hindu holy book to convince those to whom he was preaching that the teachings of the Catholic Church had been taught centuries earlier by Hindu gurus. In Latin America, festivals dedicated to pagan goddesses continued to be observed, with the same statue that had been carried through the streets for generations now designated as the Virgin Mary. On the other hand, Protestant missionaries in the Golden Age of missionary expansion (and European imperialism) in the nineteenth century were often guilty of founding churches that looked, sounded, and functioned much like those back home in England, causing natives to conclude that Christianity was "the white man's religion" and leading critics to accuse the missionaries of cultural imperialism. How, then, should any culture, including our own, influence the way in which we worship God? Note the following:

- Culture *always* influences the way we worship God. If any of us were to go through a time warp back to the first century, we would find the house churches in Corinth looking, sounding, and functioning very differently than our Sunday morning worship services. We must then ask, not whether culture should influence worship, but how and to what extent.

- Distinguishing between the unalterable essence of the Christian faith and those aspects of it that are subject to varying cultural expression is vital. We cannot make decisions about cultural accommodation among those to whom we seek to minister if we do not first recognize the extent to which our own worship of God is a product of the culture in which we live.

- Rejection of sinful and unbiblical practices is mandatory. Every culture has sinful aspects to it, and living as a Christian means in those ways being countercultural. We should be just as concerned about eliminating materialism and secularism from the operation of our churches as we are about the danger of incorporating pagan practices into newly-planted churches on the mission field.

- Care must be taken to consider that a cultural adaptation that may seem perfectly acceptable to an outsider may be inappropriate to one inside the culture because of associations of which the missionary may not be aware. For example, playing drums in worship is not sinful in itself, but if in a given culture drums are associated with summoning evil spirits, one would not want to use them in the worship of God.

- It was in dealing with the question of cultural accommodation that Paul wrote I Corinthians 9:19-23 - "I have become all things to all people, that by all means I might save some."

As we conclude our study of the Second Commandment, the most important thing to remember is that we should consider God's desires in worship rather than our own. The questions raised here are ones that high school students rarely ask. We all need to ask them rather than simply engaging in the kind of worship that pleases ourselves.

4

THE CHRISTIAN AND GOD'S NAME

Exodus 20:7 - "You shall not take the name of the Lord your God in vain, for the Lord will not hold him guiltless who takes his name in vain."

James tells his readers that "anyone who does not stumble in what he says . . . is a perfect man" (James 3:2). Attempting to control what comes out of our mouths is a challenge for all of us, and it is also vitally important, both for pleasing God and in our relationships with others. Thus, as we turn to the study of the Bible's teachings concerning speech that honors God, we need to give special attention to what for most people is a source of daily sin and failure.

As we move on to consideration of the Third Commandment, we need to look briefly at the key words that make up this short verse. The main verb, translated "take," literally means "to lift up." The basic idea here is to put something on display. Though the focus of the Third Commandment is clearly on language, we should note from the beginning that the proscription is really much broader. After all, we put God's name on display by more than our words. Anyone who bears the name of Christ puts His name on display in everything he does simply by virtue of that profession. We must therefore recognize that all we do has a bearing on the reputation of Christ in the world, and should be a matter for our concern.

Secondly, the commandment speaks of the name of God. In our modern culture, many people have no idea why they have the names they do or what those names mean. Often, names are chosen because parents like the sound, even to the point of making up names that have no meaning at all. This was not the case in Bible times. Then, names had great significance. In many ways, names were thought to define a person's character, so that the father was believed to be exercising a prophetic function when he named his child. Think of some of the names in Scripture that were intended to speak of character or special birth circumstances: Adam, not surprisingly, means "man"; Isaac, because of his mother's response to the announcement of his coming birth, means "laughter"; Esau was "hairy," while Jacob was "a supplanter"; Moses was "drawn from the water," while Joshua, the leader of the Conquest, was named "the Lord delivers" - a name shared with Jesus; Barnabas was "the son of consolation."

We also find in Scripture that names are given to exert authority in redefining who a person is. God changed Abram ("Ram is my father") to Abraham ("father of many") and Jacob to Israel ("a prince with God"); Jesus changed Simon to Peter ("the rock"), and promised to give all who belong to Him a new name (Revelation 2:17). Pagan rulers also tried to redefine followers of God when they brought them into their courts - Joseph was renamed by Pharaoh (Genesis 41:45), and

Daniel and his three friends were given new names by Nebuchadnezzar's chief of the eunuchs (Daniel 1:7).

Why is this important to our understanding of the Third Commandment?

- God's name is inseparable from God's character. His names, given throughout Scripture, tell us who He is. Misuse of the name of God is an insult to His character, and disrespect for His character is a violation of His name.
- When the names of God appear in Scripture, they are always revealed rather than given by people. Only God has the right to define Himself; we have no such privilege.

The Third Commandment refers specifically to the name "of the Lord." The name used here is יהוה - Yahweh, also known as the Tetragrammaton. The interpretation of this command by the Jewish rabbis gives interesting insight into Jewish thought, and also sheds light on how we are to apply the Third Commandment. Rather than seeing in the Third Commandment an insistence that God's name should be treated with respect in all its forms, rabbinical scholars saw here an indication that this particular name of God was more sacred than all others, and thus was to be treated with special reverence. Jewish commentators also practiced what they called "fencing the law." The basic idea behind this effort was that the best way to keep someone from breaking a law was to make sure he would never get himself into a position where he could even think of doing so (this practice was the source of many of the unbiblical traditions of the Pharisees of which Jesus was so critical).

With regard to the sacred name of Yahweh, the fence constructed by the rabbis was a fairly simple one - the best way to avoid using the name improperly is not to use it at all! Thus Jews were taught that the name Yahweh was too holy to pass human lips. Even when the Scriptures were read in the synagogue, Yahweh was replaced by Adonai, another of God's names, whenever it appeared in the text.[29] Furthermore, scribes who were copying the Scriptures had to use a fresh pen whenever they wrote the holy Name and discard it immediately afterward. A reflection of this practice of replacing the name of God with other words may be seen in Matthew 5:34-36, which we will discuss at considerable length later in the chapter. Needless to say, Jesus' criticisms of such an overly literal approach to the commandment indicate the breadth with which it should be interpreted and applied. All of God's names are to be equally held in reverence, as are all the ways in which He reveals Himself to man and displays His glory in His creation.

The last key word in the Third Commandment involves the use of God's name that is forbidden - it is not to be lifted up "in vain." What does this mean? When we use the word *vanity*

---

[29] This practice had an interesting and unexpected consequence. When the Hebrew language began to pass out of common use, scholars introduced vowel points - diacritical markings around the consonants in which the Hebrew language is written to indicate proper pronunciation. In connection with this, the vowel points for Adonai were placed around the consonants for Yahweh to remind readers to make the substitution. Centuries later, when Christian scholars discovered ancient Jewish copies of the Bible, they were not aware of what had been done and thought that the consonants of Yahweh accompanied by the vowels of Adonai actually made up a Hebrew word. When they tried to pronounce the result, what they got was "Jehovah," which is not a Hebrew word at all.

today, we usually mean pride or conceit. In Scripture, however, the term refers instead to emptiness or meaninglessness (cf. Ecclesiastes 1:2; 2:1,11). It can also refer to falsehood (Leviticus 19:12), or even serve as an oblique way of speaking of false gods (Psalm 24:4). What does it mean to use God's name in a meaningless way? Certainly we ought not to use it "for emphasis" - the application of the Third Commandment with which we are most familiar. But do we not also use the name of God in a meaningless way when we speak it without paying any attention to what we are saying - when we sing praises to God with our minds a thousand miles away, or when the name of God becomes little more than punctuation in our prayers ("Oh, Lord, I thank you so much, Lord, for being who you are, Lord, and I pray, Lord, that you would hear the petitions we bring before you today, Lord . . . "). Thus the commandment requires that we shun not only swearing, but the perfunctory use of God's name with little thought when we are engaged in prayer and worship.

OATHS AND VOWS

While the Third Commandment has a broad application to all our speech, the specific practice that the commandment addresses is the practice of swearing oaths and vows. The circumstance in which the Lord's name was most frequently "lifted up" in ancient Israel was when someone called upon God to bear witness to a promise or to the truthfulness of a statement. We must then consider this application of the commandment before we proceed to broader issues of language.

THE PROPRIETY OF OATHS AND VOWS

Some who take the Bible seriously have problems with the use of God's name in swearing oaths and taking vows because of Jesus' words on the subject in the Sermon on the Mount. He addresses the issue in Matthew 5:33-37, and His words include the rather clear statement, "Do not take an oath at all" (cf. James 5:12). Some groups such as Anabaptists, Quakers, and Jehovah's Witnesses have concluded as a result of this that any oath-taking is a sin against God, even to the point of refusing to take oaths in court.

Is this how Jesus intended us to respond to His words? Not at all. The rest of Scripture indicates that oaths, rightly taken, are right and proper. God Himself takes oaths (Genesis 22:16; Psalm 110:4; Hebrews 6:17-18), He requires oaths (Deuteronomy 6:13; 10:20), and Paul often swore to the veracity of what he said (Romans 1:9; II Corinthians 1:23; Philippians 1:8; I Thessalonians 2:5, 10). God even made provision for people to take the Nazirite Vow (Numbers 6:1-21), and several biblical figures did so, including Samson (Judges 13:5), probably John the Baptist (Luke 1:15), and Paul again (Acts 18:18). Clearly, then, what is being prohibited by Jesus is not any taking of oaths at all, but doing so in some inappropriate manner (see below).

THE SANCTITY OF OATHS AND VOWS

If oaths and vows are permissible, the Bible also indicates that they are to be taken very seriously. One who swears an oath or takes a vow is required to keep it (Numbers 30:2;

Deuteronomy 23:21-23; Joshua 9:18; Ecclesiastes 5:4-5, which speaks of an oath-breaker as a fool; Zechariah 8:17, which says that God hates those who swear falsely). Note that Psalm 15:4 goes even further in its characterization of the man of integrity who is honored by God, describing him as one "who swears to his own hurt and does not change." The natural conclusion we should draw from this is that one should be very cautious about making promises, since the future is not under our control (cf. James 4:13-16) - the phrase "God willing" should not be an empty cliche, but a recognition of God's sovereignty and our utter dependence on Him to fulfill the simplest of our plans and promises. Too often we go back on a previous promise because something more attractive comes along. We call back a friend and cancel plans, or beg off from going to work, or rescind an invitation because we like the new opportunity better. But if God honors someone who keeps his promise even when it hurts, we should not so blithely make such changes in plans.[30]

THE ABUSE OF OATHS AND VOWS

How, then, are we to understand Jesus' seeming prohibition of oaths in Matthew 5? In order to answer that question, we must remember the context, which clarifies what Jesus was trying to accomplish in the latter part of Matthew 5. In verses 17-20, Jesus is responding to an unstated accusation that He was contradicting or nullifying the Old Testament law. He states in no uncertain terms that He is doing no such thing; He is fulfilling it, while the righteousness of the scribes and Pharisees falls far short. His intention is not to "relax" God's commands, but to expand the understanding of them to include matters of the heart as well as outward behavior. When Jesus uses the words, "You have heard that it was said to those of old," He is not saying that the Old Testament law was wrong and He is about to correct it. Instead, He is contradicting the rabbis' *interpretation* and *application* of the law and telling the people what it *really* means.

Thus we must ask ourselves, as we will do frequently in the course of this book, what is the mistaken rabbinical teaching that Jesus is contradicting, and what is the true interpretation of the commandment with which He is replacing it? In the case of the Third Commandment, the issue was a hierarchy of oaths devised by the Pharisees. They argued that the sacredness of an oath depended on that by which it was sworn. Thus, while one should never speak the sacred name of Yahweh, oaths sworn by other names of God were of the utmost seriousness. On the other hand, if one swore instead by heaven, the earth, Jerusalem, the Temple, his own head, or, in modern parlance, "crossed his heart and hoped to die," the oath was decreasingly binding according to the importance of that by which the oath was sworn.

Now imagine how you would respond, if you lived in that society, to someone who said to you, "Could I please borrow a shekel for a hamburger (or perhaps falafel) for lunch. I swear by my own right hand to pay you back next Tuesday." You could probably count on waving your shekel goodbye. In other words, the hierarchy of oaths became in the hands of the teachers of the law nothing more than a pretext for breaking one's word. As a consequence, anyone who sought

---

[30] An extreme example of one who "swears to his own hurt and does not change" is Jephthah, who in Judges 11:29-40 foolishly promised to sacrifice the first thing that met him when he got home if God gave him victory in battle, and wound up sacrificing his own daughter - a difficult incident that would require more time for discussion than we have here.

to affirm a promise by swearing an oath, unless he swore by the name of God, tended to generate suspicion rather than confidence. This was why Jesus told His followers not to swear at all, but simply to be known as men of their word.

What gives us the right to interpret these words within a cultural context and conclude that, when Jesus said "Do not take an oath at all," He really meant, "You are allowed to take oaths as long as you don't use them as an excuse for deception"? The reason is simple - the numerous examples of acceptable oaths given above. The Bible does not contradict itself, and that foundational truth must always guide us in our interpretation of difficult passages and seeming discrepancies, allowing us to bring the complete teaching of God's Word to bear on confusing or uncertain passages.

THE MARRIAGE VOW

Besides the oath taken in a court of law, marriage is probably the vow with which high school students are most familiar. When two people get married, they swear an oath of fidelity to one another before God (Malachi 2:13-16). This oath, as all other oaths mentioned in Scripture, is of the utmost seriousness and is not to be broken (the fact that some sins are of such a serious character as to dissolve the covenant is a matter to be considered under the Seventh Commandment). The thing to remember here is that "for better or for worse" means that God honors one who keeps his oath even when it hurts. Contrary to the prevailing attitude in our society, marriage vows cannot easily be dismissed or disregarded when people or circumstances change, when spouses get tired of one another, or when the grass seems to be greener on the other side of the fence.

The seriousness of the marriage vow is a very important part of preserving any marriage. Beyond the obvious fact that one who takes a vow seriously will determine to keep it no matter what, the marriage vow plays a key role in resolving marital conflicts. After all, if one has the attitude that "I'm in this for life," he will approach conflicts with the recognition that things have to be worked out no matter what it takes because there is no way of escaping the promise that has been made. On the other hand, one who considers the marriage vow flexible will confront conflict with the attitude, "Well, we'll try to work things out, but if not, perhaps we would be better off going our separate ways." Thus every conflict is a potential marriage-buster, and the alternative of divorce hangs over every argument and dispute. One who does not give marriage vows the seriousness they deserve is thus setting himself up for divorce before the marriage even begins.

PURITY OF LANGUAGE

The application of the Third Commandment that most frequently comes to the minds of Christians is the matter of purity of language - to most, it means that Christians should not curse. As we consider this aspect of the Third Commandment in more detail, however, we should first note that the prohibition against misuse of God's name also implies a positive command - that speech is to be used for edification rather than destruction (Ephesians 4:29). Honoring God with our speech doesn't just mean avoiding bad language, but also speaking to build others up.

THE LORD'S NAME

Everyone understands that the Third Commandment forbids the use of God's name "for emphasis," but why is this so? Clearly, exclamations that involve the name of God "take His name in vain" because the speaker is not thinking of God at all, but is merely expressing emotion, whether positive or negative, strong or as part of everyday speech patterns. Though this may be obvious, such language has become so deeply ingrained in the surrounding culture that even many Christians say "O my God!" when something surprises them without a second thought. This ought not to be; it is a direct violation of the Third Commandment, but is certainly not the only way in which God's name is dishonored by people's words.

CIRCUMLOCUTIONS

Some people who try to be sensitive to God's prohibition think to avoid the problem by the use of minced oaths or circumlocutions. These occur when an offensive word is replaced by another word that sounds similar (because it is a corrupted form of the original) and means the same thing, but is considered more socially acceptable. Examples would include saying *gosh* or *golly* instead of *God*, *gee* or *geez* instead of *Jesus*, *heck* instead of *hell*, or *darn* instead of *damn*. But do these really absolve one of the guilt of taking God's name in vain? Jesus' comments to His followers in Matthew 5:33-37 indicate that merely substituting another word for the name of God in no way lessens the seriousness of what is being said; this is especially true when the word that is being substituted is derived from the word the speaker is trying to avoid and means the same thing. The English language is rich enough to allow people to express their emotions without calling on God's name or some variation thereof to do so.

Fine, some of my students respond, that explains why we should try to break our long-standing habits of speech that really involve subtle insults to God's name (sadly, most make no effort to change such speech patterns, while others pay lip-service to the need but make no serious effort to alter their expressions), but what about words like *heck* or *darn*? They don't have anything to do with God's name. They may not be names of God, but they speak of spiritual realities that should not be taken lightly. One who really believes in an eternal Hell to which all who reject Christ will be consigned will not lightly speak of it, or of sending people there. Any who do so minimize the seriousness of God's judgment.

EXCLAMATIONS

By this point in the discussion, my students are usually starting to get frustrated. "Well, what *can* we say then?" is the typical response, as if somehow my teaching threatens to deprive them of the bulk of their vocabulary. Obviously, many words exist in the English language for the purposes of expressing emotion. Exclamations are many and varied, and most involve no blasphemy or vulgarity (see below). How, then, should we evaluate biblically expressions of emotion such as *Good grief!* (Charlie Brown's favorite), *Rats!*, or *Fiddlesticks!* When dealing with the use of exclamations, two aspects must be considered. The first is the meaning of the word being used, and the second is the emotion being expressed. If the word is for one reason or another sinful, no acceptable emotion can justify the use of it as an exclamation. If the word itself is harmless (or even meaningless), the exclamation must be judged solely on the basis of the emotion being expressed - if it is godly and edifying, then the exclamation is acceptable; if not, then it should be avoided. Thus the Christian need not stifle his emotions for fear of accidentally blurting out something sinful, but should seek God's help to regulate his speech so that the words that come from his mouth honor God and build up others.

VULGARITY

While Ephesians 4:29 clearly rules out the use of any "corrupting talk," this becomes a bit more difficult to define when we move to the subject of vulgarity. The problem here is that vulgarity is culturally conditioned - it varies from place to place and from one time in history to another (the KJV translation of I Samuel 25:22 gives one example of language that was considered acceptable in 1611 but is thought vulgar now). While the Bible is quite clear about avoiding misuse of the names of God, it doesn't provide for us a list of words that constitute "corrupting talk."

First of all, the subject matter of vulgarity is generally derived from two aspects of human experience - sexual and excretory functions. Words describing these universal aspects of human existence are considered vulgar because such things are by their very nature private, and ought not to be mentioned in polite conversation; the culture defines them as "unmentionables." Yet not all words for the same body parts or functions are considered equally vulgar. One can speak calmly of excrement or talk about a baby pooping in his diaper, but other words for the same thing ought not be spoken by one who seeks to practice pure speech and edify those around him. Similarly, one may discuss sexual intercourse in a clinical fashion without embarrassment, but we all know that certain other words for the same behavior simply ought not to be said. Why is this true? Why should one spelling for an idea be condemned while another is accepted? Does this make any sense at all?

Again, we must turn to the culture for an explanation. In English, the vital distinction goes back to the Norman Conquest in the eleventh century. When William the Conqueror won the Battle of Hastings in 1066, the Normans settled in England and became the new aristocracy, reducing the native Anglo-Saxons to serfdom. Over time, through living together and as a result of intermarriage, the two peoples merged into one, as did their languages.[31] The original class distinction was preserved, however, in the way synonyms were treated. When speaking of almost anything, those with wealth and education would naturally use words with Latin roots, while the peasants would favor Anglo-Saxon. As far as words for sensitive subjects were concerned, the way the Norman French talked about such things was "polite," while the words used by the serfs were common or "vulgar."[32] Thus the words considered vulgar are defined as such because of the roots from which they came hundreds of years ago.

---

[31] This is why the English language has such a large vocabulary - almost everything can be said in at least two ways, derived from both Latin and Anglo-Saxon roots.

[32] Check it out in a dictionary. The rude words always have Anglo-Saxon roots, while the polite ones come from the Latin.

The obvious question that arises at this point is, "Why should our language be limited by the sensitivities of the medieval English aristocracy? Such distinctions mean nothing today!" This may well be true, but the identification of these words as vulgar continues to characterize the larger social consciousness, no matter how freely such words enter popular conversation and the media today. The issue is not whether the identification of such words as vulgar is legitimate; the only matter the Christian should care about is avoiding offensive speech, no matter why it might be offensive.

Another frequent response is, "But such words are part of the culture in my neighborhood. Everybody talks that way and thinks nothing of it; no one gets offended by such language." Besides telling such respondents to ask their mothers if they agree with such sentiments, I always note that we live in a culture that is much broader than our families, our neighborhoods, or our racial or ethnic groups. Our constant desire should be to make our speech as honoring to God as possible, completely devoid of offense, rather than seeking justifications for speaking like everyone else or getting as close to the line of sinful speech as possible.

TEASING AND RIDICULE

What about humor at the expense of others? Surely such sarcastic and hurtful speech is unedifying and fails to show love to our neighbors. Yet much of the interaction that occurs among teens (but not only teens) is of this variety, encouraged and presented as a source of entertainment by the vast majority of the dialogue in television situation comedies. Why do people seem to take pleasure in such speech? In many cases it stems from following bad examples in the media, but it also often has its roots in personal insecurity - I can somehow feel better about myself if I can get people to laugh at what I say and bring someone else down in the process. Yet some still seek to justify it. Note the following:

- "It's just done in fun. Nobody takes it seriously, and no one is hurt by it. Lighten up!" In some cases this may be true, but the fact is that we never know how our words affect others. Someone who seems to have no trouble laughing when others make fun of him may be hiding pain inside him, and this pain may shape his outlook on life and himself for years to come, and no one will ever know it.[33]
- "Criticism administered through humor is kinder than direct confrontation." Attitudes like this show why teasing is often so hurtful - those who profess to mean nothing by it really have a hidden agenda, and mean exactly what they say. Besides, the Bible advocates honest confrontation and constructive criticism (Matthew 18:15; Galatians 6:1), not subtle messages that may hurt without helping. Teasing as disguised criticism is really the coward's way out grounded in the fear of man, shows no respect for the ability of the other person to accept criticism, and assumes that I know better than God does about how to deal with people.

---

[33] I grew up in a large family, and brotherly banter was part of the normal routine around the house. Not until my youngest brother, who naturally was the target of many of the barbs, reached adulthood was he willing to admit how hurtful those interchanges "just in fun" had been.

HUMOR

In Umberto Eco's mystery novel *The Name of the Rose*, an elderly monk named Jorge of Burgos argues that humor is sin because Jesus never laughed, and because it teaches people not to take life seriously. Certainly not all humor is vulgar or blasphemous, nor is it found in ridicule and putting others down. What about humor in general? Is it something that can be edifying?

WHAT IS HUMOR?

Humor derives from many sources, but the foundational one is incongruity. We find things funny when they simply don't fit, or when they go contrary to our expectations. Humor also takes the forms of exaggeration (verbal or visual), plays on words such as puns (Shakespeare used these with great frequency), or slapstick, where pratfalls and incidents that in normal life would be harmful are funny because we know they are not (e.g., the Three Stooges). Why we laugh at such things is basically unknown - scientists and psychologists have tried to figure it out, but have been unable to do so. They have determined, however, that laughter is good for our physical and emotional health (e.g., the scene in *Mary Poppins* where the supremely serious bankers begin floating toward the ceiling when they begin to laugh), though the nature of that humor differs widely from one culture to another.

THE BIBLE USES HUMOR

Scripture gives no warrant for the dismal conclusions of Jorge of Burgos. The Bible uses humor for a variety of purposes. Note the following:

- Jesus used hyperbole (Mark 10:25) when illustrating the negative impact of riches on a person's spiritual life.
- The description of the fate of the seven sons of Sceva in Acts 19:14-16 is an example of visual slapstick, though one could hardly argue that the pain in the story was not real.
- Jesus (Matthew 16:18) and Paul (Philemon 11) used puns, and Scripture contains many other examples of plays on words in its poetic passages.
- Sarcasm was sometimes a weapon of choice for the prophets of God when they ridiculed wicked kings or idolaters (I Kings 18:27; 22:15-16; Isaiah 44:9-20).
- God Himself is said to laugh at the folly and pretensions of the wicked (Psalm 2:4; 37:13; 59:8).
- Passages such as Ephesians 5:4 and James 4:9 refer to vulgar humor and frivolity when solemnity is called for, and should not be seen as condemnations of humor in general.

CHRISTIAN USE OF HUMOR

How, then, should Christians approach the question of humor?

- Vulgarity, blasphemy, and verbal put-downs are not suitable sources of humor for the Christian. We should neither speak in such ways nor encourage those who do by our responses, nor should we seek out such humor as a form of entertainment.

- Incongruity is beneficial in pointing out the reality that we live in a fallen world where things simply "don't fit." Such humor has the serious purpose of exposing sin, making us look clearly at the absurdity of a sinful world, and encouraging us to long for the perfection we can never find in a life made foolish by the Fall.
- Wickedness deserves to be held up to ridicule. God and His prophets did it, and we should not be afraid to show in humorous ways the follies of the world around us.

LITERATURE AND DRAMA

We have concentrated most of our attention under the Third Commandment thus far on the words we speak. But what about other uses of language? If the Christian is not to let certain words pass his lips, what about his eyes and ears? In the final section of this chapter we will consider the application of the Bible's teaching about language to what we read, to participation in dramatic performances, and to the use of language in creative writing.

READING

The basic question here is, "Should a Christian read a work of literature that contains sinful language?" Note that the same fundamental principles apply to music to which one would listen and television and movies one chooses to watch. After all, if we are to think on those things that are honorable, just, pure, lovely, commendable, excellent, and praiseworthy (Philippians 4:8), does this not rule out filling our minds with what is vulgar, blasphemous, and dishonoring to God? Several points should be noted here:

- It is impossible to isolate oneself from the sinful world (I Corinthians 5:9-10). Jesus surely heard plenty of unsavory language when He mingled with tax collectors and sinners, and He did not for that reason shun their company.
- Benefits are to be gained from knowledge of the world and its ways of thinking. Shared cultural experiences can provide openings for conversation that might lead to opportunities to present the Gospel, knowledge of how the world views life can equip a Christian to speak into that perspective, and Christians can appreciate the literary or cinematic talents God has given to unbelievers and praise God for them.
- Note that each of the comments above implies *purposeful* interaction with the works of the world. Jesus didn't hang around with publicans and sinners because He thought they were fun guys.
- The above also imply *critical* interaction with the world. One of the great dangers of quality literature (or even bad literature) is that we are drawn into the action and language and absorb the worldview and values of the author without even being aware of it.
- Christians should not take pleasure in what is vile and blasphemous. If you can sit down and enjoy a movie or a book filled with sex and bad language, you need to ask yourself about your values and what your heart really seeks after.
- Saturation with evil is to be avoided. Sometimes exposure to evil for good reasons can be justified, but the line is soon crossed where we are influenced by the images we see, read, and hear. The old computer adage GIGO - "garbage in, garbage out" - is relevant here

(How bizarre that one could speak of a computer adage as *old*!). What we put into our minds will stay there (despite the fact that what we study for a test never seems to), and eventually help to shape our thinking and behavior.

- Not everyone will make the same decisions about what movies to watch or what books to read. Different people are sensitive to different things. One person may be able to read a book with one sex scene and skim over it with little effect, while another may, after finishing the book, remember nothing else. Some can distance themselves from the impact of what they read, see, or hear and give a biblical critique, while others become so emotionally involved that critical thinking becomes virtually impossible. Knowing yourself, your strengths and weaknesses, and being honest about your besetting sins is vital if you are to please God in this area.

PARTICIPATION

This question is of particular interest to me since I started acting in school productions in high school and continued through college, and have for more than thirty years directed plays at The Christian Academy. This question consequently has been one with which I have had to deal frequently from a variety of perspectives.

The standard argument here is that the conventions of the stage require one to separate the actor from the character, and thus the actor ought to speak in the way the character speaks, even if the character uses language that the actor would never use outside the environment of the play. To do anything else would be dishonest, both to the artistry of the playwright and to the reality of the character. And besides, if an actor can act out a murder on stage without being a murderer, why should we not conclude the same about blasphemy? As both an actor and director, however, I have refused to use bad language or ask others to do so. My reasoning, with which my actors are very familiar, is as follows:

- Divorcing himself from the character he plays is not easy for an actor. If this were not the case, why then do so many star actors and actresses wind up having affairs with those with whom they do love scenes in a play or movie? Some directors even advocate "method acting," where identification with the character is encouraged and the actor is taught to "get into" the part so far that he feels what the character feels, thus allowing the dialogue to flow naturally from within.
- Swearing is the only sin that cannot be portrayed on the stage without committing it. One who acts out a murder on stage can do it without murdering; the same is true with theft, anger, ridicule, or slander. But blasphemy is by its very nature a sin of the spoken word, and one simply cannot swear on stage without swearing.
- Audiences typically view plays only once, but actors practice, sometimes for months, to pound their lines into their heads. Every year when we finish a play, the cast members have a tendency to spout lines from the script at every opportune (or sometimes inopportune) moment in class or in the hallway. This is called saturation, and the warnings above apply. We ought to be careful about what we impress upon our minds.
- The idea of separating character from actor on the part of the audience is fine in professional theater or in movies, but is not as likely where my students live. Whether in

high school or college, many in the audience know the actors personally, and when a certain character does something unexpected (like kiss on stage, which always draws a reaction), the audience sees the actor, not just the character. Because of this, what an actor does on stage can easily have an impact on his testimony, especially if he is on a secular campus and is known to be a Christian. Such a person should never risk being seen to speak out of two sides of his mouth if he wishes to honor Christ.

- Other aspects of this issue are even more difficult. For instance, should a Christian accept a part in a play containing blasphemous language if his part does not? The intrinsic worth of a play and the amount of bad language are factors that need to be considered here (e.g., Shakespeare's *Macbeth*), though not all will make the same decisions.[34]

WRITING

What about a Christian who is a creative writer? Should he include sinful language in a novel or short story in order to give a faithful portrayal of the character and his environment? This is difficult question, but the following should be noted:

- The Bible accurately records examples of blasphemy in the mouths of the godless (Genesis 4:23-24; Psalm 14:1; Matthew 12:24), and of course in the words of Satan (Genesis 3:4-5). The length of the list in the previous sentence also indicates that such uses of language are exceedingly rare in the Bible.
- Scripture accurately records evil, but never sensationalizes it or uses it for mere entertainment purposes. It always clearly portrays evil as being evil.
- Christian authors who have produced some of the most realistic and powerful portrayals of evil in the history of literature have managed to do so without having to resort to bad language. Works that come to mind include C.S. Lewis' *That Hideous Strength*, J.R.R. Tolkien's *The Lord of the Rings*, and John Milton's *Paradise Lost*.
- An author who chooses to write vulgar or blasphemous words is responsible for putting those words into the minds of his readers. If so, is he guilty of being a stumblingblock, of causing others to sin?
- Lastly, motive matters. Why does a writer feel the need to include sinful language in what he writes? Is the purpose for edification or for effect? Each writer must answer this question for himself.

As we conclude our study of the Third Commandment, we should again remember where we started - this is a problem with which all struggle, and that struggle will only be won if we really desire to please God in our speech and if we daily acknowledge our dependence on the grace of God to send out of our mouths those words that honor Him and lift up those around us.

---

[34] I had to struggle with this in college and am not at all certain that I always made the right decisions. In one case I am sure I did not, when a friend was directing a student production and was having trouble finding actors; the language in the script was appalling, but he pleaded with me to take a small but important part that had no lines at all, and I agreed. Today I would not have done so.

5

THE CHRISTIAN AND GOD'S TIME

Exodus 20:8-11 - "Remember the Sabbath day, to keep it holy. Six days shall you labor, and do all your work, but the seventh day is a Sabbath to the Lord your God. On it you shall not do any work, you, or your son, or your daughter, your male servant, or your female servant, or your livestock, or the sojourner who is within your gates. For in six days the Lord made heaven and earth, the sea, and all that is in them, and rested the seventh day. Therefore the Lord blessed the Sabbath day and made it holy."

The Fourth Commandment is perhaps the most controversial part of the Decalogue among Christians. Disagreements over the Sabbath, its continuation, and its proper observance have created frequent divisions in the history of the church and continue to be barriers to fellowship among some today. As we enter into our study of the Fourth Commandment, however, we will see that it speaks to us on issues far beyond the usual controversy on which people focus their attention.

THE SABBATH AND CREATION

Exodus 20:11 connects the setting apart of the Sabbath to God's creation rest in Genesis 2:2. Why is this significant? First of all, God intended man to imitate Him in the way he structured his life; in the same way that God worked for six days and rested one in His act of creation, so man is to structure his life around the practice of working for six days and resting one. Secondly, the connection of the Sabbath to the work of creation means that the institution of the day of rest was intended for all people, and is not simply a matter of Jewish ceremonial observance, as some Christians have claimed over the years. The Fourth Commandment is, like the other nine, moral law intended for all mankind (why do both Christian and non-Christian societies measure time in *weeks*?) rather than ceremonial law that has been fulfilled in Christ and serves only as a helpful picture that is no longer relevant to our daily living.[35] Thirdly, the focus of the Sabbath, both in Genesis 2 and in its appearance in the Decalogue, is on rest rather than on worship (*holy* means *set apart*), though elements of worship are later associated with Sabbath observance (Leviticus 23:3). The significance of this will become apparent later.[36]

---

[35] Note that the incorporation of the Sabbath principle into the regulations concerning the gathering of manna in the wilderness also occurred before the giving of the Ten Commandments (Exodus 16).

[36] A fourth area of significance that is often pointed out is the power of the parallel as an argument for a literal six 24-hour day creation.

THE SABBATH AS A PATTERN

The six-and-one cycle characterized other areas of Jewish life besides the week. The Jewish agricultural calendar also incorporated a sabbatical year in which the land was to lie fallow after six years of farming (Leviticus 25:1-7); the purpose was to provide a Sabbath rest for the land. Furthermore, after seven such cycles had been completed, the fiftieth year was to be a Year of Jubilee, a time of great celebration,[37] in which the land would again be given rest (Leviticus 25:8-55). Not only that, but in the Year of Jubilee all property was to be returned to its original owners and debt slaves were to be freed.[38] Jeremiah 34:17 even indicates that the failure of the people to observe the sabbatical years and the Year of Jubilee was one of the reasons for the Babylonian Captivity - you did not give the land rest, so I will give it rest from you; you did not liberate your slaves, so I will liberate you to destruction by the sword (see also Leviticus 26:34-35; II Chronicles 36:20-21).[39] The cycle of six and one thus appears to be part of the rhythm of God's creation; those who do not observe it will be departing from the way they were made to live and the way the world is intended by God to work.

THE SABBATH AND GOD'S DELIVERANCE

In the version of the Decalogue given by Moses in his farewell sermon, we see another connection involving the Sabbath. Deuteronomy 5:15 indicates that the observance of the Sabbath is not only related to God's work of creation, but also to His deliverance of the Israelites from bondage in Egypt. The connection here is obvious - when you were slaves, you never got to rest, but had to work all the time, but now that you are free men because of God's work of deliverance, you have the privilege and blessing of resting one day out of seven. The mindset here is, sadly, one that is far different from the way people today often view the Sabbath. Too often young people and adults alike view the Sabbath as a burden - "Why *can't* I do _____ on Sunday?" - rather than viewing it as a blessing - "Finally, a day when I don't have to work. Isn't God good to us?"

Note also that the curse that fell upon man at the Fall was directly related to work (Genesis 3:17-19), which became burdensome rather than a matter of pleasant fulfillment. Thus the Sabbath rest may also be viewed as a temporary respite from at least one of the consequences of the Fall. God blesses His people by giving them rest (Psalm 127:2; Matthew 11:28-30; Revelation 14:13), while the wicked have no rest (Isaiah 48:22; 57:21).

------

[37] The description of the beginning of the Year of Jubilee in Leviticus 25:10, "proclaim liberty throughout the land to all its inhabitants," is inscribed on the Liberty Bell.

[38] The legislation surrounding the Year of Jubilee is a good example of the way in which the Jewish civil law illustrates God's concern for social justice; we find here that land ownership is not absolute, and that Old Testament "slavery" was more like indentured servitude.

[39] The fact that the Babylonian Captivity lasted seventy years is an indication of how long it had been since the sabbatical year or the Year of Jubilee had been observed. The fact is that the Old Testament gives no evidence that the Israelites *ever* observed these provisions of God's law.

THE SABBATH AS A TYPE

We have already seen that the Sabbath points back to the beginning of time - the work of God in creation. Hebrews 4:1-10 also shows that the Sabbath observance is intended to point forward. After all, the rest we have on this earth is brief and limited. But the Sabbath is intended to point forward to the never-ending rest the Christian will experience in Heaven. Thus the Sabbath in a sense is a foretaste of Heaven on earth, a blessing from God that reminds us of the glories that are to come. If you find it trying to worship God for one hour on Sunday morning and can't wait to get home so you can do what you really want to do, will you really enjoy the eternal worship of Heaven?[40]

THE SABBATH AND THE JEWS

Specifics of Sabbath observance were incorporated into Jewish civil and ceremonial law, and violations of these regulations brought heavy punishment along with God's judgment on Israel (Exodus 31:12-17; 35:1-3; Leviticus 23:3; Numbers 15:32-36; 28:9-10; Nehemiah 13:15-22; Isaiah 58:13-14; Jeremiah 17:19-27; Ezekiel 20:9-26). These punishments led the rabbis and teachers of the law during the Intertestamental Period to erect fences to keep people from breaking the Sabbath, and thus incurring the wrath of God. Traditions included restrictions on travel on the Sabbath to about three-fifths of a mile[41] (cf. Matthew 24:20; Acts 1:12), the prohibition of picking grain for breakfast (Mark 2:23-28; the rabbis had determined that this simple act constituted harvesting and threshing, and thus was forbidden), carrying one's bedroll (John 5:10), and of course healing someone.

These man-made traditions were not only a bone of contention between Jesus and the religious leaders of His day, but also have continued to multiply among orthodox Jews ever since. The prohibition against lighting a fire on the Sabbath (Exodus 35:3) not only led to the practice of Jewish women preparing the Sabbath meal the previous day, but also has produced an odd situation where most Orthodox Jewish synagogues hire Gentile janitors so they have someone to turn on the heat and lights for Sabbath worship!

These manifestations of nit-picking legalism are far from the intent of the Sabbath. We have already seen that God intended it to be a blessing. Jesus added that the Sabbath rest was not to be viewed as one of tightly-enforced complete inactivity, but rather as an opportunity to show mercy to others.

---

[40] C.S. Lewis, in *The Great Divorce*, argued that, if those in Hell visited Heaven and were given the opportunity to stay, they would turn it down because their hearts simply did not yearn for heavenly things.

[41] Those who made the laws also managed to find loopholes. The Sabbath day's journey was defined as about three-fifths of a mile from one's home, but since one's home is where one's possessions are, someone who wanted to take a longer trip could simply have a servant scatter worthless possessions at intervals along the road he intended to travel on the Sabbath so he would never be more than a Sabbath day's journey from his "home."

THE CHRISTIAN AND THE SABBATH

As noted earlier, the Sabbath has been a source of controversy among Christians for many years. How are we to understand and apply this commandment to our lives today? Several questions arise when considering this matter.

THE CHANGE OF DAY

Some groups on the fringes of the Church such as Seventh-Day Adventists, Seventh-Day Baptists and the Worldwide Church of God have objected to the whole idea of Sunday worship on the ground that the rest and worship required by the Fourth Commandment is to occur on the seventh day, i.e., Saturday. Is this conclusion warranted in Scripture? What does the Bible tell us about the day that is to be set aside for rest and worship? Surprisingly, the New Testament tells us very little on the subject. Some argue that the post-Resurrection appearances of Jesus often occurred on the first day of the week (Matthew 28:1-10; Luke 24:13; John 20:19-23), and that this justifies Sunday worship. We also see that the practice of the early church was to gather for worship on the first day of the week (Acts 20:7; I Corinthians 16:2). By the end of the first century, one day was designated as the Lord's Day (Revelation 1:10), which by then is assumed to be Sunday.

Though the change of day is supported by relatively little biblical evidence, what appears to have happened is that Christians began to gather on Sunday as a way of celebrating the Resurrection of Jesus, which had occurred on the first day of the week. As long as the majority of Christians were Jews, some continued to attend synagogue worship as well as worshiping on Sunday, especially in towns where large numbers of Jews had been converted (the earliest church buildings were converted synagogues). However, by the end of the first century, Gentiles predominated and the change of the day of worship was complete and widely accepted. The literature of the early church bears witness to this change, and shows no evidence of significant disputes on the matter. The fact that Sunday was made a legal holiday by the "Christian" emperor Constantine, which is often used as an argument by advocates of Saturday worship, is really irrelevant; the practice had been long-established by the time of Constantine's reign in the early fourth century.

MUST THE CHRISTIAN KEEP THE SABBATH?

This question rather than the previous one is the main source of controversy among believers concerning the Sabbath. Those who view the Fourth Commandment as ceremonial law tend to reduce the Decalogue to a "Nonalogue" and divorce Old Testament teaching on the Sabbath from the life of the New Testament Christian. On the other hand, those who see the Fourth Commandment as moral law tend to emphasize the strict restrictions found in the Old Testament legal and prophetic writings and insist on careful observance of a Christian Sabbath. What should we conclude concerning these matters? Note the following:

- Because the Sabbath extends from the beginning of creation and serves to point Christians to the eternal state in heaven, it is moral law. Those who ignore the Fourth Commandment as irrelevant to Christians today are not being faithful to the teachings of God's Word.

- One must distinguish between the foundational moral principle contained in the Fourth Commandment and the civil and ceremonial outworkings of it in Jewish life. We no longer offer sacrifices on the Sabbath, nor do we stone those who gather sticks or prohibit the cooking of food.

- What is the basic moral principle contained in the Sabbath command? It is that one day out of seven is to be set aside for rest and worship. Because Christian worship involves participation in community, I don't have the option of choosing my own Sabbath and deciding to work on Sunday and have my day of rest on the golf course on Saturday.[42]

- Strict Sabbatarians such as the Puritans saw in the Fourth Commandment one moral principle rather than two. The Sabbath, they believed, was to be a day of worship wholly set apart for God; the rest required was the "rest of worship," therefore recreation was prohibited and only godly activities could occupy one's time (cf. Isaiah 58:13-14).[43]

- As already noted, the Sabbath was spoken of in terms of rest long before worship was even introduced on the day. I would thus argue that two principles are relevant here, and that rest from labor, even if not specifically religious in character, is part of the blessing that God gives His people on the Sabbath.

- The legalism of some strict Sabbatarians sometimes approximates that of the Pharisees. Is watching television or playing in the back yard on Sunday a sin? One would think so to hear some people discuss the subject.

- Jesus opposed a legalistic approach to the Sabbath. He argued in His confrontations with the Pharisees that works of necessity (Matthew 12:1-8; Mark 2:23-28) and works of mercy (Mark 3:1-6; Luke 13:10-17; 14:1-6; John 5:1-17; 7:20-24; 9:13-17) were both appropriate on the Sabbath.

- Of course, this leaves open the question of what constitutes a work of necessity (works of mercy somehow do not enter the debate as often). The clear intention of the Fourth Commandment is that the Sabbath is to be different from all other days, and that the ways in which it is to be different involve gathering for corporate worship and not engaging in normal work. In the same way that Jesus' disciples picked grain on the Sabbath and David's men ate the consecrated bread in the Tabernacle, it obviously is not wrong to prepare meals on Sunday - eating is a necessity. In the same way that Jesus healed on the Sabbath, those who are engaged in medical practice often must work on Sunday because medical emergencies do not wait for the calendar. In the same way that the priests in the

---

[42] Though some Christians in non-Christian societies are forced by the laws and practices of the culture to gather for worship on a day other than Sunday. Christians in Israel find it necessary to worship on Saturday because workplaces are closed on that day and Sunday is a normal work day.

[43] In 1618, Europe became enmeshed in the Thirty Years' War, and James I wanted to be prepared in case England was drawn into it. He therefore issued the Book of Sports, which encouraged all young men to play games and exercise on the village greens on Sunday afternoons in order to be physically fit. Pastors were ordered to read the proclamation from the pulpit on Sunday mornings. Puritan pastors, however, after the reading, under the heading of "Thus saith the King," followed with the statement, "But thus saith the Lord," then read the Fourth Commandment.

Temple did not profane the Sabbath when they offered sacrifices, so preachers, Sunday School teachers, and worship leaders do not violate the Sabbath by doing such work on Sunday - their tasks are both works of necessity (without their labors, corporate worship could not take place) and works of mercy (ministering to God's people).

- Labors that are optional are not appropriate for Sunday, as they ignore the force of the commandment and also reject God's intended blessing for the day. *What if the only job I can find requires me to work on Sunday?* But can't you trust God to give you a job that doesn't violate His law? *I'm a student, and weekends are the only times I have to work!* But can't you trust God to provide for your needs when you obey Him, especially when the income from your job is spent on luxuries rather than necessities? *The way you load us up with homework, I have to work on Sunday or I would never get it all done!* This is likely to be due to bad planning and lack of discipline. The bottom line is that the Christian must trust God rather than seeking justifications for breaking His law.

- What about choices that make others work? Should a Christian take his family out to a restaurant on Sunday in order to keep his wife from having to make dinner, or should he refrain in order to avoid encouraging someone else to break the Sabbath? This is not an easy question, and even Christians who take the Sabbath seriously differ on the proper approach.

- The central problem with most American Christians today is that they are more interested in doing what they want on Sunday rather than pleasing the Lord, and thus they seek justifications for what they have already decided they want to do.[44]

- Rest and worship are intended by God to be blessings, not burdensome restrictions to be avoided or circumvented. God knows what we need, both physically and spiritually, better than we do, and we need to submit to His love and wisdom.

THE CHRISTIAN AND LABOR

Most people, when looking at the Fourth Commandment, see only instructions regarding one day out of seven. This happens largely because we tend to learn the Ten Commandments in their shortened forms. What we often miss is Exodus 20:9 - "Six days you shall labor and do all your work." This sentence does not exist merely to set the seventh day off from all the others; it also is God's command for how the rest of the week is to be used. Thus the Fourth Commandment deals with all of our time and how we ought to be using it to honor God.

---

[44] This section of the course generates far more heated responses from my class than almost any other - students become defensive as they seek to rationalize their own choices. Challenging them to think about these things, which they often have never done, is essential to focus their minds on the real root of their own desires. How much do they really *want* to please God?

WORK IS COMMANDED

If God commands us to work six days, how are we to understand this with regard to the daily details of our lives? Does this mean that a five-day work week (or a five-day school week[45]) is wrong? Does the requirement negate vacations, relaxing Saturdays with family or friends, or even retirement? Note the following:

- When the Fourth Commandment requires six days of work per week, it is not necessarily speaking of remunerative labor. The Old Testament economy was based more on agriculture and barter than on money, and the idea of getting paid for work was not part of the experience of many people; certainly, it was not part of the lives of most women. It is better understood as requiring six days of productive activity. The number of hours is not specified; instead, we should see the commandment as describing the basic makeup of daily life as one of labor.

- Thus the five-day work week is not a violation of the commandment as long as the sixth day is used productively - working around the house, doing homework, etc.

- With regard to vacations, God recognized the need to set time aside periodically from the daily grind in ways that went beyond the stated Sabbath rest. In the Old Testament, annual feasts provided breaks from daily labor (Leviticus 23), and we have already seen the instructions concerning the Sabbatical Year and the Year of Jubilee. In the New Testament, even Jesus recognized the need for occasional rest (Mark 6:30-32), though He never turned away anyone who sought His help, even in such times.

- As far as retirement is concerned, Social Security didn't exist in Bible times, so people would work at their means of making a living as long as they were able. When they could no longer work, they would be supported by their families (in Mark 7:9-13, Jesus criticized the Pharisees for *not* doing this), or if no such help was available, by the church. Today, many who see retirement as a time to relax and turn from labor find that they do not live very long; man was made for work, and, despite our constant longing for relaxation, does not function very well without it.

WORK IS CURSED

Too many people misunderstand the account of the Fall in Genesis 3 to teach that work is the result of human sin. This simply is not true; Adam and Eve worked in the Garden of Eden, tending the garden and enjoying the fruits of their labor (Genesis 2:15). Furthermore, this labor is one of the designated purposes for which God made man in the first place (Genesis 1:26-28). What, then, was the impact of the Fall on human labor? In simple terms, because of man's rebellion against God, what had been pleasurable and fulfilling became burdensome, and the created world that had freely yielded its fruits now had to be worked by man with the sweat of his brow. In other words, work is not the result of sin, but because of sin, work is hard and it isn't fun!

---

[45] Westminster Theological Seminary, where I studied and where I took the course from which this book is derived, in its early history held classes six days per week because of their understanding of the Fourth Commandment. Mercifully, that practice had been discontinued a number of years prior to my enrollment!

The importance of this biblical truth cannot be overestimated. It affects our entire outlook on life. In the first place, it affects our expectations. People who don't understand the impact of the Fall on work often get the idea that, if I can only find just the right job, I'll love going to work every day and life will be a perpetual joy. What usually happens to such people? Their expectations fail to be fulfilled, so they are dissatisfied. They either live life in misery, or else quit and look for another job, which will surely bring them the fulfillment they desire. They change jobs every few years and live in a perpetual state of frustration.

The Christian who understands the reality of living in a sinful world, however, will have no such false expectations. He knows that he is a sinner, as are those around him, and that one of the consequences of that sin is that work will be hard and often unpleasant.[46] This reality will therefore not surprise him, and he will recognize that his task is to glorify God as best he can in an imperfect world.

WORK IS TO BE VIEWED AS A CALLING

The fact that work is part of what it means to be human, but that labor is also cursed by sin, does not mean that work is to be avoided, but that it is to be redeemed. Labor is not a necessary evil, but a means of accomplishing God's purposes in the world. We often think of "callings" as being restricted to pastors and missionaries, who speak of God calling them to their ministries, but, as the Protestant Reformers recognized when they spoke of Genesis 1:26 as the Cultural Mandate, a businessman or full-time mother is every bit as much called by God as those involved in vocational ministry (in fact, the word *vocation* comes from the Latin word for calling). We also must reject the attitude of our society that jobs that require higher levels of education, for instance, are of more inherent value than those done by those with nothing more than high school diplomas or less.

This, too, is important in shaping our attitudes toward work. Work is not simply something we do to pay the bills. Someone who looks at work in that way will value it less and put less effort into it than one who recognizes that God has called him to the job he occupies. After all, if I am fulfilling God's calling, I can look at the beginning of every work day, whether spent taking care of the children or commuting to the office, as an opportunity to do God's work in the world.

WORK IS TO BE CONSTRUCTIVE

If all we do is to glorify God (Romans 14:7-8; I Corinthians 10:31; Colossians 3:17), our choice of vocation must obviously reflect that. While any honest labor can and should be done as a form of ministry, some jobs simply cannot be done to the glory of God no matter how one

---

[46] The obvious question always comes up at this point: "Mr. Walton, is your job hard and unpleasant?" God has blessed me with a job I love - I would never want to do anything else - but the marks of sin rest on it every day (grading research papers, anyone?).

looks at them (see pages 33-34).[47]   One must therefore choose a job, or decide how one will occupy his or her time, with the question of loving God and loving one's neighbor in mind.

SOCIAL IMPLICATIONS

If the Fourth Commandment is indeed moral law intended to apply to all people at all times and all places, we may conclude that it has implications for the broader society. What are the consequences when a society ignores the mandates contained in this commandment?

FAILURE TO OBSERVE A DAY OF REST

Today's secular society clearly is not driven by any desire to worship God, so keeping the Sabbath "holy" means nothing to most people. Our nation has changed greatly since the colonial era in Puritan New England, or even since the nineteenth century. One simple and relatively insignificant example of the rapidity and extent of social change in America in this regard is that, when I was growing up in the sixties, baseball teams often played doubleheaders on Sundays. League rules, however, required that no inning could begin after 6:00 in order to allow fans at the game to get to evening church services on time. Today, no one would think of caring about such things. Even children's sports teams think nothing of scheduling games and practices on Sundays.

But what are the social consequences, even if the requirement to give oneself to worship is ignored (the history of the Old Testament shows us clearly that God will surely judge those who refuse to give Him the worship He deserves)? A society that ignores the six-and-one cycle that God has built into His world will surely suffer for it.[48] But how? Note the following:

• Working all the time fosters materialism and greed. The workaholic must keep working harder and longer in order to have more and more, and views rest as nothing more than a necessary hiatus that recharges his batteries so he can get out and make more money (cf. Luke 12:13-21).
• Failure to rest one day out of seven contributes to the breakdown of family life. In our society, even those who take plenty of time off often give inadequate attention to their families, but the situation is worse for the one who is never home or never has time to spend with family members.
• Failure to get adequate rest is personally destructive, both physically and psychologically. This in the long run is not good for business or the economy.
• Overworked people tend to do shoddy work.

---

[47] Overtly immoral vocations are not the only ones that fit into this category. What about businesses that make their money by turning out useless or exorbitantly-priced products that are of no possible value to anyone?

[48] The importance of this issue can be seen by looking at a radical group during the French Revolution, the Hebertists, who made a deliberate effort to destroy Christianity and the Church by designing a new calendar that replaced the week with the *decade* - a ten-day period with nine days of work and one of rest, the idea being that, without Sunday, Christianity would fade away, and besides, more work would get done. The attempt was an utter failure.

For much of American history, states had "Blue Laws" that mandated the closing of most businesses on Sundays. Over time, authorities failed to enforce these laws, and ultimately most of them were stricken from the books. Can a Christian argue that American society would be better off if they were reinstituted, though the chance of such a thing happening is very slim indeed, since anyone who proposed any law that even hinted at a connection with Sunday rest would immediately be attacked by groups like the American Civil Liberties Union on the grounds of preserving separation of church and state?

I have already tried to lay out the social costs of ignoring the mandate of Sabbath rest, but one can also make the case that it carries economic costs as well, and not just because of tired and inefficient workers and shoddy workmanship. Let's take a simple example. Suppose, back in the era of the Blue Laws, a certain small town had two hardware stores. Each is competing with the other for the business of the residents of the town. One day, one owner gets the bright idea that he can gain an edge on his competition and earn a greater share of the hardware business if he opens on Sunday afternoon. The sheriff is a friend of his, and he assures him that he will turn the other way with regard to enforcing the law. So he announces Sunday hours, and soon finds that, as he expected, he is selling more and making more profits. What is the consequence? The owner of the other hardware store, in order to keep up with the competition, decides that he, too, must open on Sunday. Soon the hardware business in the small town is back to the original equilibrium, with both stores making about the same number of sales.

Think about what has happened in the preceding illustration, which is in many ways a microcosm of American society. Both stores are now open seven days a week instead of six, paying more in overhead, utilities, and salaries. But are they selling more hardware? Will the people in the town buy more hammers in seven days than they had been buying in six? Of course not. The result is that *both* owners have to settle for greater costs and decreased profits because their greed drove them to want more than the other guy.

On the other hand, God honors those who honor Him. One clear example of this in American society today is that of *Chick-Fil-A*, a fast food corporation owned by a Christian who refuses, despite enormous social pressures (exerted by malls, among others, who want every store to be open whenever the mall is open), to open his stores on Sundays. His testimony and his profit margin alike show the practical value of taking God's law seriously. Also, in central Pennsylvania west of where I live, the countryside is heavily populated with Mennonites and Amish. Here, one rarely finds a business, even a restaurant, open on Sunday, yet the people there seem to be thriving despite their refusal to give in to the pressures of the larger society.

FAILURE TO VALUE WORK

What about the other side of the coin? How does society suffer if it ignores the requirement to work six days per week? When work is not valued, certain obvious consequences can be expected:

• People who don't value work don't work very hard, so productivity will suffer.

- Quality will suffer as well when all people are interested in is getting out of work as soon as possible; they will settle for whatever is "good enough."
- The whole mindset with regard to work will become perverted. Instead of the "Puritan work ethic" that valued hard work as a godly virtue, people come to view work as nothing more than a way to finance leisure, which is what is really important in life. They thus "live for the weekend."
- This has moral consequences for society every bit as much as the greed and materialism of the workaholic. The tendency here is to seek increasingly stimulating forms of leisure. The law of diminishing returns dictates that the buzz of pleasure from an activity will gradually wear off over time, so more extreme forms of excitement must be sought. Is it any wonder that the entertainment provided by our society becomes more and more debased each year? One need not look far in popular culture, whether involving television, movies, or music, to see the consequences of the constant craving for more by people whose lust for pleasure can never be satisfied.

Finally, we must recognize that neither work nor leisure exists for its own sake or for the sake of the other. Instead, both exist for the glory of God. Anyone who makes work or relaxation the center of his life is looking for ultimate meaning in something that is incapable of providing it, and is guaranteeing a life of frustration and disappointment. The same is true of any society.

PERSONAL IMPLICATIONS

If the Christian is really serious about using his time in a way that pleases God, he must recognize that the small decisions of everyday life and the habits and patterns we build into our lives play a vital role in doing so. The obvious starting point is to recognize that laziness, which is the greatest enemy of good stewardship of time, is clearly condemned in Scripture (Proverbs 6:6,9; 10:26; 12:24,27; 13:4; 15:19; 18:9; 19:24; 20:4; 21:25; 22:13; 24:30; 26:13-16; Matthew 25:26; Romans 12:11; II Thessalonians 3:6-12 only begin to scratch the surface). Wasting time is a *sin* (Ephesians 5:16), but few people take this problem seriously. If they did, they would find time management much easier. How, then, can the Christian become a good steward of the gift of time that God has given him? After all, our time doesn't belong to us any more than our money or any other aspect of our lives. It belongs to God. What ways of approaching time management can help us to be better stewards?

ORGANIZATION

God is not a God of confusion, but of order (I Corinthians 14:33, 40). We should be like Him in this aspect of our lives as in all others. What does good organization require? Simple practices like "a place for everything and everything in its place" help enormously. Think about how much time you spend trying to find things. If you develop habits of putting each thing you use regularly in the same place each time, you will always know where to find it - glasses, keys, homework, cell phones, remotes . . . How much time could you avoid wasting each day if you never had to look for such things?

Another simple habit that most people find helpful is making to-do lists. Are you the kind of person who goes to the grocery store and forgets what you came for?[49] Effective list-making with regard to something like a Saturday to-do list does require that you know yourself, however. People who do not do a good job of estimating how long a job will take tend to make lists that are too long, and wind up living in constant frustration because they can never get everything done and jobs are always hanging over their heads. Good stewardship of time requires ruthless realism.

DISCIPLINE

Good stewardship of time also requires discipline. The best-made list in the world will do no good if you can't stick to it. Poor stewards of time are invariably characterized by weak self-discipline. Are you the kind of person who, while working on the computer, is constantly switching to chats with your friends? Distractions are the greatest enemy of disciplined work habits, which is why for years, education experts have insisted that parents provide a quiet space without distractions for their children to do their work. In the computer age, this becomes much more difficult because the same technology that has become the tool on which we do most of our work is also that through which we access the distractions that pull us away from it.

Obviously, procrastination is another major problem in this area. Anyone who leaves work until the last minute rather than getting it done as soon as possible will *never* be able to do his or her best, despite the frequent claims of my students that "I work best under pressure."

This also requires you to know yourself. Are you the kind of person who works most effectively by staying at your desk until the work is done, or are you the kind who needs periodic short breaks in order to do your best work (be honest, now; was that last break really necessary)? A disciplined person goes through life often knowing the satisfaction of having the work demanded of him completed. At the end of the day, he feels no guilt or pressure because everything he needed to do has been accomplished.

PRIORITIES

Good stewardship of time also requires the ability to set right priorities. Note the following:

- Your priorities should be shaped by what is important to God rather than by your pleasures or the expectations of those around you.
- Again, know yourself. Some people do best when they take on the hardest jobs first (these tend to be morning people), while others like to knock off the easy ones so they can give the tougher jobs their full attention.
- Distinguish between what is necessary and what is optional, and give priority to the former.

---

[49] At my age, I inevitably find that I go down into the basement with two things in mind to do, and promptly forget one of them. Though I don't make a list before going down to the basement, I do use them for grocery shopping.

- Avoid pushing the important aside in order to give attention to the urgent.
- Recognize that God will feel free at any time He desires to interrupt or delay your plans (James 4:13-16). God's distractions do nothing more than indicate *His* priorities for your life, and you should embrace them without complaint or fear.
- Have confidence that God will never expect you to do anything for which He will not provide the strength. If you find yourself unable to accomplish everything on your plate, either you are overcommitted and need to reduce your responsibilities in order to be a faithful steward, or else you are not doing a good job of time management and need to examine the ways in which you are using (or wasting) your time.

One who lives faithfully in the area of time management will find a great reduction in stress and an ability to do much more for the Kingdom of God than he thought possible. When the great evangelist George Whitefield told his friends who were worried about his health and told him he needed to slow down, "I would rather burn out than rust out," he was not advocating the life of a workaholic; he was determined to give everything he had, all his time and energy, to the cause of Jesus Christ. This is good stewardship of time.

6

THE CHRISTIAN AND GOD'S ORDER

Exodus 20:12 - "Honor your father and your mother, that your days may be long in the land that the Lord your God is giving you."

One of the ideas we have been emphasizing in our survey of the Ten Commandments is the universal applicability of the principles found in them. God alone is God, He alone deserves worship and has the right to determine how that ought to be done, and He claims the right to regulate all our speech and time. As we arrive at the Fifth Commandment, we encounter another broad aspect of life with which every human being struggles, and that is the matter of authority. Simply put, we don't like it. We want to do what we want to do when we want to do it. As we sample some of the possible applications of this commandment, we will see again how extensive is its reach in setting forth the basic principles of godliness.

THE POSITION OF THE FIFTH COMMANDMENT

We noted in the introductory chapter that the Decalogue follows rather neatly the pattern of the two great commandments enunciated by Jesus in Matthew 22:37-40, with the first table of the law dealing with what it means to love God and the second speaking about loving one's neighbor. While people often think of the Fifth Commandment as beginning the second table, it really serves as a transition between the two. The fundamental concern of the Fifth Commandment is with authority, but not human authority alone. The reason for this is that all human authority is *derivative*, delegated by God and therefore never absolute. Submission to human authority is simply a manifestation of submission to divine authority, thus the honor commanded here is first and foremost honor given to God, which motivates and provides the foundation for honor toward those He has put in positions of authority on earth. As a result, submission to God's authority will lead to proper relationships with other people, starting with those who in various ways rule over us.

THE PERSPECTIVE OF THE FIFTH COMMANDMENT

The wording of the Fifth Commandment sets it apart from the others in the Decalogue. In what sense is this true? First of all, it is the only one of the Ten Commandments that is expressed in purely positive terms (even the Fourth Commandment, which begins with positive wording, goes on to say, "on [the Sabbath] you shall not do any work . . . "). Why is this significant? At this point I always ask my students what kinds of rules are more restrictive, positive ones or negative ones. They usually give the expected response that negative ones are more burdensome - nobody likes being told not to do something. I then ask them to consider modifications in our school's dress code over the years. At one time, we had a dress code in the high school that consisted of a list of things students were not allowed to wear to school. After a while this became long and tedious, as fashions kept changing and students continued to find new ways of annoying the authorities with their appearance. Finally the school went to uniform dress, consisting of a fairly short list of things among which students could choose when dressing for school. This has caused far less trouble, and has been helpful to administrators, parents, and students. But which code was more restrictive, the negative one that listed what could not be worn or the positive one that listed what must be worn? The answer is obvious - the positive code is the more restrictive one. So it is with the Fifth Commandment. It does not merely require that a person not dishonor his parents, but insists on the positive response of honor - benign neglect and indifference simply are not acceptable. God does not permit us merely to tolerate, learn to live with, or endure authority; what He requires is active respect and honor.

WHAT IS HONOR?

This is another one of the commandments where understanding the key words is vital. The main verb in the sentence is the same word that is often translated *glory* when referring to God. If we are to reverence God, we must also respect the God-given authorities that bear His image. Thus the relationship of children to parents is fundamentally a spiritual relationship (Ephesians 6:1; Colossians 3:20). Matthew 15:4-9 makes this connection very clearly. Jesus here is criticizing the Pharisees for a tradition they had developed called *Corban*. The idea went something like this: someone could declare part or all of his property to be *corban*, or dedicated to the Lord. Once he had done so, that property would technically belong to the Temple treasury, which is where it would go when the person died. During his lifetime, however, he enjoyed full use of it and could do with it as he pleased. The loophole that developed in connection with this tradition was that, when some wealthy Pharisee was asked by his infirm or destitute parents for assistance in their old age, he would sadly deny their request for help by telling them that his property had been dedicated to God, and it simply wouldn't be right to take what was God's and give it to his parents, no matter how much he loved them; it was a matter of principle, you see. In the meantime, of course, the Pharisee could continue enjoying the income from his property himself.[50]

But what about passages like Luke 14:26, which speaks of the need to "hate" family in order to be Jesus' disciple? Is this not establishing a strong dichotomy between honoring God and honoring parental authority? Jesus clearly here is using hyperbolic language, but nonetheless He is affirming the priority of loyalty to God over loyalty to any human authority. As we will see as we look at some of the implications of the Fifth Commandment, loyalty to God takes precedence over obedience to any earthly authority, but this does not mean that some vague allegiance to God can be used to dismiss in a cavalier manner our responsibility to love and honor those God has placed over us.

---

[50] What was going on here should remind us of Joseph Fletcher's attempt to set the second great commandment against the Decalogue, insisting that love for man would require disobedience to God. Here the opposite was occurring - the purported desire to honor God became an excuse for not honoring one's parents.

The Fifth Commandment thus requires respect, but it requires more than that. As Jesus made plain when people paid lip-service to God's authority or His, honor means nothing apart from obedience (Matthew 21:28-31; 23:1-3; Luke 6:46-49; John 14:15; see also I John 2:3-6). This is true of earthly authorities as well as divine ones, as Ephesians 6:1 makes clear.

The third component of honor in addition to respect and obedience is one that we often don't consider, and that is material support. Those who honor God will give Him their tithes and offerings (Malachi 1:6-8; 3:6-12). Material support is also required for earthly authorities. We have already seen how Jesus scorned the attempts of the Pharisees to avoid supporting their parents in their old age (see also I Timothy 5:3-8), but other earthly authorities fit into this category as well. For example, the Bible requires both paying taxes (Matthew 22:15-22; Romans 13:6-7, where paying taxes is specifically linked to honor) and supporting those engaged in vocational Christian ministry (I Timothy 5:17-18).

"FATHER AND MOTHER"

The Fifth Commandment clearly concerns one's relationship to his biological parents. The family is not merely a social construct, but is ordained by God, and thus maintaining it is vital. But the Fifth Commandment should not be restricted in its application to biological relationships alone, since Scripture uses similar terminology to require honor in the following relationships:

- Man to God (Ephesians 3:14)
- A wife to her husband (Ephesians 5:22-24, 33; I Peter 3:1-6)
- God's people to religious leaders (II Kings 2:12; 13:14 use the term "father" in reference to Elijah and Elisha, I Peter 5:5 speaks of honoring elders, and Acts 23:5 indicates the need to give respect even to godless and hypocritical religious leaders who have authority over you)
- Citizens to rulers (Genesis 45:8 and Judges 5:7 use the terms "father" and "mother" to describe political leaders, and Romans 13:1-7 and I Peter 2:13-17 require obedience to them in general)
- Servants to masters (Ephesians 6:5-8; Colossians 3:22-25; I Peter 2:18)
- Students to teachers (Proverbs 5:13, where the foolish boy ignores the wisdom of his teachers)

CONFLICTING AUTHORITIES

Thus the Fifth Commandment extends broadly to all human authorities, but we should not think that these authorities are to be viewed as equal. One of the central difficulties encountered in the application of the Fifth Commandment involves the problems that arise when different authorities under which we are placed conflict with one another. God's authority clearly comes first (Acts 5:29), but what of human authorities, which inevitably come into conflict? By considering the order in which God established the family, the church, and the state, we can gain at least some sense of His priorities regarding them. We find that the family was established first (Genesis 2:24), and for many generations, even into the patriarchal era, the family fulfilled the functions of all three institutions, with the father serving as both priest and king (Job offered sacrifices for his family in Job 1:5 and Abraham led his clan to war against other clan leaders in Genesis 14). The next formal authority structure to be established by God was the priesthood; Exodus 29 represents the first time God sets apart a religious authority distinct from the family, though priests had existed in pagan lands for centuries before this. Finally, God establishes a political institution separate from religious authority with the inauguration of the Israelite monarchy in I Samuel 9 (the Judges, who fulfilled political functions, but usually only within specific tribes, served as a transition to the national monarchy), though again kings had existed in other nations for many years previous. Does this mean that in conflicts among family, church, and state, the family is to take priority over the church and the church over the state? Scripture certainly does not draw such a conclusion in any overt way, but the sequence nonetheless is of some use in understanding God's priorities for human relationships.

THE PROMISE OF PROSPERITY

We saw earlier that the Fifth Commandment is unique because of its positive wording, but it also is set apart because it is the only commandment that contains a promise, as Paul reminds his readers in Ephesians 6:2. Yet does not the promise given in the commandment seem problematic, especially given the extent to which it contradicts everyday human experience? How often have we known good and godly people who have died young and miserable wretches who have lived to plague the world well into their nineties? How, then, are we to understand this promise? Several points should be noted:

- The promise is a conditional one, based on obedience. Those who obey will enjoy the promised blessing, while those who disobey will not. This, of course, is part of the problem in our attempt to understand it.
- The conditional nature of the command is *not* based on the quality of the person in authority. Contrary to those who would argue that honor and obedience are owed only to those authorities who merit it, ungodly authorities are to be honored along with those who are righteous (Acts 23:5; I Peter 2:18). Thus we are to honor imperfect parents, less-than-outstanding teachers, and even government officials from the other political party, not because of who they are, but because we love and trust the God who put them over us.
- The promise given in the Fifth Commandment is corporate rather than individual - it is given to the nation of Israel and relates directly to their possession of the Promised Land. God tells them clearly that if they honor God and those He places over them, their tenure in the land will be long, but if they refuse to do so, they will be defeated by their enemies and ultimately sent into captivity.
- This does not, however, solve the problem of the use of the commandment by Paul in Ephesians 6:1-3. Paul is addressing mixed congregations of Jews and Gentiles who have not possessed the Promised Land for a long time. What, then, is this promise worth? If nothing else, we can see that one who obeys God-given authority will live a longer and happier life than he would be likely to do if he dishonored it and lived in perpetual conflict.

GENERAL PRINCIPLES FOR DEALING WITH AUTHORITY

The Bible points us to at least five basic principles for dealing with the difficult situation of submitting to the authority of sinful human beings. First of all, as we saw on the previous page, one who is to respond in a godly way to human authorities must be able to distinguish between the individual and the position he occupies. Someone who holds a position of authority is to be respected by virtue of that position, even if his personality, character, and competence are not especially deserving of respect. This is another one of those areas where the godly person must be careful to guard his tongue. How easy is it to denigrate those in authority, whether parents, pastors, teachers, or government officials, in our conversations with others?

Secondly, we need to recognize the sovereign purposes of God at work, even when He places us under difficult authorities. His goal is to glorify Himself and sanctify His people, and often He chooses to do so by placing those He loves under the authority of those who are incompetent or even wicked. Why would He do this?

- Sometimes God does this as a form of punishment. The Israelites were conquered by their enemies and sent into captivity because of their disobedience. The effectiveness of this punishment can be seen in the fact that, despite their perpetual dalliances with idolatry before the Babylonian Captivity, they never again turned to idols afterwards.
- Sometimes God does these things in order to produce sanctification and maturity (Romans 5:3-5; Hebrews 12:3-11, especially verse 10). Not everyone who is suffering under a miserable authority figure should conclude that God is punishing him for some evil He has done.
- God sometimes does this so that His people can bear witness among unbelievers (Joseph and are obvious examples - both Pharaoh and Nebuchadnezzar recognize the presence of God in their lives; see also Acts 9:15; I Peter 3:1-2).
- Failure to submit to the lesson God is teaching may extend the trial - consider that the failure of the Israelites to submit to God's authority when Moses sent spies into the land of Canaan led to forty years of wandering in the wilderness (Numbers 14:34).

Thirdly, it is important to try to understand the motives and intentions of those in authority. This is not natural, since we always tend to view the decisions of those over us in the light of how they affect ourselves. For instance, when our principal makes an announcement of some change in the schedule or a new policy, my immediate thought is, "How will this affect me and my classes?" Since the answer to that question, at least in my mind, is not always a positive one, this tends to produce a spirit of complaining. But if I take the time to try to understand the reason why such a decision might have been made in the context of its impact on the school as a whole, I find it is easier to accept the decision and cope with whatever inconveniences it might create for my narrower field of endeavor. One must remember that anyone in authority is responsible for making decisions that affect a larger number of people and a broader range of activity than you might be able to see in your limited area of experience.

Fourthly, the ability to look for creative alternatives is important if one is to deal in a godly way with those in authority. For example, in Daniel 1, Daniel and his friends were faced with a problem; their captor, Nebuchadnezzar, wanted to prepare them for service in his government, and thus wanted to make sure that they were healthy and well-educated. His chosen method for doing so, however, was to feed the fortunate chosen ones with food from his own table, the best the kingdom of Babylon had to offer. He had no knowledge, of course, that this food violated God-ordained dietary regulations. How did Daniel and his friends respond? Did they gripe and complain, or rebel and put up a fight? Not at all. Instead, they proposed a creative alternative. Since the goal was health, they suggested a way that would produce what Nebuchadnezzar sought without requiring them to violate God's law or their own consciences, and God honored their integrity by granting them favor with the supervisor the king had placed over them.

Finally, the most important principle to keep in mind in dealing with authority is the importance of trusting God. We can be sure that He wants the best for His children, even if the situation at the moment might be painful. Those who pray to God under difficult authorities have often seen God make unexpected changes in the hearts of those in power (Nehemiah 1:4-2:8; Esther 4-7; Daniel 6), but even if He chooses not to do so, God can be trusted (Daniel 3:16-18). We are not justified in taking matters into our own hands and rebelling against those over us simply because we are being mistreated.

ADULTS AND THEIR PARENTS

When we think of the specific focus of the Fifth Commandment, our minds generally go immediately to the responsibilities of minor children who live under the authority of their parents in the home. But what about adult children? Since the commandment gives no age limits, what does it mean in practice for adult children to honor their parents?

RESPECT

All older people are to be respected because of their age (I Timothy 5:1; I Peter 5:5). If this is true in broader human relationships and within the church, how much more is it true within the family? Consider, for example, the respect shown to patriarchs like Isaac and Jacob by their adult children (though they did not *always* behave in a very respectful fashion). Our youth-oriented society has lost much of the emphasis on respect for age that has characterized earlier cultures (but see the next topic) and television situation comedies revel in disrespectful behavior toward parents and others in authority, but Christians should not display such attitudes.

PRIORITIES

When a person marries and begins his own family, that family takes priority over the old. The man who marries becomes the head of a new household, and is responsible directly to God rather than to his parents; similarly, a new wife must leave her father and mother (Genesis 2:24). Especially in our society, which emphasizes the nuclear family, the extended-family structure where the head of the clan continues to exercise authority over all is no longer relevant.

But what of the single adult? The key factor here would seem to be financial independence. As long as the single adult lives under his parents' roof and receives support from them (even while away at college), he is under their authority and must obey them. One cannot claim the privileges of adulthood while living in dependence on parents. While high school students often absurdly seek to assert their independence from their parents while being totally dependent on them for virtually everything, the common claim of those away at college to be free to make their own decisions over their parents' objections while depending on them for financial support is every bit as ungodly. College may be the greatest time of freedom in a person's life because he is away from home yet does not bear complete responsibility for supporting himself, but too many use that freedom to "sow their wild oats" and become involved in all kinds of immoral behavior.

Note that this basic principle of establishing independence also has something to say about the problems that can arise when a young married couple continues to depend on parents for financial support. This leads often to divided allegiances and authority conflicts that seriously hinder the growth and maturity of the newlyweds.

SUPPORT

Finally, as we have already seen, the responsibility of adult children toward their parents extends to the requirement of material support when such help is needed. I Timothy 5:8 has some very strong words to say to those who fail to take care of elderly parents in their time of need.

COURTESY AND ETIQUETTE

Perhaps one of the most basic ways of showing honor to others is by displaying good manners. Our society sometimes seems to revel in rudeness, but the Fifth Commandment would imply that one of the ways to love our neighbors is to be *polite* to them (note the polite form of address used by Daniel before Darius in Daniel 6:21). While courtesy is a simple way to show love, we should also recognize that rudeness is essentially self-centered. Too often, however, the media picture rudeness as funny, and we have a tendency to mimic what we find humorous.

We must also recognize, however, that honor can be taken too far. In some societies, it can even degenerate into worship. Many cultures have worshiped their rulers as gods (Daniel 6:7 provides an example in the decree to pray only to the king during the designated month), including the ancient Egyptians, who worshiped the pharaohs, and the Chinese and Japanese, who worshiped their emperors.[51] In addition, Asian religions such as Buddhism and Shintoism promote ancestor worship - an example of the Fifth Commandment run amok. Whenever the honor given to human authorities puts them in a place equal to or above God, the result is not godly courtesy, but idolatry. This becomes problematic for Christians in some non-Christian cultures where common courtesies are sometimes related to pagan religious practices, making compromise hard to avoid.

---

[51] This is not just ancient history. The militarists who controlled Japan during World War II used the worship of Emperor Hirohito as a means of uniting the people in the war effort.

Finally, one must recognize that courtesy, as we saw earlier with vulgarity, is culturally conditioned. The Bible tells us to honor those in authority, but doesn't say how. The main reason for this is that manners vary greatly from time to time and place to place. A long list of such cultural differences can be compiled with little difficulty (for some reason the first thing my students always mention is belching at the table . . .). Differences affect greetings (shake hands, bow, kiss on one cheek, kiss on both cheeks, make eye contact or not?), forms of address, clothing (standards of modesty differ greatly from place to place), and, yes, table manners. While understanding what manners in any particular country or culture are is sometimes challenging, the Christian must take the time to find out these things if he is serious in avoiding offense, showing honor, and giving a good testimony for the Lord in an alien environment.

EMPLOYERS AND EMPLOYEES

The first authority relationship we will consider under the Fifth Commandment is that between employers and employees. While the economic structure of society today is very different than it was in Bible times, basic principles in Scripture still apply. The obvious passages to which we should turn are those that describe the relationships between slaves and masters (Ephesians 6:5-9, Colossians 3:22-4:1; I Peter 2:18). Though the parallel is hardly perfect, the principles continue to be valid.

RESPONSIBILITIES OF EMPLOYERS AND EMPLOYEES

The above passages indicate that those in authority in the workplace are not to be tyrannical, but are to recognize that God holds them accountable for how they treat those under them (Ephesians 6:9), and that remuneration is to be just and fair, so that workers are to be paid according to their value (Colossians 4:1). Obviously, employers are also responsible for running their businesses honestly and according to the law.

Employees, on the other hand, are to obey those in authority over them and show them respect (Ephesians 6:5; Colossians 3:22). They are also to give their best effort, whether their bosses are watching them or not, because they are really working for the Lord and not for man (Ephesians 6:5-8; Colossians 3:22-24). The worker who performs differently when his boss is in the room is motivated by the fear of man or the desire to please man, and has forgotten that the omnipresent God is his real master.[52]

The parable told by Jesus in Matthew 20:1-16 also contributes something to our understanding of this issue. While Jesus had a completely different purpose in mind in telling the parable, which deals with the nature of eternal rewards, the story nonetheless can help us here.

---

[52] A somewhat humorous illustration of this took place one day in class. While I was going over this section of the curriculum, the principal walked into the room and sat down in the back. I took advantage of this to ask the students if I taught my class any differently with my supervisor watching, and they admitted that I didn't. I then asked them if they *behaved* any differently with an administrator in the room, and got some rather sheepish glances and a few snickers in response. They got the point.

Note first of all that the employer made a fair arrangement with his workers - a denarius was considered a normal day's wage - and treated the contract as binding. This is as things should be. The workers, on the other hand, were dissatisfied, not because they were treated unfairly in the original contract, but because they compared what they received with what had been given to others. Had the workers who were hired first taken their pay and gone home without peeking into the pay envelopes of those hired later, they would have been completely content. But their insistence on comparing themselves with others made them unhappy and led to complaining and dissatisfaction. Like the professional athlete who negotiates an obscenely rich contract and then wants to hold out and renegotiate as soon as someone else gets a better one, the worker who judges his treatment by comparing his salary with others is setting himself up for constant frustration.[53]

LABOR UNIONS

An examination of the principles in these Scripture passages makes it obvious that many of the practices and resulting conflicts associated with the Industrial Revolution would never have occurred had employers and workers alike lived according to God's Word. Yet those abuses did occur and conflict did result. One of the consequences was the formation of labor unions. These obviously are not mentioned in Scripture, yet the role they have played in modern history requires us to consider how they relate to the standards of behavior with regard to authority found in the Bible. Note the following:

The abuses practiced by factory owners during the Industrial Revolution were very real and devastating to workers and their families. Workers could be fired from their jobs without notice and without cause, workplaces were often dangerous, especially textile factories and mines, workers who were injured or disabled were simply released and replacements were hired, and pay was as low as the employers could get away with. Furthermore, work hours were long - often 12-14 hours per day, six days per week, and women and children were subjected to mind-numbing and body-destroying drudgery.[54] When workers tried to organize to protect themselves, they were often met with mass firings and violence at the hands of hired thugs. Such practices are clearly contrary to biblical teachings about the way employers should treat their employees.

On the other hand, when labor unions gained legal status in the latter part of the nineteenth century, they soon sought to use their power to get as much as they could for workers. The threat of a strike was held over the heads of employers in negotiations to the point where they had little choice but to give in to what often became legalized extortion; unions, too, were not shy about

---

[53] This leads to another helpful illustration. Every year, the Philadelphia *Inquirer* puts out a special edition called the Report Card on the Schools, which includes tables with all kinds of information about all the schools in the Delaware Valley, both public and private. Included in the charts is information about teacher salaries. How easy it would be to become discontent when reading this information is easy to guess for those who have any notion of the salary scales in Christian schools in relation to those enjoyed by public-school educators.

[54] We should also note that some outspoken Christians worked against these abuses, including Robert Raikes, the founder of the Sunday Schools intended to provide a rudimentary education for child laborers, and A.A. Cooper, the Seventh Earl of Shaftesbury.

engaging in violence. Employers soon found that they had lost the ability to fire redundant,[55] lazy, incompetent, or even dishonest workers because the unions protected them. Union contracts drove salaries so high that businesses found it hard to compete with those overseas in a worldwide market (it is unions more than government policies that have driven factories overseas). Unions became politically powerful, contributing to candidates that would advance their agenda, and thus were given privileges that often excluded non-union workers from the job market. Employees in so-called "closed shops" or "union shops" were forced to join and pay dues to the union even if they disagreed strongly with its policies.[56] Reactions against such practices have led to a significant reduction in the power of unions in modern America, though they still have an important voice in business and politics.

How are we to evaluate these things? A few thoughts:

- Unions, to the extent to which they sought biblical principles of fairness rather than the authority of employee over employer, are not in themselves wrong.
- Trying to get as much money for the least amount of work possible is just as wrong as trying to get as much work as possible out of an employee for as little money as possible.
- Collective bargaining, though it can help to prevent abuses, also works against fairness in the workplace to the extent that it insists that every worker be treated the same regardless of his ability or the quality of his work.[57]
- Consider the example of paying, promoting, and laying off on the basis of seniority. While one might legitimately argue that experienced workers are good for a business and that employers ought to do all they can to retain them and develop company loyalty, others might argue that younger workers have more energy and a higher education, and ought to be given precedence over those who lack those skills. A further problem is that racial prejudice in the past has prevented the hiring of racial minorities, and where government policies have forced such hiring, minorities tend to have less seniority than others. Should the government then require that they cannot be laid off in order to maintain some sort of racial balance?
- The bottom line here is greed (I Timothy 6:10; Exodus 20:17). If employers and employees followed the teachings of Scripture and sought the good of one another, seeking the benefit of all inside the company and out and promoting the prosperity of the business, labor disputes would be far rarer than they are. One of the things I like about working in

---

[55] Unions of railroad employees in the age of steam engines required railroads to hire a fireman for every train, but refused to drop the requirement when trains became entirely electric, resulting in the necessity of employing one worker on each train who spent his whole time sitting in the back of the train doing nothing.

[56] Most unions today, for example, take positions in line with the extreme left wing of the Democratic Party, but workers who, for instance, oppose abortion are helpless to prevent their union dues from going to politicians who support it.

[57] This is why unions have often been accused of promoting socialism or even communism. The charge in the first case has merit, since the socialists were the first to promote unions during the Industrial Revolution and unions have become prominent advocates of the welfare state. The latter connection is ironic, for despite the claims of communists to champion the cause of workers, communist states have routinely outlawed union activity because their societies have already supposedly become workers' paradises.

a Christian school is the fact that faculty and administration live in harmony in pursuit of the same goal - the glory of God and the good of the students and their families - without the adversarial relationship that is so common among my public school acquaintances.

CHURCH AND STATE

Although we often think of this controversy as being unique to the United States, where so much debate centers around the meaning of "separation of church and state," the relationship between church and state has been matter of concern in all areas of the world throughout human history.

HISTORICAL BACKGROUND

For most of recorded history, the idea of separation of church and state has been unthinkable. Religion was rightly considered so important to society that to govern without reference to it would have been thought absurd. As a result, priests in ancient civilizations tended to exercise a great deal of power to the extent that they served sometimes as advisers to kings, and sometimes as their rivals. Kings would not think of making important decisions without consulting the relevant gods or goddesses though oracles or omens and offering the appropriate sacrifices.

When God set up the government of Israel, it was intended to function as a theocracy. This meant, primarily, that God was acknowledged as the real king and that all other authorities were delegated by Him and functioned according to His Word and His will. Kings were not absolute monarchs (unlike the later rulers who advocated Divine Right), and prophets and priests were often involved in political affairs as advisers; of course, when the kings strayed from God's path, the true prophets warned them of God's coming judgment while false prophets became enablers in their unfaithfulness. The theocracy fell with the destruction of Jerusalem by Nebuchadnezzar in 586 BC, and has never been restored.

This is not to suggest that many have not tried to restore it.[58] The Maccabees, after overthrowing the Seleucid in the middle of the second century BC, set up the Hasmonean dynasty, which lasted for about a hundred years. The ruling family was a priestly clan, but any connection between these men and enforcing God's law or submitting to God's authority was extremely remote. The coming of Christianity was followed by two and a half centuries of persecution. Then came the conversion of Constantine in 312 and the beginning of Christendom. The Christian emperors wanted a Christian society, but they wanted it on their terms. This led to centuries of

---

[58] Most people today who use the term "theocracy" have no idea what a theocracy is. Is it a form of government where church leaders rule the state or where the church dictates policy to political leaders? If the first, one has never existed in Christian or Jewish societies; if the second, no example may be cited other than the role of the prophets in Ancient Israel. Protestant attempts to create "theocracies" involved establishing a society where church and state each had its own realm of authority, but both sought to follow Scripture. Thus those who cry "theocracy" every time a Christian makes a political pronouncement or seeks to inject moral values into the national discourse completely miss the point of what those speakers intend, and are simply using the term to try to generate fear of a dictatorship where narrow-minded Christians impose their values on others.

infighting between popes on the one hand and kings and emperors on the other over who would wield ultimate power.

When the Reformation arrived, the Protestants continued to assume the validity of a Christian society, but they wanted it to function according to the Scriptures. In Geneva, John Calvin, with the encouragement of the magistrates, rewrote the law code of the city and reworked the educational system to promote godly living and Christian truth. John Knox tried to do the same thing for an entire country in Scotland, while the English Puritans sought, through control of Parliament, to finish the Reformation in England; when they failed, many migrated to America and tried to set up a Christian civilization in New England. The big problem with Christian societies is that they tended to impose civil penalties on all whose views differed from their own, while eagerly going to war against any who wanted a different kind of Christian society (most notably Catholics).

The result of all this was a general disenchantment with the whole idea of a Christian society and the promotion of secularism in the Enlightenment. Our American idea of the separation of church and state is among the more radical consequences of Enlightenment secularism. Even then, all our Constitution does is prohibit a national church - Massachusetts and Connecticut had state-sponsored churches until the second decade of the nineteenth century. The First Amendment certainly was never intended to muzzle religion in public life, whether in the schools or in government.

By the way, to say that America was founded as a Christian country is to distort the truth. While Christian standards of morality were generally accepted, most of those who began our nation were, as Francis Schaeffer has put it, "living on borrowed capital." Most of them were Deists, and the major founding documents demonstrate clearly the Deist thinking of the Enlightenment.[59]

One might argue that, in the years since the beginnings of Christianity, four different relationships have existed between church and state:

- Persecution - This has ranged anywhere from legal disabilities (e.g., Protestants in some Catholic countries and vice-versa) to civil penalties to attempts to eradicate the church altogether (e.g., under some of the early Roman emperors such as Diocletian, in some Communist countries since the twentieth century, and in some Muslim states today).
- Toleration - This involves freedom for the church to operate without restrictions from the government.
- Separation - The state may not involve itself in church affairs, either by hampering its operation or by officially favoring one church over another.

---

[59] The first sentence of the second paragraph of the Declaration of Independence is a good example: "We hold these truths to be self-evident, that all men are created equal, that they are endowed by their Creator with certain unalienable Rights, that among these, are Life, Liberty, and the Pursuit of Happiness." Acknowledgment of God as the Creator, the language of natural law, and the dependence on the political theory of John Locke (his phrase, altered slightly by Jefferson, was "life, liberty, and property") make this statement in many ways unbiblical, as a careful analysis will demonstrate.

- Establishment - The government recognizes and supports with tax money one particular church (the Roman Empire after 381, when Christianity was declared the official religion of the state; Catholicism in the Middle Ages and in many countries in southern Europe, including France, Italy, Spain, and Portugal, and Latin America in the early modern period; the Anglican Church in England; the Presbyterian Church in Scotland; the Dutch Reformed Church in the Netherlands; the Lutheran Church in much of Scandinavia).

Note that several of these can exist and have existed in conjunction with one another. When one church is established, others might be persecuted or tolerated, while separation of church and state is theoretically accompanied by toleration, though given the direction of recent court decisions in the United States, that is by no means assured for the future.

BIBLICAL DATA

In examining what the Bible has to say about these different kinds of relationships between church and state, we must focus our attention on establishment and separation, which are the two positions over which Christians usually argue. Everyone would choose to see Christianity tolerated rather than persecuted (I Timothy 2:1-2), though no one can question that times of persecution have also been times of growth and strength in the church.[60]

Those who argue in favor of establishment tend to find support in the Old Testament. No one can question that the form of government established by God was one that openly acknowledged His authority and enforced His law. But did God intend Christians for the remainder of history to seek to duplicate such a state? We see no such teaching in the New Testament. We should also note the dismal failures that have accompanied attempts to reconstruct theocracies among Christians. Even societies that began with a large majority of believers committed to the cause of a Christian state, such as the Puritans of Massachusetts Bay, failed to sustain it because it was sabotaged from within. After all, just because the founders of the religious experiment are Christians doesn't mean their children will be; as a result, almost every serious and sincere attempt to build a Christian society has failed within one generation.

Those who argue in favor of separation have a much more difficult task on their hands. The basic problem here is that, because the idea of separation of church and state first appeared in history near the end of the eighteenth century, not only does the Bible not mention it, but the authors of Scripture would have found the concept inconceivable. What slim biblical defense they are able to manage consists largely of Matthew 22:21 and some arguments from silence, such as that Jesus sought no political influence, the New Testament church sought no involvement in politics, and first-century Christians made no attempt to challenge the government on the broader social issues of the day. Pragmatic arguments can be brought to bear here as well, largely by pointing out that attempted theocracies have not only come to a rapid and bad end, but have led to religious wars and persecutions. Furthermore, the more the church has become involved in the

---

[60] When Tertullian asserted that "the blood of the martyrs is seed," he meant that those who gave their lives for the cause of Christ during the Roman persecutions bore such a powerful witness that many were converted by it.

state, the more it becomes corrupted by the lust for earthly power (e.g., the medieval and Renaissance popes).

In short, Christians are to seek to live peaceable and godly lives under whatever form of government God places them. They are to bear witness, realizing that their citizenship is in heaven (Philippians 3:20), not on earth, and their primary loyalty should be directed upward. We will conclude this section of the chapter by considering a few specific church-state issues that have become questions in the news in recent years.

DEFINING A CHURCH

Does the government have the right to do this - to determine what is a legitimate church and what is not? The reflexive response is that no, of course the state has no such right. But we might consider, for example, the responsibility of the government to protect its people from fraud. Does the state have the right to put a stop to someone who forms what he calls a church in order to defraud the ignorant and naive of their money, offering certificates of ordination and Doctor of Divinity degrees for $25 over the Internet (people do this and the government has *not* stopped them)? Does the government have the right to say to a man who declares his house a church, himself the pastor, and his family the congregation in order to claim exemption from property taxes that what he has formed is not a legitimate church (someone in our area years ago tried to do exactly that)? What about those who wish to use religion as a shield for illegal drug use? Though one can easily see the dangers inherent in the exercise of such governmental power (if it were turned against Christians, as it sometimes has been in denying tax exemptions to churches that engage in political advocacy and schools that refuse to measure up to state-mandated forms of inclusiveness[61]), appropriate uses of it are clearly necessary in order to protect people from predatory, dishonest men who hide behind the veil of religion.

TAXATION OF CHURCHES

While some religious organizations have lost their tax-exempt status for a variety of reasons, churches generally are tax-exempt. Some argue, however, that such tax exemption is a form of establishment contrary to the First Amendment because it favors religious organizations over non-religious ones and uses public tax money to support religious organizations by default because it collects no taxes from them.[62] Such an argument is absurd on the face of it. First of all, churches are tax-exempt, not because they are religious, but because they are non-profits. They are not taxed for the same reason schools, colleges, hospitals, and even the ACLU are not taxed, and it has nothing to do with religion.

The basic idea behind making non-profits tax-exempt is that they perform a service of value to the community, and can do so better than the government. Taxes would simply inhibit the

---

[61] Bob Jones University in Greenville, South Carolina lost its tax exemption because of this.

[62] Liberals in Colorado have sought to make this argument and get it on the public ballot as a referendum, but thus far have gotten nowhere.

organizations' abilities to perform those services, and society as a whole would suffer. Would it thus be unbiblical for governments to tax churches? Of course not, and if something like that ever happened, Christians should submit and pay the required taxes. Though it might not be unbiblical, however, it would be terribly foolish on the part of the government. The good done in society by religious non-profits, including churches, would leave a vacuum that the government could never hope to fill, even with twice the increased tax money.

AID FOR RELIGIOUS SCHOOLS

This has been a major source of contention in recent years, particularly with attempts to create educational vouchers that would allow parents to take a portion of their tax money and apply it to tuition at any school of their choosing, including religious ones. Note the following:

- Some forms of aid to religious schools already exist and have been accepted by the courts. In Pennsylvania, for instance, where Catholic schools are numerous, the state provides money for textbooks as long as those books are not religious in nature and are also used in similar public schools. The state also requires school districts to transport all children living within the district to any school they choose to attend as long as it is within ten miles of the district boundary and as long as the district buses children of the same age to its own schools. The federal government also provides free or reduced-cost lunches for students whose parents qualify.

- The argument behind such benefits given to religious schools is that the aid is not going to the schools, but to the taxpayers, so that their children deserve the same benefits as other taxpayers who send their children to public school. While some see this as a sophism, noting that parents who receive such aid are thereby enabled to pay tuition to the school by choosing to send their children there, other argue that, if these things are true of books, buses, and lunches, why is the same not also true of tuition? Why should those who choose Christian schools be forced to pay tuition twice, once in their monthly checks to the private school and again in their taxes that support public education?

- Those who oppose such aid trot out the usual argument about separation of church and state, but refuse to admit that forced secularism is every bit as much religious indoctrination as biblical instruction. They also argue that government aid in the form of vouchers would deprive the public school of needed funds, and would thus hurt the poorest among us, who could not afford private education, even with vouchers (which usually only cover a small fraction of tuition). While this may be true if vouchers were applied to those who already attend private schools, for whom some of the money that now goes to public schools would be diverted, the argument does not make sense at all for those who are now in public schools but would be able to switch if vouchers were instituted. Suppose, for instance, that vouchers were established to cover up to $2000 of tuition at the school chosen by the parents. The average cost of an education in public schools today is more than $10,000, however. What would happen to the remaining $8000, which would still come in as tax money from the community? It would continue to go to the public school, which would get money for a student it no longer had to educate. Thus in the long run public schools would actually *benefit* financially from a voucher system, and get the smaller classes for which teachers' unions are constantly agitating at the same time.

- We should also note that many Christians are opposed to the idea of vouchers. The reason for this is that they fear that government money always comes with strings attached, and that accepting anything at all from the state would open the door eventually to government interference with curriculum, admissions, and hiring, though such things have not yet happened in states where forms of government aid presently exist. Becoming dependent on state money is always a risky proposition, and some Christian schools refuse to take that chance.

CIVIL DISOBEDIENCE

The second topic under the Fifth Commandment that concerns conflicting authorities is civil disobedience, which involves the purposeful and deliberate violation of the law in support of a principle or cause. It need not be non-violent (*civil* here refers to the fact that it is the government that is being disobeyed, not to the manner in which that disobedience is carried out; even non-violent protesters are often anything but civil).

Civil disobedience is also another topic that requires the difficult task of line-drawing. Again, the extremes are easily eliminated; Romans 13:1-5 rules out anarchy every bit as much as Acts 5:29 rules out lockstep acquiescence to the state. The problem thus is not *whether* the Christian should ever violate the law, but when and under what circumstances disobedience to government is justified. Over the centuries of Christian history, believers have taken three basic stances on the issue.

WHEN THE GOVERNMENT IS SINFUL

This is the most radical position, and argues that, because all human governments are sinful, the believer owes his allegiance to none. While this might seem to be a recipe for anarchy, and in some cases has been,[63] for the most part those who espouse this position choose isolation rather than active disobedience; in fact, they are more often than not pacifists. Groups like various Anabaptist sects (including the Amish), along with the Jehovah's Witnesses, prefer to avoid contact with civil authorities as much as possible and want nothing more than to be left alone.[64] Despite the integrity with which its advocates hold to this position, it is clearly contrary to the teaching of Scripture. Romans 13:1 teaches that "[the authorities] that exist have been instituted by God," thus can hardly be described as Satanic (remember that, when Paul wrote these words, the Roman Emperor was Nero).

---

[63] Some survivalist groups unconvincingly claim biblical justification for living in the mountains of the West and threatening to shoot any government agent who dares trespass on their property.

[64] Jehovah's Witnesses, who teach that all human governments are Satanic, may succeed in being left alone in the United States, but have faced severe persecution in countries whose rulers are less secure.

WHEN THE GOVERNMENT DOES SOMETHING SINFUL

This approach is less radical than the last, and argues that, though the government has been instituted by God, that government may disqualify itself as a legitimate government when it does something sufficiently sinful. Scottish Covenanter Samuel Rutherford (1600-1661), in his book *Lex Rex*, argued that Charles I of England had so disqualified himself because of his departure from the true (Presbyterian) church in attempting to introduce bishops into Scotland. A similar argument, though without the same biblical foundation, was made by John Locke (1632-1704) in his defense of the Glorious Revolution in England; this argument in turn was adopted by the Founding Fathers in the Declaration of Independence, where they argued that "whenever any form of government becomes destructive to these ends, it is the right of the people to alter or to abolish it, and to institute new government."

In modern times, this approach to civil disobedience has supported the ethic of protest. Any who wish to oppose government policies argue that, because [racism, war, the draft, nuclear power, etc.] is unjust, the people are justified in breaking the law in order to protest that injustice. This was an important tactic used by participants in the Civil Rights Movement, antiwar movements from Vietnam to Iraq and Afghanistan, those fighting for environmental causes, and even pro-life protesters seeking to close abortion clinics. Is breaking the law to protest government policies biblical? We can best answer that question after reviewing the final alternative.

WHEN THE GOVERNMENT MAKES YOU DO SOMETHING SINFUL

This is the most conservative of the three positions. Those who argue this approach insist that the Christian may only break the law when to keep that law would be sin; in such cases, he obviously "ought to obey God rather than man" (Acts 5:29). Notice that such a stance would rule out civil disobedience for the sake of protest - laws against trespassing or disturbing the peace do not cause the Christian to sin, and therefore ought not be broken. But what about laws requiring blacks to ride in the back of the bus and use segregated bathrooms and water fountains? Is it a sin to obey these?

In my opinion, the third position is the biblical one for the simple reason that all examples of civil disobedience in Scripture fit into this category. The Hebrew midwives would have sinned had they obeyed Pharaoh and killed the male children who were born to the Israelite women (Exodus 1:15-22); Moses, however, would *not* have sinned had he refrained from killing the Egyptian overseer (Exodus 2:11-12), thus was in the wrong. Daniel (Daniel 6) and his friends (Daniel 3) would have been guilty of idolatry had they obeyed the commands of Darius and Nebuchadnezzar, but Esther delivered her people by using the laws of the land to her advantage. Peter and the other apostles would have sinned against Christ's direct command (Matthew 28:19-20) had they refrained from preaching (Acts 5:29), and were right to disobey the Sanhedrin. Thus civil disobedience is permissible only when to obey the government would be to sin against God; in fact, in that case it is *required*. Disobedience, however, may occur only at the point of conflict; one should not feel justified in breaking other laws if the state passes one that you consider to be unjust.

REVOLUTION

This topic is actually a special case of the previous one. If Scripture lays down guidelines for disobedience to God's ordained authorities, what does it tell us about the legitimacy of overthrowing them? Note first that the three positions described under Civil Disobedience each lead to different conclusions with regard to revolution.

- Those who believe that human governments are by their very nature sinful could in theory justify revolution at any time, though most don't because of their pacifist convictions. Survivalists, however, have no such restraints, and are quite willing to use violence and revolutionary rhetoric, though they only very infrequently put that rhetoric into practice.
- Those who believe that lawbreaking is justified to protest sinful government policies and practices also will usually draw the conclusion that, if the government is *terribly* sinful, it may be overthrown. Precisely this justification was used by Puritans who went to war against Charles I, Covenanters who rebelled against Charles II, English Protestants who overthrew James II in the Glorious Revolution, American colonists who fought George III, and Confederates who broke away from the Union by initiating the Civil War. As recently as the twentieth century, the World Council of Churches attempted to justify supporting communist revolutionaries attempting to overthrow what they considered to be unjust governments in Latin America and South Africa.
- Those who believe that civil disobedience is only justified when to obey the government would be to sin against God would naturally arrive at the conclusion that revolution is never justifiable.

Must we then conclude that revolution is always wrong? What about instances in Scripture where God appears to have sanctioned or even commanded rebellion against the government? Moses led Israel to repudiate Pharaoh's authority, Othniel overthrew the Mesopotamian king Cushan-rishathaim (Judges 3:7-10), Ehud *assassinated* Eglon (Judges 3:15-23), and so on throughout the book of Judges, with violent rebellions against oppressive rulers being led by Deborah and Barak, Gideon, Jephthah, and Samson (though he was not so much a military leader as a one-man wrecking crew against the Philistines). On the other hand, when some in Judah advocated armed resistance against Nebuchadnezzar, God told them through Jeremiah to submit instead (Jeremiah 27:5-8).

While the biblical examples undoubtedly complicate the question, certain observations are worth considering:

- Overthrowing the government by violence in Exodus and Judges was in each case initiated by God. The leaders of the revolts didn't simply decide on their own that the government was oppressive and therefore had to go.
- The oppressive Canaanite rulers were no better and no worse than Nebuchadnezzar, so what made the difference? In each case, Israel fell under foreign control as God's judgment against their sins, and was delivered, not because the rulers had suddenly become oppressive, but because of their own repentance. All these examples, of course, occurred in a theocratic setting.

Another possible way of looking at the problem must be considered. In John Calvin's *Institutes of the Christian Religion*, he addressed the question of revolution by first arguing that it was never acceptable for God's people to overthrow their God-ordained authorities. However what about situations where legitimate rulers were at odds with one another, such as the Holy Roman Emperor and the magistrates on the town council of Geneva? In that case, he said,

> So far am I from forbidding these officially to check the undue license of kings, that if they connive at kings when they tyrannize and insult over the humbler of the people, I affirm that their dissimulation is not free from nefarious perfidy, because they fraudulently betray the liberty of the people, while knowing that, by the ordinance of God, they are its appointed guardians.

The basic idea here is that local authorities, who are responsible for protecting the welfare of the people, may resist higher authorities should they practice tyranny, and the people must then choose to follow the legitimate authority that is more biblical (though they may not choose to follow neither). This view, sometimes called the Case of Competing Authorities, was used by some who were influenced by Puritanism and Reformed theology and had no interest in the natural law arguments of the Deists to support the American Revolution by asserting that the lawful colonial legislatures like the Virginia House of Burgesses had the right to oppose king and Parliament when they acted unjustly, and in fact would have been neglecting their duty had they *refused* to do so. Note that one might also use this argument to justify the actions of the Judges, who, like the evil rulers they overthrew, had been placed in positions of authority by God.

With regard to the American Revolution, we must note that devout Christians stood on both sides of the conflict and believed their stances were biblical. Those who supported the Revolution made some of the following arguments:

- Any government that violates God's covenant forfeits its right to obedience.
- Religious freedom is possible only where there is political freedom, so we must fight to defend our God-given religious liberty.
- God-given unalienable rights (Deists).
- Fear of Anglican establishment - being forced to support the Church of England.
- Fear of religious persecution.
- Calvin's influence - following colonial assemblies against king and Parliament is our God-given duty.

On the other hand, those who opposed it said things like:

- God requires that we submit to political rulers, even if they are unjust.
- Oaths of loyalty to the king may not biblically be broken.
- John Wesley's influence - in his *Calm Address to the American Colonies*, he argued that the Revolution was nothing more than a tax revolt, and as such was unbiblical.

The complexity of the question makes simple answers impossible, though I personally am inclined to accept Wesley's reasoning and doubt that the Revolution can be justified biblically.

CRIME AND PUNISHMENT

The last topic under the Fifth Commandment will bring us to the question of the state's administration of justice. If the God-given role of the state is to be "an avenger who carries out God's wrath on the wrongdoer" (Romans 13:4), we must consider what guidelines the ruler is to follow in pursuing this mandate. This leads us to two fundamental questions.

HOW IS CRIME TO BE DEFINED?

If the state is to administer justice by punishing those who do wrong, rulers must of necessity define what constitutes wrong behavior. How are they to do this? Three basic answers have been given in the Christian era:

- Crime is to be defined according to God's law. We can certainly justify this on the basis of the argument made earlier that the moral law is intended for all people at all times and all places, but those who have taken this approach have often wanted to implement the Old Testament civil law as well. No one can deny the extent of the influence of God's moral law on the legal codes of Europe and America, for which it is foundational, though often unacknowledged today. We should also note that such an approach is difficult to maintain in a pluralistic society. People today would be likely to scoff or even threaten lawsuits should anyone come close to suggesting such a thing. Actually, the clearest examples today of people trying to shape law on a theocratic basis are not in Christian countries at all, but Muslim ones, where believers aggressively promote the enforcement of *sharia* in their own lands and attempt to impose it on others as well.
- Crime is to be defined according to natural law. This was the answer of the Enlightenment, and the one that had the greatest influence on the legal system of the United States. Natural law is, according to Enlightenment thinkers, law that has been built into the universe by the Creator; this law is discernible by human reason, and all reasonable men will naturally arrive at the same conclusions. The problem here is that Deists had a stubborn tendency to ignore human sin. Yes, God has given all men consciences, but those consciences are corrupt and cannot in unaided fashion lead to a foundation for social justice (see page 7). Besides, natural law has long been repudiated by American legal scholars, who cannot tolerate even such a limited reference to God as the source of law.[65]
- Crime is to be defined by the will of the ruler. This approach is often termed *civil law* or *positive law*,[66] and is certainly the most popular approach in the Western world today. In the same way that advocates of the Divine Right of Kings in the seventeenth century argued that, because the king is God's representative, his word is law, and he need listen to no

---

[65] When Clarence Thomas was being questioned by the Judiciary Committee of the Senate prior to his confirmation as a Supreme Court justice in 1991, he said he considered natural law to be the foundation for a just society. Needless to say, the media had a field day ridiculing anyone who would dare to say such a thing.

[66] Positive law, not in opposition to negative law, but as that which is *posited* rather than derived from a fixed standard.

higher authority or take the advice of anyone, so advocates of positive law today argue that those who have been chosen by the people to make the laws are free to legislate whatever they believe to be best for the people without reference to any external standard.

In considering these approaches, we should note the following:

- We have already argued that a theocracy is untenable and not to be anticipated according to the teachings of Scripture (see page 87).
- This does not mean that Christians should not seek to have God's moral law shape the rulings of government, since good standards are better than bad standards for everyone, believer and unbeliever alike.
- Should Christians try to do such a thing, the cry of "separation of church and state" will soon be accompanied by the cry of "legislating morality." Christians, or so the argument goes, are trying to impose their (narrow, old-fashioned, bigoted) views on everyone else, and this should not be tolerated. The problem here, of course, is that *any* laws involve legislating morality. The question is not whether morality *ought* to be legislated, but rather *whose* is to be legislated? Those who object to Christian opinion simply want to clear the field for their own ideas by eliminating the competition before the discussion even begins, and Christians should not be intimidated by such charges.
- One of the problems with seeking to incorporate biblical values into law is that we simply cannot expect unbelievers to act like Christians. While outward behavior can to some extent be regulated by law, matters of the heart cannot be. Even if Christian morality did have greater influence in the field of law, we would accomplish little more than promoting hypocrisy, though some would still, with some legitimacy, argue that moral behavior, even if the heart is not in it and it has no spiritual value, is better than immoral behavior for the well-being of society.
- Most legal matters are by their very nature questions of positive law. Scripture simply does not tell us what the speed limit ought to be on a certain road. Most of the work done by legislators involves specific regulations for which the Bible provides no specific guidance. We must, however, recognize that the approach taken by a legislator to issues with obvious moral components indicates much about the condition of his own heart and his desire to do what pleases God in carrying out the responsibilities of his office.

HOW IS PUNISHMENT TO BE MOTIVATED?

We also need to consider, not only *what* behavior is to be punished by those in authority, but *why*? What is the purpose of punishment? What is it intended to accomplish? Five major motives have dominated thought and practice in this area:

- Deterrence - In this view, the primary purpose of punishment is to keep the criminal from repeating the undesirable behavior, and at the same time discouraging others from doing it as well. Those who emphasize this motive have argued endlessly over the deterrent value of capital punishment, though it obviously deters repeated criminal behavior in at least *one* person.

- Rehabilitation - Here, the primary purpose of punishment is to change the criminal, making him a better person and equipping him to be a contributing member of society. This is particularly popular today, and we see in our criminal justice system significant involvement of social service agencies in order to accomplish this. It is worth noting in passing that this motive directly contradicts the first one, since this requires creating a positive environment for the treatment of the criminal, which is hardly a deterrent to someone on the outside.[67]

- Restitution - The idea here is to make the criminal pay back society for the damage he has done. This could take the form of paying back the injured party, fines, or community service.

- Quarantine - The basic idea here is to protect society by getting the criminal out of circulation. This, of course, is the primary motive for imprisonment, but can also be seen in earlier years in the practice of sending those who had committed crimes into exile.

- Retribution - This means that punishment should primarily be determined by what the criminal deserves as a result of his behavior. This has fallen out of favor today, when humane treatment of criminals has often totally obscured the idea that someone who does wrong *deserves* to be punished for it. Such thinking is closely related to a refusal to recognize the fundamental sinfulness of man.

In considering these different motives, we should first of all note that *all* of them are biblical. Deterrence is found in Proverbs 19:25, where even the punishment of the fool is seen as instructive to others, and in many prophetic writings where God's judgment is intended to teach His people not to sin. Rehabilitation is seen in Hebrews 12:10, Proverbs 22:15, and many other places. Restitution is often found in the Old Testament civil law (Exodus 21:36; 22:7), as is exile (e.g., Numbers 12:14), though imprisonment was not often used in Israel. Retribution is found in passages such as Exodus 21:23-25.[68]

If all five motives are seen in Scripture, the final question we must ask concerning these things is, "Which one is the most foundational, the one on which all others must rest?" My students, who, like all of us, are children of their age, tend to favor rehabilitation and cite the mercy of God to support their conclusion. I would argue, however, that retribution should be the most fundamental motive for punishment, not only because it is cited as the basis for legal justice in the Old Testament,[69] but also because, without the sense that the punishment should fit the crime, all four of the other motives can be horribly abused. Note the following:

---

[67] In fact, many criminals have found prison preferable to the streets, and have benefitted from job training and drug rehabilitation so much that they sometimes return rather than live in a dangerous world.

[68] Note that the phrase "an eye for an eye and a tooth for a tooth," sometimes called the *lex talionis* or "law of the tooth," which conjures up grim images of amputation and mutilation, simply means that the punishment should fit the crime, and was actually intended to *limit* the extent to which the authorities could mete out penalties.

[69] We will look at Jesus' comments on this subject in Matthew 5:38-42 in the next chapter.

- If deterrence is the main consideration of those in authority and they have no concern for what a person really deserves, punishment quickly becomes extreme and brutal. If draconian penalties are assessed, no one would dare resist those in power. Furthermore, deterrence might be even more successfully accomplished by punishing the innocent (dictators who wield secret police forces to intimidate the population have long understood this).

- If rehabilitation were the main concern of those in power, it could quickly become a euphemism for brainwashing or other forms of social conditioning, as it often did for political dissidents behind the Iron Curtain.[70]

- If restitution were the primary goal of rulers, and they had no concern for justice, they could simply arrest wealthy people, trump up charges against them, and seize their property.[71]

- If quarantine were the primary motive, it would be the easiest thing in the world to imprison or exile anyone who spoke out against government policies or even sought to run against the person in power in an election. Again, the Soviet Union before the fall of communism is an example of this, as are many African countries today (Zimbabwe is a notable example), where anyone who tries to run against the President suddenly finds himself and his friends in jail.

Thus justice must be primary, or man's best intentions can lead to horrible forms of tyranny, to which history and today's news bear witness. And what determines justice? Rulers could do worse than to consider the implications of "an eye for an eye and a tooth for a tooth."

This concludes our survey of the Fifth Commandment. Submission to authority is a challenge for all of us, and the application of biblical principles by those who rule, and especially by those who find themselves under authority, is essential, not only for a just and peaceful society, but also in order to please and honor God.

---

[70] See also the arguments made by C.S. Lewis in the last novel of his space trilogy, *That Hideous Strength*, where he asserts that social conditioning is even more cruel and more dangerous than corporal punishment.

[71] Machiavelli, in *The Prince*, advocated both this and the practice described under deterrence above.

7

THE CHRISTIAN AND THE
SANCTITY OF LIFE

Exodus 20:13 - "You shall not murder."

The Sixth Commandment tends to be the one that my students find most interesting; here we deal with the life and death issues that are so controversial in modern American society. But before we begin to deal with those issues, we must first be sure we are clear about what the commandment actually means.

THE MEANING OF THE WORD

In Hebrew, Exodus 20:13 consists of just one word - a verb in the imperative mood with a negative prefix. Thus the meaning of that word matters a great deal. The root word here is *ratsach*, which is used to describe what we would call murder or manslaughter, whether premeditated or unpremeditated. While modern translations handle the word correctly, the KJV translation of the commandment, "Thou shalt not kill," has been the source of untold mischief and misinterpretation, with people arguing that because of this God forbids everything from capital punishment to war to the killing of animals, all of which are clearly approved elsewhere in Scripture. When the Bible speaks of these things, however, different Hebrew words are used. This is really no different from English, where we have many words to describe the taking of life (the students have a good time coming up with a long list, including slang terms), each of which has a slightly different meaning or connotation. Thus the Sixth Commandment forbids the unlawful taking of human life.

THE SANCTITY OF HUMAN LIFE

But why is human life so special? Animal rights activists today argue that "animals are people too," and apart from the teachings of Scripture, one would be hard-pressed to defend human uniqueness as a matter of kind rather than degree. But the Bible gives us the fundamental reason why human life is sacred - because man, alone among God's creatures, is made in God's image (Genesis 1:26). Genesis 9:5-6, a passage we will be examining in more detail later in the chapter, connects the image of God in man with the severe penalty - capital punishment - to be meted out to those who take human life. One who strikes out against man, who is the image of God, strikes out against God Himself. Not only that, but human life is pictured as the direct gift of God (Genesis 2:7), and only God has the right to take it away (a right that He is perfectly free to delegate should He choose to do so, of course). When God threatens death to Adam and Eve should they eat the forbidden fruit in Genesis 2:17, we ought not to conclude that therefore human life is cheap; instead, this threat should tell us something about the seriousness of sin.

Even after the Fall, we find that God consistently acts to preserve human life despite man's rebellion against Him. After they sinned, God preserved the lives of Adam and Eve so they would have an opportunity to repent; He even kept them from eating of the Tree of Life so they would not be confirmed forever in their sinful condition (Genesis 3:22-24). When Cain committed the first murder, God preserved His life and even made sure that no one else would kill him (Genesis 4:15), though He later instituted capital punishment when the size of the population demanded formal restraints. Even with the extreme wickedness that elicited the judgment of the Flood, God determined to preserve life, even to the point of giving man 120 years' warning (Genesis 6:3).

Israelite law also worked to preserve human life despite more than a dozen capital offenses listed in the civil law of the theocracy. One notable example of this is the establishment of the Cities of Refuge (Numbers 35:22-34; Deuteronomy 19:4-13; Joshua 20). These were six cities scattered throughout the Promised Land where someone who had caused the death of another accidentally could flee to escape the Avenger of Blood (someone designated by the family of the deceased to pursue justice). Once the person arrived safely at the City of Refuge, he would face trial to determine whether the death he caused had really been an accident. If not, he faced the full penalties of the law, but if it had been a real accident, he was required to stay in the City of Refuge until the death of the high priest; here he would be safe from the Avenger of Blood. When the high priest died, he would be free to go. Note that this system, which strikes us as somewhat arbitrary, especially in the nature of the penalty, served to preserve human life in two ways - not only did it protect someone who caused the death of another accidentally from losing his own life, but it also discouraged carelessness with regard to the lives of others - it provided a severe enough penalty that a person who went out to chop down a tree when his neighbor was nearby would make very sure that the head of his axe was tightly fastened.

The best example of God's determination to preserve human life, of course, is the death of Christ on the cross. God cared so much about the lives of His rebellious creatures that He was willing to sacrifice the life of His only Son so that those who put their trust in Him could enjoy eternal life when what they really deserved was eternal death and separation from God.

BROADER APPLICATION

This is another commandment that Jesus addresses in the Sermon on the Mount and, as we would expect, He goes beyond matters of outward behavior to examine the attitudes of the heart. In Matthew 5:21-26, Jesus insists that the attitudes, motives, and words that lead to murder - hatred, anger, insults - are just as much violations of the Sixth Commandment, and just as worthy of God's judgment, as the overt act of ending the life of another. Thus, as we consider issues associated with the Sixth Commandment, we will examine, not only questions directly related to the taking of human life such as capital punishment, war, and abortion, but also those that involve assaults upon the image of God in man, such as racial prejudice and slavery.

QUALITY OF LIFE

Another issue that often enters into discussion of Sixth Commandment topics is that of the quality of life. In John 10:10, Jesus says, "I came that they may have life and have it abundantly," so God clearly cares about the quality of human life. But what tends to happen with regard to the life and death issues before us is that people try to play the quality of life off against the existence of life. They point to deformed, suffering people - infants with birth defects, comatose accident victims, elderly people in constant pain from cancer or unable to interact effectively with the world around them because of dementia, and argue that such "life" is not worth living because the quality of life is so low. Scripture, however, never allows us to conclude that any human life is "not worth living." While God cares about the quality of life, it should never take precedence over the existence of life.

CAPITAL PUNISHMENT

The first issue before us under the Sixth Commandment is perhaps the practice against which the Sixth Commandment is most frequently directed - capital punishment. The death penalty has existed from the earliest recorded law codes and has been common to almost every human society, but has been challenged increasingly in modern times. Today, most of the nations of Europe have outlawed the death penalty, even to the extent that a country like Turkey has faced barriers in its efforts to join the European Union because it still executes criminals. Needless to say, pressure has been mounting in the United States to discontinue the practice, though in most states many men are on death row, but few executions are actually carried out.[72]

SECULAR ARGUMENTS

Though I intend to give most of our attention to biblical arguments on both sides of the issue, we should at least mention in passing some of the secular arguments that one often hears today. Those in favor of capital punishment usually speak in terms of protecting society and giving vicious murders what they deserve. Those who oppose capital punishment, on the other hand, citing the "cruel and unusual" clause of the Eighth Amendment, argue that seeking vengeance is not fitting for a civilized society and lowers the state to the level of the criminal ("two wrongs don't make a right"). They also maintain that capital punishment is often administered unfairly, not only because innocent people are sometimes condemned to death, but also because death penalties are disproportionately given to the poor and minorities.

The question of deterrence is raised by both sides. Those who oppose capital punishment point to statistics to show that murder rates have not decreased when capital punishment has been reinstituted, while those in favor trot out their own statistics to show that they have. Part of the problem here, of course, is that deterrence is difficult to measure - how can anyone hope to gain

---

[72] Despite having hundreds on death row in state prisons, some for decades, Pennsylvania has not executed anyone in the last thirty years except for two mass murderers who *requested* that their penalties be carried out.

reliable statistics concerning how many people decided *not* to commit a murder because of the possibility of execution? Furthermore, any such measure is bound to be corrupted by the long delay and low probability of someone sentenced to death actually facing execution. If "justice deferred is justice denied," murderers in America today face nothing even vaguely approximating justice, which seriously inhibits the deterrent value of any executions that actually do happen.[73]

BIBLICAL ARGUMENTS FOR CAPITAL PUNISHMENT

Many arguments and examples could be cited, but we will consider five, along with the responses of critics of capital punishment:

• The Covenant with Noah (Genesis 9:5-6) - God formally instituted capital punishment after the Flood. Given the wickedness that had motivated the Flood originally, something had to be done to restrict the evil in men's hearts (but note that animals are included as well, in much the same way that pit bulls that attack children are destroyed according to law today). While the command here may seem obvious, opponents of capital punishment have a way of trying to explain away the clear sense of the passage. They argue that we have here, not a command at all, but a mere statement of fact - "Don't shed human blood, because if you do it will start a blood feud and the bloodshed will never end." Such a reading of the passage is absurd because it is contradicted by the context, both before and after. Verse 5 does not allow for the conclusion that verse 6 reflects a regrettable statement of fact because it clearly states that God *requires* the life of the one who kills. As far as the following context is concerned, the reference to man being made in God's image eliminates the interpretation of critics, which would then make verse 6 state something along the lines of, "Don't shed human blood, which will lead to an endless blood feud because man is made in God's image!"

• The Law of Moses - To use the Sixth Commandment *against* capital punishment is absurd for one who has any confidence in the coherence of Scripture. Why would God forbid something in Exodus 20 that He turns around and commands six times in Exodus 21? In fact, the Old Testament law requires capital punishment for over a dozen offenses besides murder, including striking a parent (Exodus 21:15) or even cursing father or mother (Exodus 21:17), juvenile delinquency (Deuteronomy 21:18-21), kidnaping for slave trading (Exodus 21:16), accidental death of an innocent bystander in a fight (Exodus 21:22-25), owning an animal known to be dangerous that kills someone (Exodus 21:29), bestiality (Exodus 22:19; Leviticus 20:15-16), child sacrifice (Leviticus 20:2), witchcraft (Leviticus 20:27), adultery (Leviticus 20:10), incest (Leviticus 20:11-12), homosexuality (Leviticus 20:13), false prophecy (Deuteronomy 13:5), prostitution (Deuteronomy 22:21), and rape (Deuteronomy 22:25).

   God clearly views capital punishment as a way of purging evil from society. The question that Christian supporters of capital punishment must address is not why they

---

[73] Some have wondered whether the privacy surrounding the few executions that do occur today mitigates against deterrent value as well. When executions were public, they became like circus sideshows, but people could clearly see the consequences of lawbreaking. In fact, in the Old Testament, executions were to be carried out by stoning (e.g., Joshua 7:24-25); this was not only very public, but also involved the *participation* of the whole community.

advocate the practice, but why they restrict their discussion of it to murder when God clearly considers many more practices, especially those connected to sexual perversion, to be capital offenses. Here is where the nature of the Israelite theocracy enters into the discussion. What may be regulated in a society that openly acknowledges God as its King and His law as its standard may not so easily be imposed on a pluralistic society that cares nothing for God's law and objects strongly to anyone who would even suggest that the government has a role in regulating what goes on behind closed doors between consenting adults (though they have few qualms about regulating drug abuse . . .). Murder was declared to be a capital crime before the giving of the Jewish law, while the other offenses are part of the civil law.

- The Judgment of God - God's approval of capital punishment is demonstrated by the fact that He on several occasions carried it out Himself (the Flood, Sodom and Gomorrah, the rebels who made common cause with Korah in Numbers 16, Ananias and Sapphira in Acts 5:1-11) or told others to do so (the citizens of Jericho in Joshua 6:17, Achan and his family in Joshua 7, the Amalekites in I Samuel 15:3). The obvious response on the part of capital punishment opponents is that today we have no voice from God commanding the state to execute criminals; furthermore, if God wants to do it Himself, let Him do so. We should note here that, if nothing else, these passages establish the truth that capital punishment cannot be viewed as wrong *in principle*, restricting opponents who even try to take the Bible seriously to argue specific circumstances or pragmatic considerations rather than that the practice is abhorrent in the eyes of a merciful God.[74]

- The Teaching of Jesus - While the Sermon on the Mount is often used by opponents of capital punishment to make their case, as we will see a little later, it can also be used to *support* capital punishment. In Matthew 5:21-22, Jesus explicitly addressed the Sixth Commandment and the death penalty associated with it in the Old Testament. If He intended to oppose the execution of criminals, this would have been the perfect opportunity. Instead, He doesn't say that, in this age of God's grace, killers should be spared, but expands the definition of murder to include hatred, anger, and insults, stating that these, too, are worthy of judgment. While this is clearly an argument from silence, it nonetheless can perhaps keep people from imputing to Jesus attitudes that He simply did not manifest in His own teaching.

- The God-Ordained Power of the State - Romans 13:4 is the key verse here; Paul says that the ruling powers have been established in their authority by God, and that this authority includes the power of the sword to punish those who do evil. The fact that these words were written when Nero ruled Rome shows that the misuse of capital punishment by those in power in no sense mitigates against its appropriateness, as opponents would argue. The solution to the misuse of capital punishment is not to stop using it altogether, but to work to avoid the abuses that admittedly have long been part of its application. We should also note that Jesus Himself acknowledged the right of Pilate to take His life (John 19:11), as did the repentant thief on the cross (Luke 23:41); the Apostle Paul said the same with regard to Nero in Acts 25:11. These comments possess special power because, in the cases of Jesus and Paul, the contemplated executions were or would have been unjust and

---

[74] Though some would even go so far as to argue that the strict and vengeful God of the Old Testament has been superseded by the loving and merciful Father of Jesus Christ.

an abuse of state authority by a time-serving bureaucrat (Pilate) or an insane megalomaniac (Nero).

BIBLICAL ARGUMENTS AGAINST CAPITAL PUNISHMENT

Again, we will cite five out of many possible arguments, along with the responses of those who support capital punishment.

- The Case of Cain (Genesis 4:8-15) - The argument here basically goes that the case of Cain is especially important in the capital punishment debate because Cain was history's first murderer. As such, God's treatment of him should be seen as establishing a precedent, giving insight into the heart of God, as it were. Opponents of capital punishment then draw a parallel between God's treatment of divorce in the civil law (Deuteronomy 24:1-4) and His clear opposition to the practice in passages such as Malachi 2:14-16. Did not Jesus say in Matthew 19:8 that the Old Testament permitted divorce only because of the hardness of men's hearts, but that this did not reflect the heart of God? Why should we not conclude the same with regard to capital punishment?

    Supporters of capital punishment argue that God's treatment of Cain should not be viewed as a precedent, but as an exception. On what basis do they make such an argument? First of all, the sparing of Cain can be seen as an exception because of Cain's own expectations (Genesis 4:14); he clearly thought that others would kill him because of what he had done.[75] Secondly, note the assurance that God gives to calm Cain's fears (Genesis 4:15) - God not only placed a mark on him to keep others from killing him, but also promised him that should anyone kill him, "vengeance shall be taken on him sevenfold." This doesn't mean that anyone who kills Cain will be killed seven times, but is a Hebrew figure of speech - when something is to be done sevenfold, that means it will surely happen. Both Cain's response and God's thus indicate that, for whatever God's reason might have been, His decision to spare Cain was an exception to His normal mode of dealing with such offenses.

- The Argument from the Law - Some capital punishment opponents argue that capital punishment is part of the Old Testament civil law, and thus is no longer applicable in modern society. While this may be true with regard to certain specific offenses (see above), it is clearly not true in general, since God mandates the practice both before the giving of the Law (Genesis 9:6) and after the end of the theocracy (Romans 13:4).

- The Teaching of Jesus - Those who dispute the question of capital punishment often wind up citing competing passages in the Sermon on the Mount. Opponents typically go to Jesus' words in Matthew 5:38-39, where Jesus, according to their interpretation, repudiates the *lex talionis* of the Old Testament in favor of a response of mercy and not returning evil for evil.

---

[75] Skeptics often ask who was around to kill him? His parents? Like those who point to Cain's wife in Genesis 4:17 to cast doubt on the veracity of Scripture, they forget that Adam and Eve had many other sons and daughters (Genesis 5:4). Nothing in the text indicates that the murder of Abel by his brother occurred when they were young. Abel certainly would have been avenged by other brothers, in the same way that Cain married his sister.

Several points should be noted here. In the first place, opponents of capital punishment really don't believe what they argue about this passage. Do they believe that if someone kills your daughter, you should offer your son as well? Do they believe that the state should not do anything to stop the evildoer? Of course not. They are thus highly selective in their application of the verse.

Secondly, we need to remember what Jesus is doing in this section of Matthew 5. He is decidedly *not* repudiating the Old Testament law, but is rejecting the ways in which the religious leaders of His day have twisted it. How, then, were they misusing the *lex talionis*? Essentially, they had taken a principle of legal justice and turned it into a guideline for personal relationships. When the Old Testament said that one is to take an eye for an eye and a tooth for a tooth, this did not mean that, if someone punches you in the mouth and knocks out one of your teeth, you can do the same to him. Justice was to be administered by the proper authorities, not taken into the hands of the individual. Jesus is not thus objecting to legal authorities doing their job of punishing wrongdoers, much less by doing so according to principles of justice. What He opposes is people taking the law into their own hands and seeking personal vengeance when they are the victims of evil treatment.

- The Case of the Adulterous Woman[76] (John 8:1-11) - How do opponents of capital punishment use this passage to bolster their case? First of all, Jesus refuses to condemn the woman to death despite the fact that Old Testament law would have required it. Secondly, He enunciates what they see as an important general principle in verse 7 - "Let him who is without sin among you be the first to throw a stone at her." In other words, only one who is without sin himself has the right to mete out punishment to others; since we are all guilty before God, we have no right to condemn those whose sins have simply been of a different character from our own.

Several responses are appropriate here. The first is again a charge of inconsistency; those who interpret the passage in this way don't really mean that no one has the right to condemn anyone else - the result would be societal anarchy. What they really mean is that no one who is not perfect has the right to condemn anyone else *to death*, but this is inconsistent, especially with the way such people often abuse Matthew 7:1.

Secondly, again the context of the encounter is important. The target in this incident is not the woman, but Jesus (John 8:6).[77] How could this be? For centuries the Jewish ruling authorities had possessed the power to condemn criminals to death; that power passed to the Sanhedrin in the early years of Roman rule. However, when Archelaus, son of Herod the Great, died in 6 AD, the Romans replaced him with a series of appointed prefects, one of whom was Pontius Pilate. One of the steps taken by these prefects was to reserve the power of capital punishment for themselves, thus depriving the Sanhedrin of the authority to execute anyone (this is why the religious leaders simply

---

[76] In our treatment of this passage, which is surrounded by many legitimate textual questions, we will assume its canonical status and deal with the moral conclusions that may rightly be drawn from the story. Even if the passage was not originally part of John's Gospel, it may well have been an actual encounter in the life of Jesus.

[77] If they had been serious about stamping out adultery, the man involved would have been present as well, since it is rather difficult to commit adultery by oneself.

couldn't put Jesus to death themselves, but needed Pilate's cooperation). The Pharisees thus constructed what they thought was an airtight trap in which they could catch Jesus. When they brought the woman before Him, they asked whether or not she should be stoned. If Jesus said no, He would have directly contradicted the Law of Moses, and the Pharisees would have rushed away, leaving the woman alone, and announced loudly to anyone who would listen that Jesus had spoken out against Mosaic Law. If, on the other hand, He had said to stone her, they would have gone immediately to Pilate and told him that Jesus was fomenting rebellion against Rome by arrogating to himself a power that only the Roman authorities possessed.

His escape from the trap was brilliant. Not only did He avoid falling into their hands, but He turned the tables on them, putting them in the same position with which they intended to catch Him. When He said that the one among them who was sinless should cast the first stone, they had two choices - breaking Roman law (the consequences of this would have been unthinkable, since they exercised what power they had left only by Roman sufferance) or admitting their own sin. To us, this would not seem like a difficult choice - after all, we all know Romans 3:23. But to the religious leaders of Jesus' day, sin was something only done by others - "sinners" were those who failed to keep every detail of the laws and traditions of the rabbis. The Pharisees and teachers of the law distinguished themselves from ordinary people because they knew those traditions so well and kept them so carefully; in fact, such law-keeping was the basis of their moral authority among the people. So admitting to being sinners was no easy task - it was tantamount to saying to the people over whom they wielded such strict rule, "We're just like everybody else." This is why they chose to slink away as quietly and unobtrusively as possible.

What, then, about Jesus' treatment of the woman? Why does He say, "Neither do I condemn you"? The first reason is a legal one - the Old Testament law required two or three witnesses in order to hand down the death penalty (Deuteronomy 17:6), and the woman's accusers had melted into the woodwork. No legal grounds remained to condemn her. On the other hand, she remained morally culpable. Even though she was no longer in legal jeopardy, Jesus reminded her that she had a higher Judge before whom she must stand - "Go, and from now on sin no more."

In short, the incident allows us to draw no conclusions whatsoever with regard to capital punishment. The reasons for Jesus' words, both to the Pharisees and to the woman, did not involve any objection to or repudiation of the death penalty, but were completely tied to the legal climate of the day and the intentions and needs of those involved in the confrontation.

- The Argument from Grace - The last argument against capital punishment from Scripture that we will consider is the idea that, since God wants everyone to be saved (II Peter 3:9), capital punishment is abhorrent to Him because it would deprive a person of the opportunity to repent and be converted. In practical terms, the argument is absurd because at the present time, those who are condemned to death have *years* in which to repent prior to their executions, if they even occur at all. More importantly, however, this argument completely discounts the sovereignty of God in salvation. We should never imagine God looking down benevolently on the earth from heaven and seeing someone executed, then crying out, "Oh, no! But I was going to save him tomorrow!" God's will in salvation, as in everything else, can never be thwarted by human sin or folly.

WAR

The question of war is another issue that many Christians have opposed by using the Sixth Commandment, despite the fact that war plays a prominent role in biblical history and in God's dealings with His people. Throughout Christian history, three basic positions on this issue have been espoused, with significant variations within each one.

WAR IS ALWAYS RIGHT

This view is grounded in the fact that the authority of the state comes from God (Romans 13:4), including the power to wield the sword. The Christian is commanded to obey the government, so if the state says to fight, the Christian ought to fight. In the Bible, men who fought for the armies of pagan empires are not condemned for doing so; in fact, many appear in a very positive light (e.g., Naaman in II Kings 5:1-4, the centurion in Luke 7:9 who is praised by Jesus for his faith, and Cornelius, the first Gentile convert to Christianity in Acts 10:1-2). One who obeys his ruler by going to war is thus not sinning. On this basis, many Christians fought for Germany in the First and Second World Wars, including Martin Niemoller (1892-1984), a U-boat commander in World War I who later became a Lutheran pastor. Those who take this position do not argue, of course, that all *actions* performed in war are just, or even all commands. They would not, for instance, adopt the Nuremberg defense where those on trial tried to excuse their role in the atrocities of the Holocaust by arguing that they were only following orders.

WAR IS ALWAYS WRONG

The pacifist view has a long and honorable history in the Christian church. Pacifists argue that no distinction should be made between actions of the state and actions of individuals (contra. argument on page 105 regarding Matthew 5:38-39, which is a key pacifist text along with Matthew 26:52 and Luke 22:49-51); if it is wrong for an individual to take human life, it is also wrong for the government to do so. War is a consequence of sin in the world, and is always evil. Christians should seek peace at any cost, even the cost of their own lives, rather than taking the life of another. Pacifists also often cite the practice of the early church in this regard. While it is true that Christians in the first three centuries generally refused to serve in the Roman army, their reason for doing so was not a principled pacifism, but rather the fact that anyone serving in the Roman military was required to offer incense to the genius of the emperor. With the conversion of Constantine in the early fourth century, that requirement was dropped and Christians willingly served in the military. Today, various Anabaptist groups (Mennonites, Amish, etc.) practice pacifism, along with Quakers[78] and Jehovah's Witnesses.

Not all pacifists put their convictions into practice in the same way, nor do they oppose war to the same extent:

---

[78] Quakers have strayed far from any biblical roots, and today are largely defined by their adherence to pacifism and their work for peace in the world.

- Some, believing that the government has the right to take life but Christians do not, willingly serve in the military in noncombatant roles - medics, chaplains, etc. - or contribute to the war effort at home through humanitarian work.
- Others are conscientious objectors, which in the United States is a justifiable reason for avoiding military service if it is a long-established personal conviction rather than a short-term convenience in order to avoid the military draft. Many of those who take this position also actively protest against governmental involvement in war.
- The most radical go beyond the refusal to serve and also seek to avoid supporting the war financially with their tax money. Some have gone so far as to calculate the percentage of tax revenue that goes to the Defense Department and withhold that percentage of their income taxes. The government frowns on this behavior, of course; while conscientious objection may excuse someone from military service, it does not excuse him from paying taxes. Even should the government prosecute such tax resisters, pacifists will often willingly go to jail rather than paying for what they see as immoral behavior on the part of the state.

The Bible, however, contains many teachings that would contradict the beliefs of pacifists. We have already mentioned the authority of the state to bear the sword and the positive treatment accorded soldiers in foreign armies in several cases in the Bible. We should also add the following:

- God frequently commanded His people to go to war. Nothing is more obvious in the Old Testament than that war was an instrument of God's judgment against evil in the world.
- Many great men of God engaged in military activity, including Abraham, Joshua, many of the Judges, and David (though David's involvement in bloodshed kept him from building the Temple - I Chronicles 22:6-8).
- John the Baptist, when preaching repentance to the crowds, was approached by soldiers who asked him what repentance meant for them. Instead of telling them to resign from the army, he told them to avoid extortion and be content with their wages (Luke 3:14).
- Jesus told His disciples to buy and carry swords (Luke 22:36).
- Paul took advantage of the protection provided by the Roman army (Acts 22:25-29; 23:23).
- The Bible often uses military metaphors in a positive context (e.g., Ephesians 6:10-20; II Timothy 2:1-4).
- Fundamentally, pacifism takes an unrealistic view of the sinfulness of man. Jesus assured His followers that wars would always exist (Matthew 24:6-7); in fact, they would get increasingly worse as the end approached. To think that evil can be fought by negotiation and compromise is to fail to recognize the depth of human depravity.[79] The goal of pacifism is totally unrealistic and unattainable in a sinful world.

Thus, while war is evil, it is a necessary evil in a sinful world.

---

[79] Appeasement has never brought peace, as Neville Chamberlain discovered when he attempted to negotiate with Hitler, and as diplomats who seek to compromise with evil men like Mahmoud Ahmadinejad of Iran are discovering today.

WAR IS SOMETIMES RIGHT AND SOMETIMES WRONG

This view, generally called the Just War Theory, has been the most prevalent in Christian history, and the passages cited above that indicate that war is sometimes the right thing to do would support the conclusion.[80]

First enunciated by Augustine of Hippo (354-430) and later expanded by Thomas Aquinas (1225-1274), the Just War Theory contains the following basic elements, though not all who hold the position would agree on the details:

- *Jus ad bellum* - "Justice before the war" requires that war have a just cause. But what constitutes a just cause?
  - Are only wars of defense permissible, so that a nation may go to war only if it is attacked first? What if one's ally is attacked - does involvement in that situation still constitute a war of defense? This was an important issue in World War I, where webs of interlocking alliances, some of which were secret, turned a minor regional conflict into a world-enveloping conflagration. Most would agree, however, that wars of aggression, seeking to conquer one's neighbors or annex their territory, are by their nature unjust.
  - May one go to war in order to prevent greater shedding of blood? Some justified the decision to drop atomic bombs on Hiroshima and Nagasaki in 1945 by arguing that more than a million lives would be saved by bringing Japan immediately to its knees and avoiding the need for a land invasion of the island nation. When Saddam Hussein was building a nuclear reactor in Iraq in 1981 with the express intention of using nuclear weapons against Israel, the Israeli Air Force launched a midnight preemptive strike and bombed the reactor. The same response is being considered today by both Israel and the United States as Iran moves rapidly into the nuclear age with the intention of developing nuclear weapons, and has threatened both nations in the process.
  - Is it justifiable to fight a war to prevent injustice when you are not being attacked, but some tyrant is taking advantage of a weaker nation or oppressing his own people? The Persian Gulf War of 1990-1991 was fought when Iraq invaded its helpless neighbor Kuwait, while the present Iraqi War was initiated, among other reasons, because Saddam Hussein was conducting a murderous reign of terror against his own people. In fact, most United States military interventions since the Vietnam War fit into this category, including incursions into Somalia and Bosnia. But should the United States, as the world's only superpower, also be the world's policeman?
  - Though not all would agree on the appropriate boundaries here, most would affirm that war ought to be a last resort, preceded by negotiations and attempts at a peaceful settlement of grievances if at all possible.

---

[80] The fact that war is sometimes wrong can be seen in such things as Jeremiah's insistence in Jeremiah 27:5-8 that Judah not resist the Babylonians militarily, Nahum's condemnation of Assyrian atrocities, and Jesus' refusal in Matthew 26:52 to allow His followers to use the sword to prevent persecution.

- *Jus in bello* - "Justice during war" involves the manner in which the war is fought. Just War advocates would not agree that "all is fair in love and war." What does the just conduct of war involve?
    - During the Middle Ages, the Catholic Church attempted to limit the carnage of war by decreeing that fighting was forbidden on certain days and during certain seasons - Sundays, Christmas and Easter, various saints' days, and during Lent. This practice was known as the Truce of God.[81]
    - The Medieval Church also sought to protect noncombatants, forbidding violence against the clergy, peasants, women and children - the Peace of God.
    - Since the Middle Ages, many have sought to define Just War in terms of avoiding harm to civilians in general. During the eighteenth century (and even during the Civil War), military battles were viewed as spectator sports - gentry would gather on the hillsides overlooking the battlefield and watch the combat as it unfolded in the valley below, and would be fully confident of their own safety.
    - Modern warfare has complicated this immensely. With guerilla war and terrorism, the enemy combatants simply don't wear uniforms, and thus can't easily be distinguished from civilians. Terrorists use this to their own advantage, setting up operating centers and launching missiles from schools and hospitals, hoping that the enemy will retaliate and that many civilians will be killed in the process. In doing this they hope to pull off a public relations coup by accusing their enemies of atrocities against civilians, at the same time ramping up their recruiting efforts.
    - Furthermore, highly-destructive weapons launched remotely inevitably kill civilians. Both the Battle of Britain and the Royal Air Force carpet bombing of German cities like Dresden showed the impossibility of distinguishing between military and civilian targets, even had the bombers wished to do so. Atomic weapons are even worse, of course, and for that reason some Just War advocates have argued that nuclear war is inherently immoral.
    - A just war is also one in which the wounded and prisoners of war are treated humanely. The atrocities practiced by the Germans and Japanese in this regard led to the signing of the Geneva Convention in 1949, requiring certain standards for the treatment of prisoners. Much of the discussion concerning the appropriateness of using "strong interrogation techniques" with terrorists stems from this principle.
    - A just war is also one that pursues limited ends (one does not respond to a border skirmish by nuking the other nation's capital city) and uses limited means (only what is necessary to produce justice and terminate the conflict).
    - Finally, a just war is one that is formally declared by a legitimate state. Private citizens may not conduct war against their government or any other, nor may radical groups turn to violence to achieve their ends, thus rendering terrorism by definition immoral.
    - The wars of the Old Testament have complicated these matters, especially the Conquest of Canaan under Joshua. The Conquest was certainly a war of aggression, and was carried out for the acquisition of territory. Furthermore, God

---

[81] By the time the Church was done adding days on which fighting was forbidden, soldiers had a difficult time finding periods of time in which fighting could be carried on. Perhaps this was really the point.

required the complete extermination of the Canaanites - men, women, children, and even livestock - and was angry when the Israelites failed to do so. In other situations God also required the killing of prisoners (I Samuel 15:32-33 - the incident that ultimately cost Saul his throne for *refusing* the wholesale slaughter of the enemy), though at times a policy of mercy was pursued (II Kings 6:20-23, which also implies that mercy to prisoners was by then general practice). The Conquest later was used as a model and justification for such disreputable Christian military efforts as the Crusades.

- *Jus post bellum* - "Justice after the war" involves largely the search for a just peace as opposed to vengeance. The great World Wars of the twentieth century provide an excellent illustration of this principle. After World War I, Woodrow Wilson sought a just and equitable "peace without victory," but the Allies, particularly France and to a lesser extent Britain, were out for vengeance. The result was the weakening and humiliation of Germany, destroying its economy (despite the brief respite and rebuilding produced by the Dawes Plan in 1925 before the disaster of the Great Depression) and embittering the population (the infamous War Guilt Clause that forced Germany to claim total responsibility for the war), thus opening the door for the rise of a demagogue like Adolf Hitler.

  By the time World War II came along, the Allies had clearly learned their lesson. The defeated Axis Powers were rebuilt after the war, and both Germany and Japan became thriving democracies and staunch allies of the West. The exception here, of course, was the behavior of the Soviet Union, which sought revenge against the Axis by bleeding its conquered client states dry, eventually leading to the collapse of the Iron Curtain beginning in 1989.

Ultimately, the wickedness of the world, while making war a necessity at times, also makes it morally problematic. Even those who seek in good conscience to follow the teachings of the Scriptures in their involvement with and conduct of war struggle mightily with the issue. In many ways it boils down to a matter of conscience, though we should always seek to apply God's Word faithfully and carefully to this difficult aspect of human experience.

ABORTION

Abortion is *the* defining social issues in contemporary America. No other question has done more to energize people on both sides of the issue, and no question has produced more political engagement and social outreach among Christians. It is also highly emotionally charged. Because it is vital for today's students to be equipped to deal with the question intelligently and biblically, we will be devoting a great deal of space to the different aspects of the question.

BIBLICAL ARGUMENTS

When we ask ourselves the question, "What does the Bible say about abortion?" the obvious answer is, "nothing." Scripture doesn't mention abortion at all, though herbal approaches to the termination of pregnancy were practiced in some parts of the ancient world. How, then, can we hope to apply the Scriptures to the most burning issue of our day? What we need to do is go behind the practice to the underlying principle on which the whole question of abortion is based, and that is the personhood of the child in the womb; this is something that the Bible *does* address. First of all, however, we should look at two passages that are sometimes used to argue *against* the personhood of the fetus.

The first of these is Genesis 2:7. Here we are told that God "formed the man of dust from the ground and breathed into his nostrils the breath of life, and the man became a living creature." Some defenders of abortion argue on the basis of this verse that personhood does not occur until man takes his first breath; then he becomes a "living soul," as the KJV translated it. But drawing general conclusions about human personhood from the creation of Adam is dangerous, especially since he never *was* a fetus in the womb. The verse marks the transition of the first human being from nonliving to living status, not from nonhuman life to human life (not even the most violent defenders of abortion would argue that the fetus in the womb is not alive). One simply can't argue on the basis of this verse that one becomes human when he takes his first breath any more than one can argue that one becomes alive when he takes his first breath.

The second, found in Exodus 21:22-25, the passage we examined earlier in connection with the *lex talionis*, is more complex. The four evangelical Bible translations given below illustrate the nature of the problem:

> If men strive, and hurt a woman with child, so that her fruit depart *from her*, and yet no mischief follow: he shall be surely punished, according as the woman's husband will lay upon him; and he shall pay as the judges *determine*. And if *any* mischief follow, then thou shalt give life for life, eye for eye, tooth for tooth, hand for hand, foot for foot, burning for burning, wound for wound, stripe for stripe. (KJV)

> And *if* men struggle with each other and strike a woman with child so that she has a miscarriage, yet there is no *further* injury, he shall surely be fined as the woman's husband may demand of him; and he shall pay as the judges *decide*. But if there is *any further* injury, then you shall appoint *as a penalty* life for life, eye for eye, tooth for tooth, hand for hand, foot for foot, burn for burn, wound for wound, bruise for bruise. (NASB)

> If men who are fighting hit a pregnant woman and she gives birth prematurely but there is no serious injury, the offender must be fined whatever the woman's husband demands and the court allows. But if there is serious injury, you are to take life for life, eye for eye, tooth for tooth, hand for hand, foot for foot, burn for burn, wound for wound, bruise for bruise. (NIV)

> When men strive together and hit a pregnant woman, so that her children come out, but there is no harm, the one who hit her shall surely be fined, as the woman's husband shall impose upon him, and he shall pay as the judges determine. But if there is harm, then you shall pay life for life, eye for eye, tooth for tooth, hand for hand, foot for foot, burn for burn, wound for wound, stripe for stripe. (ESV)

The key phrase here is the one translated in the KJV "so that her fruit depart." This is a literal translation of the Hebrew, but these words can be interpreted two ways - as referring to a miscarriage (NASB) or a premature birth (NIV, ESV). The difference, of course, is huge when one deals with the question of the personhood of the baby in the womb. If the passage speaks of a miscarriage, then the penalty for killing the baby is a fine, but that for hurting or killing the mother is the *lex talionis* - the life of the baby does not have the same value as that of the mother;

some have used this to argue that abortion is at some times permissible (see the discussion of Hierarchicalism on pages 11-12). On the other hand, if the passage refers to a premature birth where no harm is done to mother or baby, the result is a fine, but any harm done *to either one* brings the *lex talionis* into play. Thus, there is no moral distinction between the life of the mother and that of the baby. In fact, this verse would then go beyond what most opponents of abortion would argue today in stating that the death of the baby in the womb when the mother is an innocent bystander and no harm was intended to either mother or baby (i.e., the death of the baby was a tragic accident) would still subject the perpetrator to capital punishment. If this is the case, how much more is one who deliberately causes the death of a baby in the womb culpable before God!

We have not yet resolved the question, however, of which reading is the correct one. After all, the NASB is for good reason a translation highly respected among evangelicals. Do we have any indications that the NASB got it wrong, while the NIV and the ESV got it right? Note the following:

- The main verb translated "depart" in the KJV is the common Hebrew word for going from one place to another - you would use it if you left the room at the bell to go to your next class. It is *never*, either in the Bible or in extrabiblical literature, used to describe death.[82]
- The NASB needed to augment the text to make sense out of its reading. Both the KJV and the NASB helpfully use italics to indicate words that were not in the original Hebrew but were inserted to clarify the sentence using standard English. The key word in this case is the word *further*, which appears twice in the NASB reading of this passage. While the text states that, in the first case, no harm at all was done, the NASB must insert the word in question into the translation in order for the miscarriage reading to make sense.
- The NASB was first published in 1971, before the abortion controversy came to dominate the national moral discourse. I strongly suspect that the translators did not understand the full implications of the decision they had made, or how it would be used to defend the indefensible. When a revised version of the NASB was published in 1995, the translators fixed the problem, giving it the same sense found in the other modern evangelical translations.

We will now move on to consider passages from Scripture that support the full humanity of the baby in the womb from the time of conception:

- Psalm 139:13-16 - This is perhaps the best known and most frequently used of all pro-life passages. Yet how does this passage demonstrate the humanity of the baby in the womb? It indicates that God formed the child, and that God knows the child's days before one of them takes place, but these two things could be said for any of God's creatures. The fact that all were created by God, and that, in His omniscience, He knows all about them before they even exist, is true of monkeys as well as people. What, then, is the value of this passage for the question before us? Perhaps the heart of the matter is found in the use

---

[82] Part of the problem here is that the word *depart* is often used as a euphemism for death in English. When we speak of the "dear departed," we refer to someone who has died, not one who has gone on vacation.

of personal pronouns. David continually refers to that little life in the womb as *me*. No doubt can exist that the Psalmist saw complete continuity between his existence before birth and the life he lived afterward. That baby David describes was *David*, not some pre-David or potential David, and far less a blob of tissue.

- Psalm 51:5 - David here describes himself as a sinner from conception. Only human beings can be sinners, therefore a child is human from the point of his conception. Note that this also supports the doctrine of original sin and the imputation of Adam's sin to his descendants.

- Judges 13:3-5 - When the birth of Samson is announced, his parents are told that he is to be a lifelong Nazirite (this was unusual - someone normally took the Nazirite vow for a discrete period of time). In order for him to be a lifelong Nazirite, however, his mother *had to keep the Nazirite vow for him* while he was in the womb, regulating her own food intake accordingly. This points strongly toward the humanity of the child from conception.

- Jeremiah 1:5 - This verse, often used to support the humanity of the baby in the womb, is not effective in doing so. It speaks of God's omniscience - He knew Jeremiah before his birth, and even before his conception, and appointed him to a prophetic ministry. Again, knowledge does not equal human personhood. In fact, this verse, if used to try to prove personhood, would prove too much - would anyone seriously argue that Jeremiah was therefore a person *before conception*?

- In the New Testament, several verses in Luke 1 point toward the personhood of the baby in the womb. In verse 15, John the Baptist is described as being "filled with the Holy Spirit, even from his mother's womb." Only human beings have this privilege. Jesus, in verse 35, is clearly the Son of God from conception by the Holy Spirit, and the biblical teaching of the full manhood and full Godhood of Christ would imply that He was fully man from the same point. Later, in verses 41-45, Elizabeth, under the inspiration of the Holy Spirit, ascribes the response of John the Baptist in her womb upon hearing the voice of Mary to a very human emotion - "the baby in my womb leaped for joy."

Thus the evidence that does exist in the Bible points clearly toward the full humanity and personhood of the baby from the point of conception, not from some intermediate time between conception and birth.[83] Abortion therefore is the murder of a living human being.

THEOLOGICAL ARGUMENTS

The question of original sin enters into the abortion discussion in another way as well. Theologians over the years have argued over the question of the origin of the human soul. Two basic views have emerged - *Creationism* and *Traducianism*. According to the first, each human soul is a special creation of God, made by Him and implanted in the body at some stage known only to Him. The second, on the other hand, argues that the soul comes into existence at the same time and in the same way as the body - by the union of the parents. Note the following:

---

[83] Interestingly, some abortion supporters admit the humanity of the fetus, but continue to justify abortion by arguing that the life and well-being of the mother take precedence despite the fact that abortions to save the life of the mother are extremely rare.

- Because Creationism (which has nothing to do with the contemporary use of the term in opposition to evolution) allows for the implantation of the soul into the body at any time God chooses, one might easily use it to argue that the baby is not a person from conception, but only when the soul is implanted by God. Some would date this from the time of quickening (when the baby can be felt moving in the womb), viability (when the baby is able to survive outside the womb - see below), birth, or even after birth.[84]
- Creationism generates problems with regard to the question of sin. If those who hold the position are right, either the seat of sin is found in the body and not the soul, or else God creates sinful souls. Neither of these fits the teachings of Scripture.
- Traducianism clearly leads to the conclusion that the baby is fully human from conception, because it has a soul from the moment it has a body. Note that this also fits with the Bible's teaching concerning original sin - the baby is a sinner from conception because its soul is received from its sinful parents.

SCIENTIFIC ARGUMENTS

Science also provides information that can be helpful in addressing the issue of the humanity of the baby in the womb. Note the following:

- On a very basic level, what is the baby in the womb if *not* a human being? A bird in the shell is a baby bird, not a potential bird; the same is true of people.
- Furthermore, the baby in the womb is a unique human being because of its genetic makeup. The child takes half its genetic material from each of the parents, and is thus genetically distinct from its mother or from any other person. Genetically, one cannot possibly describe the fetus as a part of the mother's body, like an appendix, that can be removed and discarded if the need arises.
- Some argue that, since spontaneous abortions, which occur before the mother even knows she is pregnant, are very commonplace, abortion is simply congruent with the operations of nature itself. This in no way addresses the moral issue involved. The child who is spontaneously aborted is still a genetically unique human being who, for reasons known only to God, dies after a very short period of existence. A tsunami in the Indian Ocean may drown thousands of people, but that does not give us the right to drown those who may be inconvenient to us.
- Viability is a question often injected into the abortion debate. Viability - the point at which a baby is able to survive outside the womb - cannot, however, be used as the dividing line between human and nonhuman. Why is this the case?
    - The genetic issue raised above shows that the identity of the individual undergoes no significant changes from conception to birth and thereafter.
    - Viability cannot be pinpointed; no doctor alive can tell a woman, "Today your baby is not viable, but tomorrow it will be, so if you want to avoid taking a human life, you need to have the abortion today." Thus to use viability as a guideline for legalizing abortion, as was the case with Roe v. Wade, is preposterous.

---

[84] Some Jewish rabbis argued that the soul was implanted by God on the eighth day after birth because that was the day designated for circumcision to occur.

- Furthermore, the point of viability keeps moving earlier as technology improves. While the survival of a six-month-old fetus was unthinkable only a few years ago, such babies survive more and more frequently today. It is even conceivable that technology might reach a point where the entire gestational process could occur outside the womb in an artificial incubator; if such were ever to occur, viability and conception would become one and the same.

METHODS OF ABORTION

The discussion of this aspect of the abortion question is extremely painful, yet it plays a vital role in the moral assessment of the practice. Modern advocates have done everything possible to sanitize the process, both in their insistence in avoiding the use of the word *baby* in favor of *fetus*, or, even worse, *product of conception*. Groups like Planned Parenthood, which reap enormous profits from doing abortions, try to picture them in neutral, sanitized terms, so that many young people today really have no idea what actually happens in an abortion. The horror of the reality needs to be impressed on our young people despite the uncomfortable nature of the discussion.

FIRST-TRIMESTER ABORTIONS

- Some forms of artificial birth control are not birth control at all, but abortifacients. This includes most forms of birth control pill, which often contain a second drug in case conception is not prevented, the IUD (intrauterine device), and the so-called "morning-after pill." All prevent the fertilized egg from continuing to grow in the mother's reproductive tract.
- RU-486 (Mifepristone) - Usually referred to as the abortion pill, it is actually a series of oral medications taken over several days that prevent the implantation of the embryo into the uterine wall.
- Dilation and curettage (D&C) - In this procedure, a sharp instrument is inserted into the woman's uterus, which is then scraped to detach the implanted baby. The child is shredded in the process, and all the body pieces must be accounted for by the abortionist in order to prevent infection.
- Suction abortion - The idea here is basically the same, except that the baby is detached from the uterine wall by a powerful vacuum device; again, the baby is dismembered and all parts must be carefully laid out and counted.

SECOND-TRIMESTER ABORTIONS

The baby is now too big for the methods used during the first trimester, so a different approach to destroying it is needed. The most common practice here is the saline abortion. A large needle is inserted directly through the woman's abdomen and into the sac containing the baby. A strong salt solution is then injected into the amniotic fluid, which kills the baby by burning off its skin. This process often takes as much as an hour, during which time the baby is thrashing around in pain. The mother then delivers a dead, shriveled-up baby.

A few babies have actually survived this horrific procedure. Normally, when a child exposed to a saline abortion is born alive, the child is set aside while the abortionist attends to the mother. By the time the doctor gets around to checking on the baby, it has died, and no record is left of the failure of the procedure, which is viewed as nothing more than a "botched abortion." In one particularly notorious case, Dr. William Waddell, an abortionist in California, performed a saline abortion in which the baby was alive when delivered. The baby was set aside, but when the nurses pointed out to him that the child was still alive, he ordered everyone from the room, then pinched the umbilical cord to cut off the baby's oxygen supply, then finally strangled the child, which then died. After being put on trial for murder, the charges were dropped because two juries wound up deadlocked over the technical definition of death in California law. In another case, Gianna Jessen, who survived a saline abortion in California and contracted cerebral palsy as a result, now travels around the country speaking against abortion and telling audiences about how the grace of Christ has transformed her life.

THIRD-TRIMESTER ABORTIONS

By the third trimester, the baby is able to live outside the womb, so the methods used to kill it increasingly come to resemble those used for live births.

- Prostaglandin Abortion - Prostaglandin is a drug used to induce labor in women who have gone past their due date or who for some other reason need to deliver the baby without further delay. In this case, the procedure is the same, but the goal is to kill the baby rather than delivering it. Toxic chemicals are injected into the womb to ensure that the baby does not survive.
- Hysterotomy - This is a surgical procedure normally called a Cesarean section, in which an incision is made directly in the mother's abdomen in order to remove the child. In a normal C-section, the baby is delivered alive, but here steps are taken to ensure that such a thing does not occur, including cutting the umbilical cord before delivering the child.
- Partial Birth Abortion (Intact Dilation and Extraction) - The most grisly technique in a grisly list, this involves delivering the child feet first until only the head remains in the birth canal, at which point the baby's skull is punctured and the brains are sucked out, collapsing the skull to make removal easier. This was banned by Congress in 2003, and the ban was upheld by the Supreme Court in 2007.

LEGAL STATUS

Despite what abortion supporters claim, abortions have been illegal throughout most of Western history, basically since the cultural dominance of Christianity. Practitioners of folk medicine over the years have performed them covertly, but they were never openly accepted. More recently, the "back-alley" abortions and self-induced terminations used so effectively as an emotional appeal by abortion advocates arose where legitimate doctors refused to perform the operations. After the middle of the twentieth century, some states in the U.S. began to loosen restrictions against abortion, and clamor arose for wider legalization. By the early seventies, a hodgepodge of state laws existed, from New York allowing abortions on demand to some Southern states that outlawed it entirely. This was the context in which the landmark Roe v. Wade case arrived at the Supreme Court.

- Roe v. Wade (1973) - A Texas woman named Norma McCorvey wanted to abort her baby, but Texas law would not permit it. Friends convinced her to claim she had been raped and get a legal abortion that way. After receiving encouragement to do so from lawyers representing Planned Parenthood, she eventually sued, under the alias Jane Roe, to have the law overturned, and the case made its way to the Supreme Court. On January 22, 1973, the Court majority declared abortion to be a legal right under the United States Constitution, in the process throwing out all state laws that regulated abortion. The Court decision was based on the Fourteenth Amendment's guarantee of due process, arguing that the "penumbra" of the amendment implied a right to privacy, on which the decision was then based. Key elements of Roe v. Wade included the following:
    - Outlawing state restriction of abortion prior to viability (which was never defined, though it has generally been interpreted to include the first two trimesters - see page 115 above)
    - Even in the third trimester, abortion must be permitted when the life or health of the mother is at stake.
    - Even after viability, the fetus is not a legal person, and thus possesses no constitutional rights.
    - States are prohibited from restricting abortions to hospitals, thus legalizing abortion clinics (from which Planned Parenthood derives enormous profits).

  Ironically, McCorvey eventually became a Christian, and is now an outspoken abortion opponent.
- Doe v. Bolton (1973) - Decided at the same time and released on the same day, this companion case of the better-known Roe v. Wade ruling overturned Georgia's restrictions against abortion. The most notable element in Doe v. Bolton was its definition of health, which required states to consider "physical, emotional, psychological, familial, and age" issues in restricting late-term abortions. In effect, this legalized abortion on demand. Again, the story of the plaintiff here is interesting. The woman on whose behalf the suit was filed, Sandra Cano, later argued that her lawyer had deceived her in order to find a plaintiff and that she was opposed to abortion, but when she tried to have the decision overturned, the Supreme Court refused to hear her request.
- Webster v. Reproductive Health Services (1989) - This case, which concerned a Missouri law, was the first of many attempts by the states to chip away at the legality of abortion by restricting the circumstances under which abortions could be performed. The law, upheld by the Supreme Court, forbade the use of state funds for abortions and prohibited state-funded doctors from counseling, encouraging, or performing abortions after viability unless the life of the mother was at stake. The Missouri law also stated that the fetus had the same rights as children who had already been born, "subject to limits imposed by the federal constitution and federal court rulings" - a strange construction indeed.
- Planned Parenthood v. Casey (1992) - This case originated in Pennsylvania, and represents the closest the Supreme Court has ever gotten to overturning Roe v. Wade. The Pennsylvania law required that a woman seeking an abortion give informed consent, thus requiring abortion clinics to provide health information and rudimentary counseling; that abortion clinics keep certain records that must be available for inspection in ways that did not compromise patient confidentiality; that a 24-hour waiting period be required before an abortion could be performed to allow for careful consideration of the decision; that

parents of minors be required to give consent before they could get abortions (this was watered down by the Court, which insisted that a girl who feared the consequences of informing her parents be permitted to get consent from a judge instead); and that the spouse of the woman seeking the abortion, if she was married, give consent for the procedure (this last requirement was struck down by the Court and has continued to be rejected, on the basis that the decision is one between the woman and her doctor in which the father of the baby has no legal standing, along with the fear that such a requirement would foster spousal abuse).

- Stenberg v. Carhart (2000) - Nebraska outlawed partial birth abortion, but the Supreme Court struck down the law.
- Gonzales v. Carhart (2003) - Nebraska tried again after Congress had banned partial birth abortion, and this time the Court upheld the law.

Pro-life activists continue to try to erode the legal standing of abortion. One recent effort in Pennsylvania outlawed the practice of taking a minor across state lines in order to obtain an abortion without parental knowledge or consent. The case originated when a school guidance counselor arranged an abortion for a high school student and took her to New York himself in order to get the operation, all without telling the parents, who were understandably furious when they found out. Meanwhile, 29 states have passed fetal murder laws under which a man who murders a pregnant woman can be charged with a double homicide (the most notorious example being the murder by Scott Peterson of his pregnant wife Laci in 2002); needless to say, because these laws strongly imply the personhood of the unborn baby and the existence of civil rights for the fetus, they have been fought tooth and nail by abortion advocates. Even such laws are forced to contain strange language, noting that the killing of an unborn baby is to be considered murder unless it is done with the consent of the mother. At the same time, a constitutional amendment affirming the full personhood of the unborn child has repeatedly been introduced into Congress, and has repeated failed to obtain the necessary support.

SOCIAL ARGUMENTS

Abortion advocates have over the years made a variety of arguments to support their case. We now turn to a sampling of those arguments, along with rejoinders.

- Overpopulation - Many have argued that the human race and the environment alike are threatened by overpopulation, and that abortion is a necessary tool in combating that threat. China has certainly taken this argument seriously by instituting a one-child policy with draconian measures taken against any who violate it. However, some population experts argue that the declining birthrate, especially in the Western world, is the real threat, producing an aging population and fewer people to support them. Even if overpopulation is a legitimate concern, however, the response should not neglect moral considerations. After all, if one is willing to murder to keep the population down, there are certainly more efficient ways to do so.
- Unwanted and unloved children - The argument here is that abortion is an act of mercy to children who are not wanted by their parents and would then be subject to abuse or neglect. Two questions must be asked in response to this argument:

- Unwanted by whom? If children are not wanted by their parents, many families are eager to adopt a healthy child. The difficulty and expense of adoption are directly related to the lack of suitable children to adopt, especially since more than fifty million babies have been murdered in the U.S. since Roe v. Wade in 1973.

- Unwanted when? Abortions are often seen as the only way out by women experiencing the shock of an unexpected pregnancy. Yet the testimony of many is that the bonding that occurs during pregnancy changes the heart, so that the child who was unwanted when the woman first learned she was pregnant is very much wanted and loved by the time he or she is born.

- Many unwanted children have, by the grace of God, led fulfilling and productive lives. This assumes knowledge of the quality of a child's future life that one simply cannot have.

- Economics - Some argue that abortion is economically beneficial, not only because of overpopulation concerns, but also because it keeps the welfare rolls down. But the end doesn't justify the means; bombing the ghetto would keep the welfare rolls down as well, but that doesn't make it right. This also assumes that most abortions are performed on the poor, which is not necessarily the case; many from well-to-do families seek abortions as a matter of personal convenience.

- A Woman's Right to Control Her Own Body - This is a constant feminist screed, but they never seem to consider the woman's responsibility to control her own body when she is in the process of getting pregnant. Furthermore, as we saw earlier, the baby is *not* her body, but a distinct individual life.

- Favoritism for the Rich - This bizarre argument goes something like this: If abortion were outlawed, it would constitute discrimination against the poor, since the rich could circumvent the law by going somewhere where abortions are legal and getting one anyway. Anyone who makes such an argument is already assuming that abortions are right and should be accessible to all. However, if they are murder, then advocates might as well argue that laws against contract killings are discriminatory because the rich can afford to hire a quality hit man and get away with it while the poor must settle for drive-by shootings.

SPECIAL CONSIDERATIONS

Here, finally, we get to the toughest cases that often occupy most of the abortion debate. Though more than ninety-five percent of abortions are completely elective, abortion advocates focus their attention on the remaining five percent, the heart-rending tragedies and difficult dilemmas the minority face, in order to support the freedom of all to kill their children:

- Rape and Incest - Horrific though these may be, only a small percentage result in pregnancy and even fewer arrive at abortion clinics. Though the federal courts have required these exceptions to be included in any restrictions on abortion, even in the last trimester, abortions for these reasons are morally indefensible. Fundamentally, abortion in these situations is punishing the child for the sin of the father, which is forbidden in Deuteronomy 24:16. Advocates like to point out the cruelty of making a woman carry to term a pregnancy that resulted from such abuse, reminding her every day of the horrors she has experienced. But a few other matters need to be considered:

- • Abortion will not take away the memory of abuse.
- • Women who have been abused often carry false guilt, thinking that they are somehow responsible for how they have been treated. What good is accomplished by adding genuine guilt to that false guilt by making the woman responsible for her own child's death?
- • That child may, by the grace of God, become a blessing to many.

- • Fetal Defects - The argument here is that defective children will lead such miserable lives that aborting them is a mercy, both to themselves and to their parents.
  - • This is a selfish "quality of life" argument that gives the quality of one person's life priority over the existence of another person's life.
  - • The assumption that only a "normal" life is worth living leads to the Holocaust.
  - • It ignores the fact that doctors and tests are not always right. How many people are told by their doctors that their babies have birth defects, decide to continue with the pregnancy, and later find that the baby is fine?[85]
  - • Handicapped and disabled people have often been a blessing to their parents and to the world, and are created by God for a purpose (Exodus 4:11).

- • Health of the Mother - Again, provisions for this have been consistently required by the courts. But note again that this is a quality of life argument, concluding that the woman's health is more important than the baby's life. If my psychological condition could be improved by eliminating my obnoxious next-door neighbor, am I justified in doing so? The insistence of the courts that factors other than physical health be included here has opened the door so wide that almost any excuse for abortion has become legitimate.

- • Life of the Mother - This is obviously the hardest case, and, like rape and incest, makes up only a very small percentage of abortions. We must divide our consideration of this final issue into two separate situations:
  - • When the threat to the mother's life comes late in pregnancy, abortion is never justified. No, I am not suggesting that the woman simply be allowed to die, perhaps killing the baby as well. What we must recognize is that the goal should be to save life *as much as it is possible to do so*. Thus the proper approach is to allow the pregnancy to continue as long as possible without threatening the mother's life, then remove the baby *with the intention of saving it if at all possible*. This is not an abortion, it is a life-saving operation that has as its goal the preservation of *two* lives.[86]
  - • When the threat to the mother's life comes in the early stages of pregnancy, such as when the fertilized egg becomes lodged in the fallopian tubes and does not continue down to the uterus for implantation, the situation is very different. If the baby continues to grow in the fallopian tubes, they will burst, and both mother and baby will die. In situations such as this, theoretically one should take the same

---

[85] A college Ethics professor described the following situation to his freshmen: "A woman is pregnant with her fifth child. Her husband has syphilis, she has tuberculosis, the first of their children was born blind, the second died, the third was deaf and mute, while the fourth was tuberculous as well." When he asked the class what they would advise, they unanimously advocated abortion. His response? "You just killed Beethoven."

[86] Rick Santorum, pro-life former Senator from Pennsylvania, and his wife faced this situation and made the decision to continue with the pregnancy against the advice of their doctors. Both baby and mother survived.

approach described above, operating to save the mother with the intention of saving the baby as well, but with current technology, such a thing is simply not possible. In this case, nothing known to modern medicine will save the baby, so the doctor should do everything possible to save the mother. This, because of the intention to save the baby if at all possible, even while knowing that it is *not* possible, is not, at least technically, an abortion, meaning that even in this extreme case, abortion is not justifiable.

GENETIC ENGINEERING

The widespread acceptance of abortion today raises the question of what might logically follow, and the warnings about starting down a slippery slope in our lack of regard for the sanctity of human life have been abundantly justified by developments in recent years that have further ingrained in society the idea that concerns for the quality of life may take precedence over the very existence of life. One of the ways this idea is being increasingly explored and implemented is in the improvement of human experience by the elimination of what is substandard and attempts to perpetuate what is viewed as superior.

METHODS OF GENETIC ENGINEERING

True genetic engineering has appeared on the scene relatively recently, but in our consideration of the topic we will take a broader view, looking at and seeking to evaluate a variety of methods designed to control in one way or another the human gene pool. We will start by listing a few examples of techniques of eliminating undesirable genetic material.

- Abortion - Performing abortions in order to destroy children who are considered for one reason or another to be defective fits into our category. Note that infanticide of seriously handicapped children is another more extreme example of the same idea.
- Sterilization - The idea here is that bearers of inferior genetic stock should not be permitted to reproduce. Hitler, of course, tried this with those he considered inferior before opting for a more drastic approach. Furthermore, few people realize that this issue was the crusade around which Planned Parenthood was originally built by its founder, Margaret Sanger (1879-1966). She not only believed that widely-disseminated birth control would allow women to have the same sexual freedom as men, but she was also concerned that certain segments of the American population, such as immigrants and minorities, were growing far too fast for the good of the country. Her response to this was mandatory sterilization for undesirables. Few recognize the racist roots of the organization that has come to have such an influential voice in a variety of social issues today. Many today continue to advocate the procedure for the mentally retarded.[87] Ironically, as abortion has

---

[87] One striking case in our area occurred when a mentally handicapped woman in an institution was raped by an orderly and became pregnant. After having the baby aborted, the woman's mother requested that her daughter be sterilized, but the court refused to permit it because the daughter was legally an adult, though she was incapable of giving consent because of her condition.

grown in popularity because of the emphasis on individual rights and freedoms, mandatory sterilization is no longer promoted because it is viewed as an affront to those same freedoms.[88]

The use of abortion and sterilization for eugenic purposes basically involves removing undesirable characteristics from the human gene pool. But we have also seen in recent years artificial attempts to perpetuate genetic material considered desirable, both among humans and lower organisms.

- Artificial Insemination - Widely practiced by those who raise animals, whether for food, for sport (horses and dogs for racing), for those seeking pedigreed pets for competition, or for conservation and perpetuation of endangered species (animals in zoos), it has more recently come to be more widely practiced as a means of human reproduction. Today, lesbians or other women who want a child without the messiness of sex or a relationship with a man will often choose this path, while others have sought to market the procedure for its eugenic potential.[89] The procedure is also used by childless couples, who have the option of choosing injection of donor sperm into the woman if the man's sperm is the problem or having the sperm of the husband artificially injected if the delivery system is the issue.

- In Vitro Fertilization - This is the practice that was dubbed "test tube babies" when it was first attempted.[90] The basic idea is that eggs are removed from the woman and placed into a petri dish, after which sperm are introduced into the solution. These sperm can be from the woman's husband or from a donor, as in artificial insemination. When the eggs are fertilized, one is implanted into the woman's uterus, while the others are destroyed or frozen. Note that such a procedure not only involves the destruction of many human embryos - tiny babies - but also is responsible for the many thousands of frozen embryos stored in fertility clinics around the country and around the world that have come to be coveted for research and for harvesting stem cells.

- Surrogacy - One of the more bizarre reproductive technologies, and one which has garnered considerable public attention because of the legal wranglings it has generated, is surrogate motherhood, which involves a woman carrying a child in her womb who is not hers (the first such incident took place in 1980). This can take place through artificial insemination, in which case the baby would be genetically related to the surrogate mother

---

[88] Czechoslovakia instituted a program of forced sterilization of Gypsy women in 1973 which was denounced as genocide. It was finally discontinued when the Communist government fell in 1989. Forced sterilizations have also been reported in China by local officials enforcing the one-child policy, though the practice is technically illegal.

[89] In 1980, Robert Graham founded the Repository for Germinal Choice and solicited Nobel Prize winners to donate sperm. Despite becoming the target of widespread ridicule, his sperm bank remained in operation for two decades, though few Nobel Prize winners chose to participate.

[90] The first "test tube baby," Louise Brown, was born in England in 1978.

but would legally belong to the couple who had hired her,[91] or by in vitro fertilization, in which case the fertilized egg would be implanted in the womb of the surrogate.[92] Legality of the practice varies from state to state, with some prohibiting it, others refusing to recognize surrogacy contracts as legal, and other having no laws on the issue at all.

In addition to the bars to reproduction for eugenic purposes and the reproductive aids intended to allow otherwise-healthy people to transmit their genetic material, we also must consider genuine genetic engineering in the sense in which the term is generally used.

- Gene Therapy - The study of the human genome has led to the identification of certain genetic abnormalities with certain segments of DNA. True genetic engineering involves cutting out the defective DNA and replacing it with healthy genetic material,[93] thus eliminating the cause of the abnormality and preventing it from being transmitted to future generations (note that the practice can also be done in such a way that it treats problems in a specific organ without affecting the germ cells).[94] DNA modification is today widely used in animals and plants that are raised for food, with the goal, not only of making them more productive, but also of making them resistant to certain pests and diseases.
- Patenting Organisms - Genetics labs have in recent years sought to produce new organisms, which have been patentable since a Supreme Court case in 1980, which involved the production in a laboratory of oil-eating bacteria.[95]
- Stem Cell Research - This has become a very controversial aspect of genetic engineering in recent years. Stem cells are undifferentiated cells that have the potential to develop into different kinds of cells in the body. They are most numerous and most flexible in embryos, but can also be found in umbilical cord blood and, less frequently, in a mature human body. Scientists believe that stem cells can be used for gene therapy because they are so flexible and can be reproduced almost endlessly. Some even argue that the use of

---

[91] This was the situation in the famous Baby M case in New Jersey in 1986, when the Sterns, a wealthy couple who feared that pregnancy would harm the wife's health, hired Mary Beth Whitehead to bear a child by artificial insemination and turn it over to them after it was born. When the surrogate gave birth to a little girl, she refused to honor the contract and fled with the child. Finally in 1988 the Supreme Court of New Jersey granted custody to the Sterns, granted Whitehead visitation rights, and outlawed surrogacy contracts.

[92] One of the more bizarre examples of this kind of surrogacy occurred in Texas in 2004 when a woman agreed to serve as a surrogate mother for her daughter-in-law, who could not have children because of a problem with her uterus. She then proceeded to give birth to twin girls, thus bearing her own grandchildren. Similar cases have been reported in Japan and Brazil.

[93] The use of such gene splicing came to public attention through Michael Crichton's *Jurassic Park*, in which dinosaurs were genetically engineered using fragments of dinosaur DNA from mosquitos trapped in amber and filling in the gaps with amphibian DNA.

[94] One tragic case of this practice gone awry occurred at the University of Pennsylvania in 1999, when a teenage boy died from the procedure, causing the closure of the genetics lab for two years, though the program is now thriving and receiving more and more applications for the technique.

[95] Naturally-occurring oil-eating bacteria played a role in cleaning up the BP oil leak in the Gulf of Mexico in 2010.

stem cells could eventually eliminate the need for organ transplants because of their ability to regenerate themselves within the body. Because extracting stem cells from an embryo destroys the embryo, many have raised moral objections against stem cell research, arguing that it is tantamount to abortion. Advocates have argued that, if discarded embryos from genetics labs are used, no harm is done, since most are never implanted anyway, and have furthermore claimed that embryonic stem cells, because of their greater potency, can do things that somatic stem cells cannot do.[96] All this is speculation, however, since embryonic stem cells have not yet been used to treat anything successfully, while somatic stem cells, which can be harvested without killing anything, have been used effectively for gene therapy. Furthermore, within the last two years, techniques have been developed to modify somatic cells so that they have the same potency as embryonic ones.

- Cloning - The asexual production of an exact genetic duplicate of an organism has become a matter of increasing controversy in the last two decades. The technique involves nuclear transfer, in which an egg cell is denucleated, after which a somatic cell nucleus containing a full complement of DNA is inserted in the egg. The difficulty was to get the egg to divide, which has been accomplished by chemical baths mimicking the chemical changes that occur at fertilization. Early experiments with lower forms of life produced a few successes, but the cloning of a sheep, Dolly, in England in 1996 was the first successful duplication of a mammal, and generated broad conversations about the potential application of the technique to human beings. Human cloning has yet to be accomplished despite claims by researchers in Italy and Korea that were later proved false, and is illegal in most parts of the world. Though advocates claim that cloning could be used to produce organ banks for transfers and even replacement limbs, most of the research in this field today is focused on cloning embryonic stem cells and developing therapies using them.

PURPORTED ADVANTAGES

Given the broad range of methods described above for improving the genetic makeups of organisms, what advantages do researchers see in the development of these techniques?

- Some see the possibility of eliminating genetically-related birth defects and inheritable diseases. They argue that illnesses like sickle-cell anemia could some day go the way of smallpox, eliminated from the list of plagues on mankind by man's ingenuity.
- One of the greatest hopes of genetic engineers, which is currently being carried out on an ever-larger scale, is the use of the technique to improve and increase the food supply, thus reducing hunger and starvation.
- The ability to treat injuries or diseases that would now require organ transplants or prosthetics is another possible application of genetic engineering.
- Reproductive techniques mentioned above allow women or couples who cannot otherwise have children to do so.
- Some still seek the ultimate goal of eugenics - to improve the human race by controlling the very building blocks of who we are.

---

[96] President Bush prohibited the use of government funds to support embryonic stem cell research, while President Obama has supported such government funding.

ESSENTIAL QUESTIONS

While many undoubted advantages have already been realized by the applications of various forms of genetic engineering, serious questions must also be asked.

- Who decides what qualities are desirable or undesirable? By what standard?
- Will the expense of reproductive techniques lead to a more highly stratified society if they become widely used? Will we have a world where the rich could buy "eternal life"?
- What about frivolous uses for cosmetic purposes? Suppose one could change body parts as easily as one today changes clothing, and these alterations became the basis for acceptable fashion?[97]
- What about the slippery slope? Will today's options become tomorrow's requirements until all of society is subject to genetic controls? This does not present a pretty picture, as seen in Aldous Huxley's famous 1932 dystopian novel *Brave New World*.
- What about unexpected consequences? Can anyone be sure that genetically-engineered food will not produce new and unanticipated cancers throughout the population twenty years from now?[98] Will the elimination of certain diseases cause new problems?[99] Science fiction and horror films have for years taken a cautionary approach to genetic research, imagining what would happen if an experiment got out of control - *The Slime That Swallowed Cleveland*, anyone?
- Experimental techniques take a long time to perfect. Gene therapy has caused deaths despite careful precautions, but what of other experiments? Dolly the sheep was produced only after hundreds of failures, and eventually developed characteristics that shortened her life and raised serious questions about whether cloned organisms are inherently unstable. Research with embryonic stem cells has killed more tiny human beings than we know.
- What if such techniques fell into the hands of an unscrupulous tyrant or terrorist? We already have seen the consequences of the first in the person of Hitler, but what if terrorists gain the ability to use genetic engineering for biological warfare?
- What about the biblical view of man? We know from Scripture that man is more than his genetic material - he is a spiritual being with an eternal soul. Those who view man as being defined solely by his genes will feel free to manipulate him for his own good or the good of society without concern for the importance of preserving and honoring God's image.[100] Such a belief is inherently depersonalizing.

---

[97] My son David Walton wrote a short story, *All the Rage This Year*, and a novel, *Terminal Mind*, both of which involved this premise.

[98] Even today, people are concerned that genetically-modified foods are causing health problems, whether because the body is unable to digest them and derive the needed nutrients or because of allergic reactions experienced by some.

[99] The genetic abnormality that produces sickle-cell anemia, for example, has also been shown to prevent those who have it from contracting malaria.

[100] The oft-asked question, "Would a human clone have a soul?" is misdirected. Clones would simply be artificially-produced identical twins of different ages, and no one questions that identical twins have souls, though primitive societies used to kill them because they believed one was a *demonic* clone.

- What about the biblical view of marriage? Our society has already gone far in the direction of separating sex and reproduction from marriage, and now seems determined to separate reproduction from sex. Marriage is not a mere social construct, and we separate marriage, sex, and reproduction at our peril.

BEHAVIOR MODIFICATION

For many years, scientists and psychologists have argued about the relative importance of heredity and environment in making people what they are. If genetic engineering is associated with a view of man that sees him as fundamentally the product of his heredity, behavior modification is advocated by those who believe him to be basically the product of his environment.[101] We will approach this topic in the same way we did genetic engineering - by looking at methods, purported advantages, and essential questions.

METHODS OF BEHAVIOR MODIFICATION

People in authority are always trying to modify behavior - parents and teachers do it all the time in rearing and training children. So why do we include behavior modification under assaults on the image of God in man? For one thing, parenting and education, if done biblically, go far beyond behavior modification. As Tedd Tripp has pointed out in *Shepherding a Child's Heart*, parents and teachers who seek no more than a change in behavior will never truly parent or teach; they will only condition and manipulate, never getting to the root issue - the motives and desires of the child's heart. Biblical child-raising and education also ultimately appeal to the will - they are conscious and seek the cooperation of the one being trained. Behavior modification, on the other hand, often is not voluntary, and those who are being manipulated may well be unaware of the fact. What, then, are some of the techniques that have been developed to change people by controlling their environments?

- Stimulus-Response Conditioning - Behavior modification traces its roots to the work of Russian physician Ivan Pavlov (1849-1936). In his famous experiment with dogs, he rang a bell whenever the dogs were to be fed. Soon he rang the bell alone, and found that the dogs salivated at the sound of the bell. The response could be sustained almost indefinitely as long as it was periodically reinforced. If the dogs were *never* fed at the sound of the bell, they soon stopped salivating, but as long as they were fed occasionally when the bell rang, they would continue to salivate when they heard it. He tried a variety of stimuli and found that all gave a similar result. When his research was published in English in 1927, it influenced the development of behavioral psychology and was greatly admired by British philosopher Bertrand Russell for the insights it gave into the operation of the human mind. Take careful note of the basic conclusion reached by Pavlov through his work - that the

---

[101] Though behavior modification has not been the subject of novels as often as has genetic engineering, a few notable examples may still be cited. B.F. Skinner's *Walden Two* not surprisingly gives a positive picture of the use of behavior modification, while George Orwell's *1984* is the best-known dystopian version of a society where all are subject to behavior modification techniques. C.S. Lewis also gives a significant critique of behavior modification in the last novel of his space trilogy, *That Hideous Strength*.

mind can be conditioned to produce a given response to a stimulus *that is not related in any way* to the response that is desired. Note that advertisers deliberately attempt this all the time when they try to link the purchase of their products to felt needs such as success, esteem, relaxation, freedom, and, of course, sex.

- Behavioral Psychology - Behaviorism built on the work of Pavlov by developing the applications of conditioning and applying them to human behavior. Probably the most notable figure in this field was B.F. Skinner (1904-1990), a Harvard psychologist. Skinner's experiments included, among other things, the development of the Skinner box, used to produce complex forms of conditioned behavior in animals. Using the Skinner box, the experimental psychologist taught rats and mice to run through complex mazes without a single mistake and taught pigeons to play simple tunes on a rudimentary piano by pecking the keys with their beaks.[102] He studied different forms of reinforcement and quantified the effects of varieties of periodic applications of positive and negative stimuli. Application of Skinner's work to human behavior influenced developments in education, particularly the emphasis on rewards and depriving students of them as opposed to punishments to produce desired responses.[103]

- Propaganda - When people think of propaganda, they normally picture one-sided information disseminated by advocates of a particular idea, whether government or the media. Propaganda, they believe, consists of half-truths and outright lies intended to promote the cause of the writer or speaker. Properly speaking, however, propaganda also requires preventing ideas other than one's own from gaining a hearing, thus controlling the mental environment rather than just the physical one.[104] The need for limiting the flow of information explains why people who engineer military coups always seize the national TV and radio stations immediately after storming the president's palace (and sometimes before). It also explains why totalitarianism cannot flourish where a free press exists (unless the press is unified in a conspiracy with the tyrant, which is hard to imagine despite criticism of the bias of the liberal American media). Note, too, that this explains why totalitarian states like China hate the Internet and try as hard as possible to control it.

- Subliminal Suggestion - The idea here is to introduce ideas into the mind without the conscious awareness of the subject, and thus influence behavior. Hypnotism is one

---

[102] One of Skinner's more unusual proposals was for a pigeon-guided missile during World War II. The idea was that properly-conditioned pigeons in the nose cone of the missile would see the target on a screen and peck the target, thus transmitting impulses that would guide the missile toward it. Skinner claimed it worked, but the military never got up the nerve to try it.

[103] One of the most notorious examples of the application of Skinner's theories to human beings was an attempt in the 1950s, based on his writings, to treat pedophilia among prisoners who volunteered for the program. They were strapped to chairs and shown pictures of naked children, then shocked with a bolt of electricity, generating an aversive reaction to something that had previously given them pleasure. The experiments were discontinued when the rate of recidivism turned out to be extremely high once treatments were stopped.

[104] Orwell's *1984* provides classic examples of this need to limit access to information. Winston Smith's job at the Ministry of Truth is to change written archives in order to make them correspond to the current reality according to the state so that no one can possibly obtain evidence that anything was ever other than what Big Brother says is true. Even more extreme is Syme's work on the Newspeak Dictionary, in which he busily eliminates words from the language so that people will never be able to express ideas like *freedom* because no words will exist to do so.

example of this. Based on the work of German physician Franz Mesmer (1734-1815), who believed it could be used for healing the body by tapping into what he called *animal magnetism*, it was later developed further by Scottish doctor James Braid, who used it to desensitize certain parts of the body in order to induce healing. Later Sigmund Freud (1856-1939) came to believe that it gave access to the subconscious mind, and as such provided a useful avenue for treatment of psychological disorders.[105] In more recent years, people have sought to use the technique in order to turn a profit[106] or as a self-help tool.[107] The practice has also generated all kinds of rumors, whether claiming that musical groups are inserting Satanic messages into their recordings by back-masking[108] or that Disney animated films contain dirty words and sexual images hidden in the artwork.

- Drugs - These are also used for behavior modification. Some, such as sodium pentothal, make the subject more susceptible to suggestion, and are thus used in interrogations. More commonly, doctors prescribe drugs such as Ritalin to control ADD and ADHD hyperactivity disorders or Prozac to treat depression and its various symptoms. The behavioral changes produced by certain drugs have also led people to self-administer them (e.g., LSD in the sixties).

- Brain Surgery - Perhaps the most radical behavior-modification treatment is surgery on the brain. The frontal lobotomy, in which the connection between the frontal lobe and cerebral cortex is severed, was developed in Europe in the late nineteenth century as a means of treating severe psychological disorders. Sadly, the patients often died, suffered seizures, or were reduced to an unresponsive condition, but at least they were no longer violent and uncontrollable. The procedure was introduced into the United States in 1935; more than 20,000 lobotomies were performed in the U.S. between 1935 and 1951, when drugs became the treatment of choice.

PURPORTED ADVANTAGES

Here, the main goal is to eliminate undesirable behavior (though only occasionally to foster desired conduct). Those who advocate it are convinced that people are simply the products of environmental influences, and Behaviorists like Skinner see nothing in man beyond the physical. The utopian belief in the perfectibility of man is strong here - an ideal society can be constructed

---

[105] Some Christians are concerned, not without reason, that hypnotism could provide an opportunity for demonic influence.

[106] In the 1960s single frames were inserted into moving pictures to get customers to buy popcorn or Coca-Cola during the intermission. An experiment by James Vicary purported to show that such images affected behavior, and on the basis of his work, the use of such images was banned. Vicary later admitted to faking his results, and more recent tests have shown no appreciable change of behavior as a result of the insertion of such images.

[107] Once infomercials claimed to be able to teach you a foreign language in your sleep or get you to stop smoking by the use of subliminal messages.

[108] Such claims, which included the notorious "Paul is dead" hoax based on the Beatles' *Revolution 9*, have become much less frequent since the advent of cassette tapes and CDs.

if people would only submit themselves to the control of the experts.[109] The application of these techniques to children and others who engage in socially unacceptable behavior is seen as producing perfect harmony in the family, the school, in society, and throughout the world if only the conditioners are given the authority to put their theories into practice.

ESSENTIAL QUESTIONS

Again, certain questions must be asked:

- What about human freedom? The entire belief system behind behavior modification is deterministic - Skinner admitted as much in his *Beyond Freedom and Dignity*, in which he denied the existence of free will and argued that, for our own good, we must choose to be conditioned [How's that for a paradox!].
- What about human responsibility? If man has no freedom, he is also not a responsible being. How often in the legal system do defense attorneys call upon psychologists to attempt to argue that, because of problems in the environment of the accused - poverty, abuse, neglect - he is not responsible for what he has done?
- What about the heart? In Scripture, the heart is the center of who we are, but Behaviorists deny the existence of the nonmaterial component of man. Those who seek to change behavior will never change the person, only his outward trappings. At best, they will produce socially-acceptable hypocrites.
- What about human sin? Behavior modification denies the whole idea, believing instead that socially unacceptable behavior is the product of the society itself rather than of the individual. Any approach to making man and society better that fails to acknowledge sin will accomplish nothing of permanent or ultimate value.
- What if the techniques are used by the selfish, immoral, and tyrannical? This has happened often enough in history through brainwashing[110] and other invasive attempts to change the mental states of those feared by the powerful.

EUTHANASIA

The word *euthanasia* comes from Greek roots meaning "good or happy death," and was used in the classical world to refer to an easy transition from this life to the next. The term first appeared in a medical context in the writings of Francis Bacon in the seventeenth century, but again in reference to easing the death of one in pain rather than hastening that death. When Hitler issued a decree requiring the forced euthanasia of sick and disabled children and the elderly, the term began to take on something closer to its contemporary meaning. The formation of the

---

[109] Skinner's *Walden Two* pictures just such a utopia, a community where all submit themselves to the omniscient Fraser, whose conditioning skills produce complete peace and harmony without conflict of any kind.

[110] One of the most notorious examples of this is the purge trials conducted by Stalin in the Soviet Union in the 1930s. All who could possibly rival him for power were falsely accused of all sorts of crimes, then brainwashed to the point that they freely admitted to what they were alleged to have done, then promptly executed (the model for Room 101 in Orwell's *1984*).

Hemlock Society in the United States in 1980 opened a new phase in the advocacy of mercy killing. As was the case with abortion, many issues must be examined when dealing with this complex topic.

DEFINING DEATH

If defining the point at which human life begins is vital in dealing with abortion, the same may be said about the importance of defining death when dealing with euthanasia (see page 117, where a doctor who committed infanticide was acquitted because of uncertainty about the definition of death). Is someone whose vital functions are maintained only by sophisticated technology dead or alive? For most of human history, the question of defining death was not a difficult one - if vital life signs like breathing and heartbeat irreversibly ceased, the person was dead. Today, technology has complicated matters considerably. While many states still hold to a definition of death based on vital signs, some have opted instead for a definition based on brain waves - a person is legally dead when his EEG flattens out. Even this definition, however, is open to question. While no one would doubt that a person who shows no reading on an electroencephalograph is indeed dead, questions have been raised about whether the *presence* of an EEG reading always indicates life. In 1969, neurologist Adrian Upton attached electrodes to a bowl of Jell-O, agitated it, and got a reading that looked somewhat like that of an adult human being. Thus technology has seriously muddied our understanding of when death actually occurs.

What about a biblical definition of death? On this question the Bible leaves no doubt - death is the separation of the soul and the body (Ecclesiastes 12:7). The problem here, of course, is that while this definition is very clear theologically, it is of no scientific value whatsoever because the departure of the soul cannot be measured by any instrument devised by man, though some have tried. In 1907, Dr. Duncan McDougall measured the weight of six dying patients, placing them on a large scale, bed and all, as they were about to expire, and concluded that the weight of the human soul was 21 ounces. Another experiment was performed in 1988 by Dr. Becker Martens in Dresden, East Germany. Using much more sophisticated instruments, he weighed more than 200 terminal patients just before and just after they died; his conclusion was that each had lost exactly 1/3000 of an ounce at death. He was quick, however, in that atheistic Communist state, to deny that his findings had any significance regarding life after death. Such experiments are clearly absurd, since the soul is not a physical entity, and thus can have no weight, nor can it be measured in any way.

KINDS OF EUTHANASIA

Another problem we encounter when considering the subject of euthanasia is the diversity of ways in which people use the term. Euthanasia can be broken down into categories based on the nature of the action involved and the nature of the consent given. The distinctions are important and need to be clarified. Note the following:

- Active Involuntary Euthanasia - This involves taking steps to shorten the life of a person without that person's consent. When Hitler used the term, this is what he was doing. Note that this can be done when consent is possible to obtain or when it is not. With regard to active involuntary euthanasia, we should also note that "pulling the plug" on a comatose patient at one time fit into this category legally, but no longer does (see below), though I would argue that it still fits here morally.

- Active Voluntary Euthanasia - This is taking steps to shorten a person's life with his consent. The physician-assisted suicide made notorious by the work of Dr. Jack Kevorkian fits into this category, as does suicide proper, which will be considered in the next section.

- Passive Involuntary Euthanasia - This involves refusing treatment that might extend a person's life without that person's consent. Improved technology has made this an increasingly-common issue, as doctors, hospitals, and family members must more often make decisions about refusing or discontinuing treatment for the terminally ill who cannot speak for themselves.

- Passive Voluntary Euthanasia - This is refusing treatment that might extend a person's life with that person's consent. The consent may be given by a patient who is aware of what is going on around him, but today is often given through a Living Will, a document in which a person can specify what kind of treatment he wishes to receive (or not receive) should he become unresponsive and should the doctors conclude that nothing more can be done.[111] Often decisions of this kind are based on the patient's prognosis, the chance that the treatment will actually accomplish anything, and the question of heroic measures - is the treatment so extraordinary (rare, expensive) and so unlikely to help that the attempt would for all practical purposes be futile? We should note, of course, that what was considered an extraordinary measure yesterday, such as an organ transplant or heart bypass surgery, is today considered common practice.

LEGAL STATUS

For most of American history, taking steps to end the life of a patient has been considered murder, though it has not always been prosecuted. The declining regard for the value of human life that has become obvious in the abortion controversy, however, has also had an impact on the way people view death. The legal environment has changed, largely because of constant pressure by various right-to-die groups, so that today, passive euthanasia is legal with certain restrictions, while even active euthanasia is gaining increasing legal recognition. Note the following cases:

- Karen Ann Quinlan - In 1975, a 21-year-old woman in New Jersey passed out at a party after ingesting a potent combination of drugs and alcohol. She was rushed to the hospital and placed on a respirator. Doctors later concluded that she had sustained irreversible brain damage and would never emerge from her coma. Months passed, and her parents sought to have the respirator disconnected, but were stymied by the fact that discontinuation of life-supporting treatment was considered active euthanasia, and therefore murder. The case went all the way to the New Jersey Supreme Court, which in 1976 ruled in favor of the parents, and she was taken off the respirator. Much to everyone's amazement, she lived for another nine years without life support, though she never emerged from her coma. The significance of this case is that the removal of life support

---

[111] The idea of a Living Will originated with Luis Kutner and the American Euthanasia Society in 1967; in 1976, California was the first state to legalize such documents, and the step created great controversy. Today, Living Wills are commonplace and most people create one at the same time they create a will to distribute their property.

now was no longer defined as murder, but such decisions were entrusted to hospitals, doctors, patients and their families, and community boards of medical ethics.

- Nancy Cruzan - An auto accident in 1983 left her in a persistent vegetative condition. The hospital connected her to a feeding tube; her life signs otherwise remained stable. As in the Quinlan case, her parents petitioned the courts, this time for the removal of the feeding tube, and were repeatedly denied. The case finally made its way to the Supreme Court, and in 1990, on the second attempt, permission was granted to remove the tube. She died twelve days later. The significance of this case is that it expanded the range of what was permissible when considering discontinuing treatment. Here the treatment was not a complicated and expensive piece of technology, but a simple feeding tube. In essence, the Supreme Court gave the parents permission to starve their daughter to death with the help of the hospital.

- Elizabeth Bouvia - A married college graduate and quadriplegic suffering from cerebral palsy since birth, she admitted herself to a hospital in 1983 and requested assistance in starving herself to death. The hospital refused, ordering her to be force-fed. She contacted the American Civil Liberties Union and sued, but lost the case. She appealed, succeeding this time by arguing that forced feeding constituted assault and battery. This time she won, and the forced feeding was discontinued. At this point, however, she decided she wanted to live, and is still alive at the time of the writing of this book.

- Jack Kevorkian (1928-2011) - The infamous "Dr. Death" fought laws against physician-assisted suicide by constructing a suicide machine, which he used to help more than 130 patients shuffle off this mortal coil, even after his license to practice medicine was revoked in 1991. He was charged with murder in Michigan when he agreed to televise one of his assisted suicides (this case was different from all his other efforts because he administered the lethal drug himself rather than having the patient push the button that released it into his bloodstream, which was the basis for the murder charge). He was convicted, resulting in his imprisonment from 1999 until his release on parole in 2007. He continued to advocate the right to die on speaking tours, TV and radio appearances, books, and a 2010 HBO movie about his life (*You Don't Know Jack*, starring Al Pacino). He ran unsuccessfully for Congress in 2008.

- Terri Schiavo (1963-2005) - The most highly-publicized recent case concerning euthanasia involved Terri Schiavo, who at the age of 26 suffered massive brain damage following a heart attack. In 1998, her husband petitioned the courts to remove her feeding tube, but was opposed in court by her parents, who insisted that she responded to their voices and made occasional voluntary movements. The legal case, which turned largely on the question of the wishes of the patient[112] and on whose rights took legal precedence (her parents had themselves legally declared her guardians), wound its way through the courts; in 2001, the feeding tube was removed, but quickly reinserted after an appeal. By 2005, the case had become a *cause celebre*, and many powerful politicians were involved, including President Bush, who prompted the Congress to pass a law forbidding the removing of her feeding tube. Later that year, however, the last appeal of the parents

---

[112] Her husband insisted they had discussed this possibility and that she would never have wanted to live in a persistent vegetative state, while her parents claimed that, as a good Catholic, she would never favor euthanasia.

failed, the feeding tube was removed, and Terri Schiavo starved to death two weeks later. The case was further complicated by the desire of the husband to receive his wife's life insurance money, to say nothing of the fact that he had begun living with another woman while his wife lay in a coma and married her shortly after Terri died.

- In the United States - Oregon became the first state to legalize physician-assisted suicide in 1994. Attorney General John Ashcroft issued a ruling prohibiting the practice in 2001, but Oregon officials sued, and the Supreme Court ruled in Oregon's favor in 2006, by which time almost 300 people had died in Oregon using the procedure. In 2008, both Washington (by referendum) and Montana (by court ruling) joined Oregon in permitting doctors to assist patients in taking their lives.

- Worldwide - Countries that now permit the practice include Australia, Belgium, Luxembourg, the Netherlands, and New Zealand. Anecdotal evidence indicates that euthanasia, where legal, is occasionally done without consent when pressures build to free up limited hospital resources (thus the concern about "death panels" in connection with recent health reform in the U.S. is not without grounds).

RELEVANT BIBLICAL PRINCIPLES

The Bible obviously does not address the issue of euthanasia directly, even as it does not speak of abortion. Nonetheless, certain biblical principles are relevant to our consideration of the topic.

- God is the giver and taker of life (Job 1:21). Despite the fact that God sometimes delegates the authority to take human life (e.g., war and capital punishment), He does not delegate that authority to physicians, family members, or to the individual himself.

- Reasons for prolonging life go beyond the possibility of recovery; reconciliation with loved ones and communication of wisdom to those left behind are both valued in God's Word (e.g., the entire purpose of the book of Proverbs).

- The assumption of the Right-to-Die movement is that pain is by definition evil, and no one should be forced to live with pain. Scripture indicates otherwise, however. We know that pain is the result of sin in the world (Genesis 3:16-19), and in that sense is bad. Yet God uses it in positive ways in people's lives, including bringing them to repentance and presenting a good testimony before the world. Drugs that remove pain but leave the person unable to communicate may not be the wisest choice for one whose desire is ministry to others.

- Euthanasia advocates also tend to believe that this life is all there is, and that any level of existence significantly below the optimum is simply not worth living. They therefore seek oblivion, which they consider preferable. Whether trying to leave what they believe to be a useless and pointless existence or seeking to cling to it with all the strength they have (e.g., Dylan Thomas' poem to his dying father, *Do Not Go Gentle Into That Good Night*), they view this life as the end. Christians, of course, cannot do that. While death is the final stroke of sin in this world, it is also something not to be feared by the Christian (Philippians 1:19-26). Thus the believer need not cling to this life as if there is no tomorrow, because he looks for a heavenly city that is far more glorious than this earthly one.

- Life is not the ultimate good, despite its sanctity. "Laying down one's life for the brethren" is seen as a virtue in Scripture, exemplified by Christ Himself (John 15:13-14;

Acts 15:26; 20:24; Romans 16:3-4; Philippians 2:30; I John 3:16; Revelation 12:11). These principles should not be used to advocate euthanasia in any way, but clearly tell us something about the way Christians ought to view death and put it in proper perspective.

CONCLUSIONS

What conclusions, then, can we draw about the complex subject of euthanasia? Note the following:

- Active euthanasia is both illegal (though perhaps not for long) and morally reprehensible. One may choose to suffer martyrdom, but may not arrogate to himself the termination of his life or that of another.
- When dealing with the question of passive euthanasia - the refusal or cessation of treatment - we must recognize that we are not obligated to choose every form of treatment available. Many experimental techniques are being developed that doctors are eager to try on willing guinea pigs, but this is often not a wise choice. While experimental procedures may help some, for others they do nothing but prolong suffering. For some, hospice treatment may be the right choice.
- There is a moral difference between refusing treatment and discontinuing it. Despite legal rulings allowing for "pulling the plug" when no hope remains, taking such an action will actually contribute to the death of the person (though this cannot always be known, as the Quinlan case illustrates) and is thus active euthanasia.
- Motives matter when deciding to accept or refuse treatment, and in the case of the dying, motives are almost always mixed. Does the patient simply want the pain to go away, or does he want to place himself in God's hands rather than those of the medical professionals? Does he need the Savior but seek oblivion, or does he long to be in the arms of Jesus? Do family members want to end the sufferer's pain, or their own? Are there financial factors involved in the decision? Do the doctors want to help the patient and the family, or are they more concerned with freeing up a bed and some expensive machinery? Are they anxious to test a new technique or medicine? These issues complicate such a decision enormously, but must be faced honestly.
- Miracles should *not* be taken into account when making decisions about end-of-life treatment. God is certainly able to do miracles of healing, as many can testify, but we are not justified in basing our planning on that possibility. Why not? For one thing, miracles are by definition rare, or they would not be called miracles. Secondly, note that if the argument were carried out to its extreme conclusion, Christians would never bury anyone; after all, God has shown that He is able to raise people from the dead![113] If God is going to heal, He can do it whether we choose medical treatments or not.

---

[113] In 2006, a one-year-old child whose mother belonged to a cult called One Mind Ministries died of starvation. The leader of the cult ordered the child's body placed on a bed in a back room, where members of the cult prayed over him with the assurance that God would raise him from the dead. Five members of the group eventually faced murder charges for refusing food to the child because the leader insisted he was demon-possessed.

- In ambiguous situations (which is the case with almost all end-of-life decisions), we are obliged to choose life over death. As we have noted before, the question of the quality of life should never take precedence over the question of the existence of life.

- Thus decisions concerning refusing or discontinuing treatment are only valid when the choice is not between life and death, but between one form of death and another. When, as far as medical professionals can tell, death is inevitable, we may not choose to shorten life, but we may choose the conditions under which life is to end (home or hospice versus hospital, for example) with clear consciences if the choices are motivated by the desire to show love to the one who is dying and to give praise to God through the testimony that is presented to the world.

SUICIDE

In my favorite novel of all time, Alexandre Dumas' *The Count of Monte Cristo*, suicide is pictured as the noble thing to do for men of integrity who have suffered shame they can no longer endure. Edmond Dantes prevents both M. Morrel and his son Maximilien from killing themselves, is gratified when the Count de Morcerf, a despicable villain, does so, and later considers taking his own life. The idea of suicide as a noble end also appears in some of Shakespeare's tragedies (e.g., *Othello*, *Romeo and Juliet*, *Julius Caesar*, *Antony and Cleopatra*). Should suicide be viewed as something noble for someone who has suffered great shame or who has nothing left for which to live? Suicide is, of course, a special case of active voluntary euthanasia, and many of the same principles apply. Is suicide *ever* justifiable?

SELFISH SUICIDE

Suicide, no matter how a person may seek to justify it, is almost always selfish. Note the following:

- Killing myself for my own benefit is self-contradictory. One cannot affirm oneself by negating oneself, nor can one assert his freedom by ending it (contrary to the claims of Existentialists). One also cannot love himself by carrying out the ultimate act of self-hatred.

- Suicide is a psychological copout. It is an effort to avoid one's problems, an act of fear rather than courage. M. Morrel should have had the courage to face his creditors and rebuild his business rather than trying to end his life when debt seemed inevitable; Maximilien should have faced the supposed death of his fiancee with determination to make something of himself in the world despite his grief rather than killing himself; Morcerf took his life only to avoid the justice he so richly deserved from the legal system for the crimes he had committed. Suicide can also be an extreme form of attention-getting behavior (or why do so many attempted suicides fail?) or a way of expressing hatred for and anger at others.[114] If we are to attack problems rather than people in our everyday interactions and conflicts, is not suicide the ultimate in dysfunctional behavior?

---

[114] "I'll show them! They'll be sorry when I'm gone."

- Suicide is contrary to Scripture. While the Bible does not address euthanasia, it does talk about suicide, and the picture it paints is not a pretty one. Suicide is seen as a pathetic, degrading action by people who are far from God and fear the consequences of being captured in battle (Abimelech in Judges 9:52-54, Saul in I Samuel 31:1-4). After all, if we are to love others as we love ourselves, how can we argue that it is sometimes right to kill ourselves when it is clearly wrong to kill others? Besides, suicide is finally an act of fear rather than one of faith. Even martyrdom can sometimes be selfish, and thus wrong (I Corinthians 13:3).

SACRIFICIAL SUICIDE

What about situations where one gives one's life for the sake of others? Is this justifiable? Note that there is a difference between taking one's life and giving one's life. Going to a martyr's death or taking a bullet meant for a comrade are not the same as falling on your sword to avoid shame and torture. Jesus, of course, came to give His life (Mark 10:45; John 10:18; 15:13-14; I John 3:16), and we are told to emulate Him. But does this justify suicide? The point of giving one's life is to live it for others and, if necessary, face death with confidence and assurance, but we should no more seek death than Jesus did during those many times in His ministry when He avoided confrontation with the words, "My time has not yet come."

DRUGS AND ALCOHOL

This is another case of assaults against the image of God in man, and an important one to consider in our drugged-out and drunken culture. We will examine it under three divisions.

DRUGS FOR MEDICINAL PURPOSES

Some fringe Christian groups over the years have argued that the use of drugs for medicinal purposes is wrong because it shows a lack of faith in God. Some faith healers have gone so far as to argue that Paul suffered from his "thorn in the flesh" and received no healing from God because he lacked sufficient faith. Scripture, on the other hand, pictures the medical profession as a worthy one - Luke was a physician who traveled with Paul on his missionary journeys and ministered to his physical needs, and was very much appreciated for doing so (Colossians 4:14). Isaiah used means to heal Hezekiah's boil (II Kings 20:7), and Paul recommended the medicinal use of wine for Timothy's stomach troubles (I Timothy 5:23). Some have even suggested that Proverbs 31:6-7 implies the value of anesthetics.

Those who take such a strong position against medicinal drugs and the medical profession in general also have a mistaken idea of what faith is. Faith does not mean sitting back and doing nothing and waiting for God to act. Furthermore, sickness should not always be viewed as a direct consequence of sin (John 9:1-3), though it sometimes is (II Kings 5:27). Those who argue that God wants His people to be healthy, and if they are not, it must in some way be their fault, do not understand the severe mercy by which God sometimes deals with His children. As Paul was told when he asked for deliverance from his physical ailment, whatever it was, and was refused, "My grace is sufficient for you, for my power is made perfect in weakness" (II Corinthians 12:9).

All this does not mean that the use of drugs for medicinal purposes is always right, of course. Too often, legal drugs are abused. Some people become addicted to prescription medicines and will do anything to get them, including lying and stealing. Others compensate for abuse of their own bodies by using drugs to avoid the consequences of that abuse. How many people can't wake up in the morning without their cup (or two or three) of coffee, and can't get to sleep at night without a sleeping pill? How many athletes use steroids to strengthen their bodies, at great risk to themselves? How many women take diet pills in order to lose weight so they can conform to an artificial (and impossible for most) cultural idea of beauty?

CONTROLLED SUBSTANCES

Some drugs are illegal, and for good reason. Though the response here should be an obvious one, we have too many apologists for drug use, both in word and example, in our society to let this pass without comment. Note the following:

- Such drugs use is wrong because it is against the law. Romans 13:1-5 clearly requires that we submit to the authorities God has placed over us; it would be difficult indeed for someone to argue that *refraining* from drugs is a sin.
- Such drugs are wrong because they harm the body, no matter what certain marijuana advocates may say. The body of the Christian is the temple of the Holy Spirit and is not to be defiled (I Corinthians 6:19-20). Bodily health may not be the ultimate priority (I Timothy 4:8), but we may not destroy our bodies for our own gratification - this amounts to slow suicide (note that this argument applies to many other sins as well, such as gluttony). Some legal drugs such as nicotine fit into the same category.
- Such drugs are wrong because they cause a loss of self-control. Self-control is part of the fruit of the Spirit (Galatians 5:22-23), and yielding control of our bodies to some "foreign substance" is forbidden (I Corinthians 6:12; Ephesians 5:18). Anything addictive is by definition an idol and has no place in the life of the Christian.
- Even though some may argue that comparatively mild drugs like marijuana really do no harm, the arguments that they are helpful, even for medicinal purposes, are highly questionable, and I Corinthians 10:23 indicates that helpfulness is to be a test for whatever I put into my body.
- Even if, as some argue with regard to alcohol (see below), "I know when to stop," others may not, so the stumblingblock issue we discussed in the first chapter is also relevant here.

ALCOHOLIC BEVERAGES

This aspect of the issue has only been a matter of controversy in the last two centuries. Throughout most of the Church's history, Christians generally agreed that the use of wine was acceptable as long as it was not done to excess, and that the abuse of alcohol - drunkenness - was wrong. Medieval monasteries even made wine for their own use and for sale, and those super-strict Puritans drank beer with no qualms of conscience. How, then, did the controversy arise so that many American Christians have been raised to believe that drinking alcoholic beverages is a sin?

Part of the problem stems from the extent to which alcohol was abused on the American frontier. Life in the West was rough and morals were low. Much of the deplorable behavior associated with the frontier was centered around the saloon, which not only promoted drunkenness, but also prostitution, both of which tended to lead to the gunfights for which the West became notorious. Thus there arose the Temperance Movement, which believed that the only way of cleansing American society was by ridding it of the scourge of Demon Rum.[115] The Temperance Movement was strengthened by the fears generated by massive immigration from the nations of Catholic Europe following the Civil War. Italians and their wine, the Irish and their whiskey, the Germans and their beer were seen as destroying the moral fiber of America.[116] Even today, the question of whether or not drinking is a sin is largely restricted to American Christians.

WORDS FOR WINE IN THE BIBLE

The first thing we should do in response to this question is to examine in some detail the words the Bible uses for alcoholic beverages. The reason we must undertake this study is because those who argue that wine is a sin must in the process claim that at least some of the words for wine in the Bible refer to non-alcoholic beverages - i.e., grape juice. A quick glance at the words the Bible uses shows that this cannot be the case. Four major words for wine are used in the Bible, three in Hebrew and one in Greek:

- *Yayin* - The most common Old Testament word for wine, it is definitely alcoholic in content (Noah got drunk on it in Genesis 9:21 and Proverbs 20:1 warns against the abuse of it), but it is also used in the worship of God (Genesis 14:18; Exodus 29:40).
- *Shekar* - Usually translated "strong drink" in the KJV; those who make the grape juice argument generally contrast the harmless fruit of the vine with *shekar*. However, this substance shares both the benefits (Numbers 28:7) and the dangers (Proverbs 20:1, where it is used as a synonym for *yayin*) of the kind of wine discussed above.
- *Tirosh* - The kind of wine most often argued to be grape juice by temperance advocates, largely because it is frequently translated "new wine" in the KJV. While in most cases it is pictured as a blessing from the Lord (Genesis 27:28; Judges 9:13), it also has its dangers; Hosea 4:11 leaves no doubt about its alcoholic content, since grape juice does not usually "take away the understanding."
- *Oinos* - The only significant Greek word used for wine in the New Testament,[117] it is also the word from which our English word *wine* is derived. *Oinos* is the wine made by Jesus

---

[115] Note the similarity between this argument and "fencing the law" practiced by the Pharisees - the best way to prevent sinful behavior is to ban the questionable practice altogether (cf. taking the Lord's name in vain).

[116] This argument played especially well during World War I, when Germany was the enemy. It is no accident that the Prohibition Amendment to the Constitution passed shortly after the war ended.

[117] Only one NT reference to wine does not use *oinos* (Acts 2:13); the alcoholic content here is obvious.

at the wedding in Cana (John 2:1-11), the wine of which He partook to the extent that His enemies described Him as being a drunkard (Luke 7:33-34), and was surely the wine used at the Last Supper. Its alcoholic content is readily attested, not only directly (Ephesians 5:18), but also by virtue of the fact that most New Testament words for *drunkenness* are compounds of *oinos*.

Thus we see that the wine mentioned so often in the Bible was not grape juice, but an alcoholic beverage.[118] Does this mean that Christians should have *carte blanche* with regard to alcoholic beverages as long as they don't get drunk? There are a few other issues we need to consider before arriving at a conclusion concerning this matter.

OF WHAT DID THE WINE IN THE BIBLE CONSIST?

Here we need the help of archaeologists, who have discovered recipes for wine-making in Bible times. They have found that, though the wine was indeed alcoholic in content, it was common practice to water the wine down before serving it in proportions anywhere from 1:2 to 1:5 parts wine to water. Anyone who drank undiluted wine was viewed as a barbarian who had nothing in mind except getting drunk, even among the Romans, who were no teetotalers. The alcoholic content was thus quite low, so that drinking the wine that served as the staple beverage in the ancient world would tend to affect the bladder long before it affected the brain (in today's terms, one would have to drink about twenty glasses of the stuff in order to get legally drunk).

Another factor was related to the issue of water purification. Today people are often warned not to drink the water when they go abroad, and for good reason. In the ancient world, people could, of course, purify their water by boiling it, but in much of the Near East, wood is hard to obtain. Mixing a little wine with the water would do the job nicely, however, since vineyards are as plentiful as forests are scarce.

WHAT IS THE BIBLICAL ATTITUDE TOWARD WINE?

As noted earlier, Scripture sees wine as a blessing while condemning its abuse. The Nazirite Vow, which we have discussed earlier, prohibited the use of wine, not because wine is too sinful for one who is dedicated to God's service, but because one who is set apart indicated his separation by not getting involved in common aspects of everyday life - cutting one's hair, having contact with dead bodies (common in an agricultural economy), and drinking wine.

---

[118] One of the more memorable parent-teacher conferences of my teaching career occurred in my first or second year when this topic came up. The father of one of my students was a pastor, and when his son told him what we had discussed in class that day, he was incensed. He asked for a conference, and in the conference, I showed him the biblical evidence above about the words for wine in the Bible. He admitted that he had never done a word study on the subject, but promised to do so, and a few days later came back and apologized, recognizing that the way to prevent his son from going astray was not to "fence the law," but to teach him to "rightly divide the Word of Truth."

WHAT ABOUT CHRISTIANS TODAY?

What conclusions should we draw on this sometimes-controversial topic? Note the following:

- We cannot argue that the use of alcoholic beverages is sinful at all times and in all places. To do so would be to accuse Jesus of sin, which is exactly what the Pharisees did when they claimed that He was a drunkard.
- Can we argue on the basis of our knowledge about the content of the wine in the Bible that drinking anything stronger than that used in Bible times would be courting drunkenness, and thus abusing God's good gift? Perhaps this argument may be made with some justification, though we should recognize that almost *everything* marketed today as an alcoholic beverage is far stronger than what people drank in Bible times as a staple beverage. Certainly we ought to make a distinction between fermented beverages, which are usually fairly mild, and distilled liquors, which are quite strong and easily lead to drunkenness.
- We should recognize the pertinence of the stumblingblock argument here. This is a topic about which Christians disagree, it can tend to be divisive, it leads to fellow believers condemning and criticizing one another, yet it is not described as sin in the Bible. Each should follow his own conscience in the matter, and should not cause anyone else to stumble.
- The tragedy of alcohol abuse in our country cannot be ignored. The role of alcoholic beverages in driving fatalities, broken families, and abused wives and children is of epidemic proportions. Does this mean that a Christian, because he recognizes these problems, should choose not to get involved with something that causes so much harm? Some might argue this way (in my opinion this culturally-based argument is the strongest one for choosing total abstinence), while others insist that a Christian testimony is most faithfully given by avoiding the common caricature of Christians as "holier than thou" and showing that believers can have a good time without having to get drunk to do it.
- We should also note that this question is to some extent cultural. We have already seen that it is largely a matter of controversy in the United States; Christians in other countries where wine continues to be a staple beverage have no problems at all partaking, and view American Christians as somewhat odd because of their scruples. In any case, we should recognize that, all cultural differences aside, we must avoid any abuse of alcohol while at the same time following the dictates of our consciences.

RACIAL PREJUDICE

Racism also involves assaults against the image of God in man, often to the point of denying the full humanity of those of another race. In modern American society, racism is decidedly unpopular. Politicians try to gain advantage over others by playing the "race card," accusing the other side of racism whenever a slip of the tongue occurs or whenever anyone says anything that can be misinterpreted as racist language. Too often, however, politically-correct language masks what is in the heart rather than revealing it; what people say in unguarded moments often indicates attitudes quite different from those displayed for public consumption. Despite significant progress in the last fifty years, no one could seriously argue that America is now a post-racial country.

The issue is an important one for Christians, not only because of the biblical mandate to love one's neighbor, but also because of the sad track record of the church on the issue in American history. The segregation of the American church remains in many ways a scandal. But the worst part of the problem is that Christians have all too often been defenders of racial bigotry. While today such attitudes are written off as the province of ignorant rednecks, in the nineteenth century many moral and upright Christians seriously attempted to argue from Scripture that blacks, in particular, were inferior to whites.[119] Thus we should note that the arguments below were not simply advocated by crackpots from the lunatic fringe, but have been seriously advanced by competent biblical scholars in the past. We will approach this subject in the same way we did capital punishment, by focusing on arguments used by Christians and taken from the Bible on both sides of the issue.

BIBLICAL ARGUMENTS FOR RACIAL DISCRIMINATION

- The Curse of Ham (Genesis 9:20-27) - Probably the best-known passage used to support racism, it has been directed explicitly against blacks, and thus became a defense, first of slavery, and later of segregation. The incident itself is a peculiar one. Noah plants a vineyard and partakes of the fruit thereof, getting himself thoroughly drunk in the process, so much so that he lies down naked in his tent and dozes off. Ham sees his father's condition and tells his brothers, who back into the tent with a cloak and cover Noah with it. When Noah recovers from his hangover, he becomes furious when he finds out what Ham did and issues a horrible curse, condemning Ham's descendants to perpetual servitude to the descendants of his brothers. This raises all kinds of questions.
    - How is this passage used to justify racial discrimination? According to Genesis 10, the Table of Nations, which describes the regions of the world where the descendants of Noah settled, the children of Shem settled in the Middle East, those of Japheth settled in Europe, while the children of Ham settled in Africa. Thus, the conclusion goes, Africans are the descendants of Ham and have been cursed by God, through Noah, to perpetual servitude, thus justifying the enslavement of millions of Africans by Arabs, Europeans and Americans. This interpretation encounters several significant problems, however.
    - Who is cursed? Strangely, Noah's fury at the behavior of Ham leads him to curse, not Ham, but Ham's son Canaan. Note that, of the sons of Ham, Canaan was the only one who did *not* settle in Africa. Thus the curse has nothing to do with Africans at all, but sets the stage for the later wrath of God against the Canaanites when He ordered Joshua to exterminate them during the Conquest.[120]

---

[119] This included great theologians like James H. Thornwell and Robert L. Dabney, the co-founders of the Southern Presbyterian Church.

[120] If you want to use this as an excuse for discriminating against Canaanites, feel free. Though the Israelites did not succeed in destroying them completely (and were condemned by God for their failure), the last remnant of Canaanite civilization, the Phoenician colony in Carthage, was destroyed by Rome in the Punic Wars.

- What did Ham do that was so bad anyway? The whole situation seems rather innocuous, and critics have struggled to explain the precise nature of Ham's sin. Some have suggested that he ridiculed his father before his brothers, not showing him proper respect, or criticize him for not covering Noah up himself. One of many explanations I have encountered over the years proposes an interesting solution, though it does not by any means answer all the questions in this difficult passage. This commentator pointed out that the phrase translated "saw the nakedness of his father" is a Hebrew euphemism for sexual intercourse (cf. Leviticus 18:6-19; 20:17-21). If this is indeed what Genesis 9 is saying, Ham was actually guilty of the homosexual rape of his father while he was in his drunken stupor, and thus Noah's rage and the resulting curse were totally understandable.
- If this is true, why did Noah curse Canaan rather than Ham, who had been the perpetrator of the nefarious deed? The only possible suggestion I can make here is that Canaan, alone among the sons of Ham, shared his father's perverted proclivities, and thus Noah did not want the curse to fall on the innocent sons. One possible substantiation for this interpretation is the later history of the Canaanites, who were surely among the most sexually perverse civilizations ever to leave their blot upon the earth. They openly practiced male and female ritual prostitution in their worship, along with child sacrifice and other abominations. In any case, however, the so-called "Curse of Ham" cannot be used to support racial discrimination against Africans.

- The Tower of Babel (Genesis 11:1-9) - This became an argument to justify segregation after the end of slavery in America. The gist of the argument is that, as a judgment against man's arrogance, God separated the different peoples of earth by confusing their tongues (resulting in the population distribution recorded in Genesis 10). Unlike the marriage ceremony, which uses the words of Jesus in saying, "What God has joined together, let not man separate" (Matthew 19:6), racists here argued, "What God has separated, let not man join together." If God intended man to live in separate groups (Acts 17:26), is it not rebellion against God to try to bring them together again? Did He not intend for them to live apart so they would no longer become arrogant and rebel against Him? Note the following:
  - If God thought separating people into distinct groups would prevent rebellion, He was sadly mistaken. Clearly this is not the case, and one might even argue that segregation is just one more pathetic example of man's infinite creativity in rebelling against God.
  - Pay attention to the basis on which people were separated - it was language, not race. In fact, one might easily argue that races arose following this division of peoples as certain groups lived in geographic isolation and recessive genetic traits emerged and became dominant, producing what we know today as secondary racial characteristics (which occupy only a very few of the myriad genes in human DNA).[121] Have you ever heard anyone argue that an English-speaking man should

---

[121] This always raises the question among students, "Then what color were Adam and Eve?" The simple answer is that we have no idea, no more than we know anything about their language, though paleontologists, operating from an evolutonary perspective, theorize that the earliest humans were vaguely Negroid in appearance.

not marry a French woman because the mixing of language groups would involve rebellion against the judgment of God?

- Besides, the judgment of Babel was reversed at Pentecost (Acts 2:1-13). Here, instead of confusing the tongues of a linguistically-uniform people, God took a linguistically diverse people and brought them together so that they could all hear and understand the same speech. God's redemptive work overcomes the consequences of His judgment of human sin.

- The Segregation of Israel (Exodus 34:11-16; Deuteronomy 7:1-4) - In these passages, God clearly orders the Israelites not to marry people from the surrounding nations. These passages have often been used not only to justify segregation, but also to support the prohibition of miscegenation - the intermarriage of people from different races. Yet several highly-visible interracial marriages are clearly blessed by God in Scripture. Joseph married an Egyptian princess (Genesis 41:45); when Moses married a Cushite woman (Numbers 12:1-2), Aaron and Miriam put up strong objections, but God silenced them, even to the point of punishing Miriam with leprosy; Rahab was a cursed Canaanite from Jericho, but she married an Israelite man, became the mother of Boaz, and is found in the genealogy of Jesus (Matthew 1:5); Boaz, in turn, married a Moabite girl named Ruth, who was the great-grandmother of David and also appears in the Messianic line (Ruth 4:18-22; Matthew 1:5). What is the answer to this apparent contradiction between the commandments of the Old Testament and the actual practice of God in dealing with His people? The obvious solution is that the prohibition of marriage with the surrounding nations had no racial intent at all, but rather a religious one; God was not prohibiting interracial marriages, but interreligious ones (cf. II Corinthians 6:14-18). As long as someone like Rahab or Ruth became a worshiper of the true God, she could be readily accepted into the nation.

BIBLICAL ARGUMENTS AGAINST RACIAL DISCRIMINATION

Again, we will look at three common arguments that make absolutely clear God's hatred of discrimination based on race.

- The Unity of the Human Race - Human beings are ultimately one, both on the basis of common descent (Genesis 3:20) and common plight. All people are alike in being created in God's image and being lost in sin. If you go back far enough, we are all related.[122]
- Jesus' Treatment of the Samaritans - Perhaps the most notorious example of racism in the Bible is the relationship between the Jews and the Samaritans. The Samaritans originated following the fall of the Northern Kingdom of Israel in 722 BC. The policy of the Assyrians conquerors was to prevent rebellion by mixing populations; they thus took many people from the Northern Kingdom and scattered them throughout their various conquered

---

[122] Note that, at least for a long time, this was a claim that evolutionists could not make. In fact, some of the racial supremacy theories of the nineteenth century were based on belief in multiple origins of *homo sapiens*, the argument that "our monkeys came out of the trees earlier than your monkeys, so we're more highly evolved, and thus better than you." Today, DNA research has confirmed what Christians have known for centuries, and that is that the human race is one.

territories and brought in people from those places and forcibly settled them in Israel. The eventual result was intermarriage, along with a mingling of languages and religions, i.e., the Samaritans. The Jews looked down on and despised the Samaritans as ethnic half-breeds and followers of a mongrel religion (they worshiped in a temple on Mount Gerazim in Samaria - see John 4:20 - and practiced religious rites that combined Jewish and pagan elements), while Samaritans hated Jews because they were despised by them. Animosity was so great that Jews going from Judea to Galilee and back again would walk forty miles out of their way to avoid going through Samaria, which was located between the two.

Jesus, however, pointedly ignored this common prejudice and did everything He could to oppose it. In His encounter with the Samaritan woman at the well in Sychar (John 4:1-39), He took the road through Samaria, asked an immoral Samaritan woman for a cup of water, and preached the Gospel to her and her neighbors; when He was asked what it meant to love one's neighbor, He told a parable about a Good Samaritan (Luke 10:25-37) - surely an oxymoron in the minds of His listeners; when Jesus healed ten lepers, Luke goes out of his way to point out that the only one who returned to thank the Lord was a Samaritan (Luke 17:11-19); even when Jesus was rejected by a Samaritan village He visited, He responded with mercy while His disciples were quite eager to call down fire and brimstone upon them (Luke 9:51-56). Later, when the Gospel spread beyond the Jews in the region of Jerusalem, the Samaritans were among the first to be evangelized (Acts 8:4-8), as Jesus intended (Acts 1:8).

- The Universality of the Gospel - We have already noted that Pentecost broke down the barriers between people resulting from the sin of man and God's judgment of that sin. The Church is intended to bear witness to this removal of sin-caused barriers - Ephesians 2:11-18 speaks of Christ breaking down the wall between Jews and Gentiles, while Galatians 3:28 speaks of other artificial barriers as well that no longer exist in the Kingdom of God. The Church should thus be a place where prejudice and favoritism are unknown (James 2:1-9).[123] This was a difficult task for the early church, as Peter's vision of the sheet lowered from heaven in Acts 10:9-16 illustrates and Paul's later confrontation with the same apostle in Galatians 2:11-14 confirms, as it is for the modern church. Progress has unquestionably been made in recent decades, but much remains to be done even though most barriers now are based more on cultural differences than on racial prejudice. The only difference that is of any importance at all for the child of God is that which divides the sheep from the goats, the Children of Light from the Sons of Darkness.

SLAVERY

The reason why this must be treated as a separate topic is that, while the Bible clearly condemns racial prejudice, it seems to tolerate or even encourage slavery. How can this be? The simple reason for this is that slavery in the Bible was not based on race, but usually on either conquest or voluntary debt servitude; thus it must be separated from the previous discussion. Generally speaking, slavery involved ownership of a person's *labor* rather than ownership of the person (but see Exodus 21:21, which implies certain property considerations).

---

[123] A beautiful example of this can be found by examining the list of elders in the church in Antioch in Acts 13:1, which displays both ethnic and geographical diversity.

SLAVERY IN THE OLD TESTAMENT

The Old Testament does not condemn slavery (Genesis 14:14; 17:12-13; 20:14; 24:35) but accepts it as a normal part of life. It does, however, seek to regulate it in order to avoid common abuses; note the regulation of Hebrew slavery in Exodus 21:2-6, the prohibition of cruelty to slaves in Exodus 21:20-21, and the regulation of debt slavery in Leviticus 25:39-46. Another indication that slaves were not simply viewed as property to be treated however the master wished can be seen in the fact that slaves sometimes shared rights of inheritance; see Genesis 15:2-3, where Abraham's servant will inherit his property if Abraham dies childless, and Genesis 30:1-13, where the sons of Leah's slaves become equal heirs with the sons of Leah and Rachel in the family of Jacob. Thus Old Testament slavery had nothing to do with racial inferiority, and in no way brought into question the humanity of those who were enslaved. Those in nineteenth-century America who used such passages to justify their treatment of Africans and their descendants apparently were rather selective, all too often ignoring the verses that spoke of the proper treatment and legitimate rights of the slave.

SLAVERY IN THE NEW TESTAMENT

Again, slavery is not condemned, but is assumed to be a part of society (the passages we have already examined in Ephesians 6:5-9 and Colossians 3:22-23 - see pages 82-83 - show that a large percentage of the early Christians were in fact slaves, and that they needed to be exhorted to submit to their earthly masters; see also I Corinthians 7:20-24; I Timothy 6:1; Titus 2:9-10; I Peter 2:18-19). The entire book of Philemon would be incongruous if slavery were sinful in and of itself. Here Paul requires the runaway slave Onesimus to return to his master Philemon, who is to receive him, forgive him, and treat him as a brother in Christ now that he has been converted. Jesus also draws much illustrative material from the institution of slavery in His parables (Matthew 13:24-30; 18:23-35; 21:33-41; 22:1-14; 24:45-51; 25:14-30; Luke 12:35-48; 14:16-24; 15:11-32; 17:7-10; 19:11-27; 20:9-18).

CONCLUSIONS CONCERNING SLAVERY

What should we then conclude concerning this practice, which has left such a dark mark on American history in general and that of the church in particular? Note the following:

- Slavery or indentured servitude are not in and of themselves wrong, and may thus not be condemned as such.
- Race-based slavery does not measure up to biblical requirements, and is thus sinful.
- Biblical restrictions on slavery and the teaching of the New Testament about the spiritual equality of all believers can and should work toward the elimination of slavery in the world,[124] which has indeed been the case, though not as swiftly as one might have hoped. One can imagine how differently Philemon must have treated Onesimus after he returned.

---

[124] In the late seventeenth century, some American slave-owners were reluctant to allow their slaves to hear the Gospel for fear that they would have to free them if they became Christians. Once the Virginia House of Burgesses passed a law stating that Christian slaves did not have to be freed, evangelism proceeded rapidly.

- Slavery as it has actually existed in history has rarely given any heed to the biblical restrictions concerning the way slaves are to be viewed and the way they are to be treated; violence and sexual abuse are wrong in any relationship, whether slave or free. No institution of slavery that denies the full humanity of the slave or condones the abuse of slaves is in any way countenanced by Scripture.
- Slavery continues to exist today, but has nothing in common with the slavery condoned in Scripture. For the most part, modern slavery involves the forced sexual bondage of young men and women from impoverished families and societies, and is one of the most neglected scandals of the twenty-first century.
- The responsibilities of masters and slaves enumerated in the New Testament apply to all situations where one person has control over the labor of another; whether slave or free, we all ultimately labor for God, who is the Master of all.

ANIMAL RIGHTS

Another common misuse of the Sixth Commandment is by people, whether vegetarians, vegans, or animal rights activists, who argue that it forbids the killing of animals. Though this is clearly not what God had in mind in giving the commandment, the argument is heard so frequently that students must be equipped to give a biblical response and present a Christian view of the place of animals in God's creation.

ANIMAL RIGHTS ARGUMENTS

Today we often hear in the news of groups like People for the Ethical Treatment of Animals (PETA) and the Animal Liberation Front engaging in violence against people and property in support of their ends, whether by throwing paint on fur coats and the people who wear them or vandalizing laboratories where animal experiments are being conducted. Writers like Princeton Professor of Bioethics Peter Singer advocate civil rights for animals, arguing that the Utilitarian principle of "the greatest good for the greatest number" and the obligation to avoid pain apply to animals as well as humans, insisting that any morality that favors people over animals involves the fallacy of "speciesism." At the same time, Singer supports abortion, euthanasia, and even bestiality on the grounds of relative measures of pleasure and pain. Let us consider some of these arguments one at a time.

- People and animals are morally equivalent ("animals are people, too"). This belief, which is at the heart of the animal rights movement, is grounded in evolutionary theory, which views man as nothing more than a highly-developed animal.
- Causing an animal pain is immoral. One might easily note here that the "nature red in tooth and claw" pictured by Darwin involved a violent struggle for survival in which animals are causing pain to their prey all the time. Even from an evolutionary perspective, how can such an argument be maintained consistently?
- Human use of animals for food and clothing is immoral. The same argument again applies with regard to food, though we see no examples of animals using one another for clothing. One might as well argue that, since animals do not wear clothing, people ought to run

around naked, since nature appears to be the model. After all, is clothing not merely a social construct based on an outmoded system of morality that simply does not fit our animal status?

- Some animal rights activists, while not objecting to the use of animals for food and clothing, insist that such activities be conducted humanely. They are thus opposed to the conditions in factory farms and slaughterhouses and oppose hunting for sport. These issues will be addressed below.

- One frequent target of animal rights activists is the practice of animal experimentation for medical purposes. This can involve trying out new drugs on animals, often by first inducing injuries or diseases, or testing the safety of cosmetics by applying large quantities of the chemicals involved to the skin and eyes of animals. One area of inconsistency that often appears here is that activists gain publicity and raise an uproar over the supposed abuse of "cute" animals, but seem to ignore experimentation with creatures generally recognized as ugly or undesirable, such as insects.

- Animal rights advocates often speak of the importance of maintaining the balance of nature by avoiding human interference with that balance. But does this not miss the point that human beings, too, are part of the natural world? Does not the "survival of the fittest" give us the right to thrive at the expense of weaker organisms?

- Animal rights advocates believe that man should go out of his way to avoid driving any animals to extinction, even to the point of opposing any building project, large or small, that might impinge in any way upon the habitat of an endangered species. But did not Charles Darwin himself argue in *The Origin of Species* that extinction is an inevitable consequence of the struggle for existence, and that the geological record gives abundant evidence that extinction is part of the normal course of nature? From an evolutionary perspective, why should we disadvantage the strong in order to perpetuate the weak, which on their own would never survive to use up the earth's resources?

BIBLICAL VIEW OF ANIMALS

How should we respond to these arguments? What does the Bible tell us about such matters? Note the following:

- Animal rights activists deny the basic biblical teaching concerning the uniqueness of man. Man is made in the image of God, while animals are not (Genesis 1:26). Human uniqueness does not reside in any physical characteristic (as evolutionists, physical characteristics are all that matter to them) or combination thereof, but in skills of communication (chimpanzees, whales and dolphins simply don't measure up) and abstraction, and in the need, desire, and ability to worship.

- Man is immortal, while animals are not. No one is quite sure what the New Heavens and the New Earth involve (Is Isaiah 11 a picture of a Millennial Earth or of the New Earth in eternity, or is it simply metaphorical?), but Scripture gives us no reason to believe that all dogs go to heaven. The use of the word *soul* in the KJV translations of Job 12:10 and Revelation 16:3 has been taken by some to mean that animals have souls, but the verses have been translated more accurately in modern versions, which show clearly that the passages speak of animals as living *beings*.

- God has given man dominion over the animals (Genesis 1:28). This means that man is free to use animals for his good and God's glory as a good steward of the world God has made. The use of animals by man for his own benefit is not therefore wrong.

- God explicitly gave animals to man for food (Genesis 9:3), though the appearance of this for the first time after the Flood surely indicates that this is one of the consequences of the impact of human sin on the created world.[125] Certain restrictions, such as avoiding the eating of blood (Genesis 9:4), reminded the people that life ultimately belonged to God, while the avoidance of unclean animals in the ceremonial law was at root a matter of health and hygiene; today we are far more advanced in our ability to take care regarding such matters. And while it was acceptable for man to kill animals, it was not acceptable for animals to kill man (Genesis 9:5; Exodus 21:28-32). But does the *way* in which animals are raised or killed for food matter? What should we conclude about the treatment of animals in factory farms and slaughterhouses? Without denying the reality and inappropriateness of unnecessary cruelty, we should recognize that too often the practices in these places are sentimentalized by describing in vivid detail the psychological and emotional as well as physical suffering of the animals involved. The real goal of activists here is not to prevent cruelty, but to push a radical agenda that objects to all use of animals by man; no modifications in the system would satisfy such people.

- The use of animals for clothing is clearly permitted. In fact, God was the first one to kill an animal for this purpose (Genesis 3:21). John the Baptist was one among many biblical figures who dressed in the skins of animals (Matthew 3:4).

- The use of animals as beasts of burden is clearly permitted, though cruel treatment of such beasts is not (Balaam's interaction with his donkey in Numbers 22:22-30 is a unique example of this; see also Deuteronomy 25:4; Proverbs 12:10).

- Killing animals for reasons other than food and clothing was also permitted, with animal sacrifice being the obvious example. Animals could also be killed to protect people (Samson and the lion in Judges 14:5-6) and livestock (David protecting his sheep in I Samuel 17:34-35).

- What about hunting? Hunting and domestication were the only ways people in the ancient world could make use of animals for food and clothing, so clearly this went on (e.g., Esau in Genesis 27:3-4) and was acceptable. But what about hunting for sport? The issue here is primarily related to the boundaries of dominion. Some hunters maim and kill for the thrill of it, leaving the wounded or dead beast where it has fallen. This can hardly be said to be dominion over the animals for the glory of God (Proverbs 12:27). On the other hand, many hunters not only use animals for food, but also pay a great deal of attention to animal conservation, culling overpopulated herds in order to allow them to thrive. Such good stewardship clearly fits within the context of the Cultural Mandate.

- What about zoos? While animal rights activists complain incessantly about inhumane conditions in zoos - one gets the impression they would be happier if all animals were free to roam and people were confined to cages - zoos have done a great deal in recent years to promote conservation and good stewardship of the environment, to say nothing of disseminating greater knowledge of and appreciation for the animal kingdom.

---

[125] Does this mean that all animals were herbivores before the Fall? This is hard to imagine, and we really have no way of knowing, but if death was a consequence of the Fall for all, this is indeed possible.

- What about animal experimentation? Here, the purpose makes a great deal of difference. While developing drugs that promote human health is a worthy endeavor for scientists, and the use of animals for testing purposes is clearly superior to subjecting human beings to serious risk through exposure to untested pharmaceuticals, the question of cosmetics is a more complicated issue. Certainly one would argue that something potentially hazardous should not be marketed to the general population, so that testing for potential health hazards is important; on the other hand, is the craving for beauty a sufficient cause for the destruction of animals? Is this really good stewardship of God's creation?

- What about pets? This one creates an interesting conflict among environmentalists. While radical animal-rights activists see owning pets as a sort of slavery, most spend their time trying to shut down puppy mills and rescuing abused pets, devoting large amounts of time and money to caring for them. On the other hand, keeping a pet is seen by some environmentalists as a huge waste of earth's resources, since the meat that goes into food for dogs and cats could be used to feed starving people in other parts of the globe. While the domestication of animals is not wrong according to Scripture, we must discern what constitutes appropriate stewardship in this area.

CARING FOR THE ENVIRONMENT

Environmentalism is often closely associated with animal rights, largely because those who advocate one often advocate the other as well. Though they have some areas of overlapping interest, however, environmentalism addresses far broader concerns. Again, this is a very controversial issue today, and one to which Christians must be able to give biblical answers.

ENVIRONMENTALIST ARGUMENTS

Environmentalists, scorned as "tree-huggers" by their critics, have exercised an increasingly powerful voice in the twenty-first century. From concerns about global warming to warnings about the disappearance of the rain forests and the polar ice caps to Al Gore's Nobel Prize to the Obama administration's push for cap-and-trade legislation that would severely restrict carbon emissions, environmentalism is news. Everyone nowadays seems to be "going green," from Citizens Bank, which pays customers who pay bills online rather than using checks, to Philadelphia Electric Company, which gives rebates to customers who allow them to restrict their access to air conditioning in periods of high electricity usage, to the Philadelphia Phillies baseball team, which proudly advertises during game telecasts all the steps they have taken to save energy and avoid waste in the operation of their ballpark. Yet environmentalists rarely approach their passion from a biblical perspective. On what basis do they argue for environmental preservation?

- Some are humanists, who believe that the fate of the world is in the hands of man, and if man fails to protect "the only earth he has," it will be destroyed, and mankind with it.

- Some are materialists, who believe that the key to human happiness is found only in this world, and therefore preservation of the material environment ought to be the most important focus of our attention and efforts.

- Some are pantheists, who argue that people and grass are morally equivalent, so that any destruction of the natural world by man is wrong. Some who take this position tend not only to be anti-technological Luddites,[126] but also would be quite happy if man passed entirely from the face of the earth so that nature could thrive without the destructive influence of the human race. Instead of raising nature to the level of man, they tend to lower man to the level of the beast.

Note that all three of these perspectives, though they differ from one another, have one thing in common - they are blatantly anti-Christian. Often environmentalists blame Christianity and its Cultural Mandate for the destruction of the earth, since to them the very concept of human dominion over nature has led to capitalism, industrialism, and all other forms of evil. While they may argue that those who seek to use the natural world are really abusing it, they are as incapable of recognizing the difference between use and abuse as are their opponents. If the Industrial Revolution turned use of natural resources into horrible abuses like strip mining and air and water pollution, groups like Greenpeace, in their battles to save whales and baby seals, are quite willing to reduce the human population in order to do so. On one side, all use is permissible; on the other, all use is by definition abuse.

RELEVANT BIBLICAL PRINCIPLES

Is Christianity, then, opposed to environmentalism? Not at all. The biblical concept of stewardship should lead Christians to be concerned for God's world and want to take good care of it. How, then, should a Christian respond to the contemporary discussion of the issue?[127]

- The Cultural Mandate (Genesis 1:28) allows man to use God's creation for his benefit and God's glory. To call this abuse is to deny the unique place of man in God's universe.
- The Cultural Mandate does not give *carte blanche* for abuse of the environment. Stewardship requires caring for something that does not belong to you. When we treat the world like it is ours, with no sense of accountability to God, abuse will inevitably result.
- Christianity caused pollution and environmental destruction only in the sense that some unbiblical variants promoted a wrong view of man's relationship to the world around him.
    - Asceticism, whether Catholic or Byzantine, taught that the material world was of no importance, therefore the Christian should have no concern for it, but should give his attention solely to spiritual things. In such an environment, those who have *no* concern for spiritual things are the ones who are taking advantage of the world's resources. This is not inclined to produce an attitude of stewardship, no matter how many people like Francis of Assisi sought to promote it.[128]

---

[126] The Luddites were nineteenth-century British opponents of the Industrial Revolution who went around vandalizing and burning factories.

[127] An excellent treatment of this subject may be found in Francis Schaeffer's *Pollution and the Death of Man: The Christian View of Ecology.*

[128] Francis of Assisi (1182-1226) wrote the famous *Canticle of the Sun* and allegedly preached to birds.

- Dualism, which separated life into the realm of the material and the realm of the spiritual, while it did not seek to restrict Christian activity only to one realm, nonetheless divided the field of human endeavor so that biblical principles applied only in the spiritual realm. The Renaissance promoted this kind of thinking, while the Enlightenment gradually pushed the spiritual realm into a smaller and smaller corner until it was eliminated altogether.

- The biblical view of technology is an interesting one. The earliest mentions of technological achievement appear in the line of Cain (Genesis 4:20-22), and the earliest technological marvel mentioned in Scripture, the Tower of Babel, was an act of rebellion against God. The same may be said of the building of cities (Cain in Genesis 4:17, Nimrod[129] in Genesis 10:8-12, Babel in Genesis 11:4). Should we then conclude that technology is inherently evil, and act of rebellion against God? While it may originally have been an assertion of human self-sufficiency, like so many other acts of rebellion, God redeemed it and used it for His own purposes. When we go to the end of the story in the book of Revelation, how do we find God's glorious redeemed church described? As a *city*, the New Jerusalem, descending out of heaven for the marriage supper of the Lamb. Technology is therefore not evil in itself, but may be used for good as much as it has been used for evil. Christians are to redeem this aspect of the world around them as well as being good stewards of the created universe.

- What, then, are the root causes of the massive despoliation of the environment that we see all around us?

  - Greed, which causes man to seek short-range benefits with no concern for long-range harm, is a major cause of pollution and environmental destruction. As long as I get my profits, I don't care what happens to the environment. A Christian should never take this attitude, and should oppose those who do (Luke 16:13). The constant desire for *more* and the refusal to be satisfied with what we have should never characterize the life of the Christian (Luke 12:13-21).

  - Consumerism, which causes people to want the newest gadget, the most fashionable clothes, and in general to accumulate an abundance of *things*. How often do people throw away something that is perfectly usable just because it is out of style or because they are tired of it? Advertisers thrive on stimulating this kind of behavior, and Christians should not be deceived by it.

  - Laziness, which contributes to littering in streets and buildings. How often do you see an empty bottle thrown on the ground within three feet of a trash receptacle? Furthermore, many people simply can't be bothered to do simple things like recycling and using reusable bags in the grocery store. This shows disrespect for God's world.

- What should a Christian do? In recent years, Christians have become much more environmentally conscious, though often unable to distinguish between a biblical approach and that of the liberal environmentalists who operate from anything but biblical principles. A few obvious steps can and should be taken:

---

[129] The phrase "mighty hunter before the Lord" is not a compliment, but describes him as a tyrant who rebelled against God (the name *Nimrod* means *rebel*).

- Realize that God is concerned about how we treat His world (e.g., Leviticus 25:1-5; Deuteronomy 23:12-13). Just because the most vocal environmentalists are anti-Christian and take positions that Christians could never support does not mean that Christians should ignore environmental questions. What is needed is a fully biblical environmentalism that puts the created world in its rightful place in relationship both to God and to man.

- Avoid waste - This is not really all that hard, and once one gets into the habit, is really quite satisfying.[130] If you would not want someone to mess up your house, why should you mess up God's world?

- Live simply - Before buying something, ask the simple question, "Do I really *need* it?" I'm not advocating living like a monk, though ascetics in the past have often spoken of the benefits of not having to worry about material things, but simply replacing things only when they're worn out or broken rather than because of changes in style or in order to have the latest technological gadget.

- Realize that those who exercise bad stewardship are potentially putting the quality of their own lives ahead of the existence of others. After all, who suffers from the shortage of resources in the world? Certainly not those of us who live in affluent America.[131]

- Set an example before the world of the full implications of living one's life before God. If no aspect of life is untouched by our desire to see God honored, the environment is included. Avoiding waste, excessive consumption, and pollution are acts of godly obedience.

---

[130] I have been subjected to endless ridicule and teasing by teachers and students alike because, for years, I have brought my lunch to school in a sugar bag. I have found that I can get an entire semester's use from one bag rather than carrying a new bag to school each day and throwing it away. This is just one small thing, but if Christians would care more about such matters, the world would be a cleaner place.

[131] This is not to suggest that only the wealthy pollute. Many of the worst polluters are those who are mired in poverty, who destroy their own environments and harm their own quality of life by actions such as dumping human and animal waste in rivers and streams or leaving it in streets and gutters.

8

THE CHRISTIAN AND THE
SANCTITY OF MARRIAGE

Exodus 20:14 - "You shall not commit adultery."

We live in a sex-saturated society. Television, movies, music videos and the Internet provide visual and mental images of sexuality unavailable to previous generations. Premarital sex is assumed to the extent that promoting abstinence is viewed as an exercise in futility, hence "safe sex" should be the goal. Those who abstain from sex until marriage are viewed as strange and are sometimes socially ostracized. In this environment, the challenge to Christian teens is huge, making a firm foundation in biblical morality essential. Before considering specific issues associated with sexuality, however, we must examine the biblical basis for understanding the role of sex in human life.

SEXUALITY AND CREATION

"So God created man in his own image, in the image of God he created him; male and female he created them" (Genesis 1:27). The first reference to sexuality in the Bible connects the fact that humanity exists as male and female with the truth that mankind has been made in the image of God. In what ways is human sexual differentiation related to the image of God? Note the following:

- The fact that the Bible uses both masculine and feminine word pictures when speaking of God indicates that the richness of who God is cannot be encompassed in a single human gender. No one can doubt that the vast preponderance of biblical imagery used to picture God is masculine - *Father*, *husband*, even *king*, along with the consistent use of masculine singular pronouns. Feminine imagery does appear on occasion, however, such as in the name *El Shaddai* (the root word behind the name means *breast*, thus referring to God as a Nurturer; see Genesis 17:1; 28:3; 35:11, all of which refer to God making promises of fruitfulness) and the passage where Jesus pictures Himself as a mother hen gathering her chicks (Matthew 23:37). Thus the salient characteristics of both manhood and womanhood are reflections of who God is.
- The fact that Israel is described as the wife of God and the Church as the Bride of Christ suggest that, in relation to the masculine headship of God, all His people are feminine. In the Old Testament, this relationship implied God's care and governance and Israel's responsibility to obey and be faithful, while in the New Testament Christ loves and gives

His life for His people, who in turn must respect and submit to Him. Some have suggested that this imagery implies that masculinity and femininity extend beyond the realm of gender because all of God's creation is feminine to His masculine. Whatever this may mean, it certainly indicates that gender differentiation is an essential aspect of God's relationship to the world He has made and the people in it.[132]

- The fact that men and women alike are made in the image of God implies that they are the same in essence while fulfilling different roles in God's economy. The whole idea of essential equality combined with role differentiation is difficult for our society to grasp. For modern feminists, any hint of role differentiation is necessarily denies equality, to the extent that even the existence of physical differences other than the most obvious ones must be repudiated.[133] Yet Scripture clearly teaches that role differentiation need not undermine essential equality. The clearest example of this is found in I Corinthians 11:3, where role differentiation between men and women is rooted in the Headship of Christ over all and compared to the differentiation of roles in the Trinity, where the fact that God is the Head of Christ in no way suggests that one is inferior to the other.

- The close connection between sexuality and the image of God shows that sexuality is a central part of who we are as people. The consequences of denying that truth and somehow seeking to picture sexuality as dirty, something to be shunned in order to seek holiness, have been devastating, whether in the monastic system of the Middle Ages or in the struggles with a celibate priesthood that have brought such shame on the Catholic Church in recent years.[134]

SEXUALITY AND THE FALL

If human sexuality is deeply rooted in who we are as creatures of God made in His image, it is also intimately connected to the Fall and its consequences. The first reaction that occurs when Adam and Eve eat the forbidden fruit is sexual shame (Genesis 3:7). Every aspect of man's nature was in that moment corrupted by sin, but that corruption first appears in the realm of sexuality. Note the following:

- In an unfallen world, nakedness is not shameful, but as soon as sin appears, perversion of sexual urges associates nakedness with shame.[135]

---

[132] An interesting take on this issue may be found in C.S. Lewis' novel *Perelandra*, where angelic beings embody the principles of masculinity and femininity in a way that transcends human gender distinctions. Note, however, that in this as in many other ways, Lewis was influenced by Plato's Idealism.

[133] Sadly, this mentality has penetrated deeply into the Christian community, not only in liberal and mainline congregations, but among professing evangelicals as well, where "egalitarians" wage war against "complementarians" in order to argue against defined roles for men and women in the home and in the church.

[134] Despite attempts to provide alternative explanations such as a recent argument that sexual abuse by clergy is rooted in the sexual permissiveness of the Sixties, the unnatural insistence on celibacy must be seen as a significant reason why so many Catholic priests have been involved in the abuse of children.

[135] This has implications for the visual arts that go beyond the scope of this course.

- Because of the intimate nature of both spiritual and sexual relationships, one is bound to affect the other. This may be seen immediately in that the gender roles assigned by God, with man as the loving leader and woman as the suitable helper, are twisted by sin so that the woman covets the leadership role and the man becomes a tyrant rather than one who lays down his life for his beloved (Genesis 3:16).

- The connection between the spiritual and the sexual may also be seen in the common practice among the prophets of referring to idolatry as spiritual adultery. Hosea 1-3 and the pictures painted in Ezekiel 16 and 23 are obvious examples; note too that this is not just Old Testament imagery - James 4:4 and Revelation 17 make the same connection.

- Historically, spiritual rebellion has been associated with sexual perversion. Not only do we have this general principle outlined in Romans 1:18-32, but we also see throughout history that idolatry frequently produces abominable fertility rites, as may be witnessed in the artifacts of many pagan cultures in the ancient world. This is not only true of pagan cultures in the ancient world, of course. No clearer evidence of the connection between the spiritual and the sexual may be seen than the sexual depravity that has increasingly overtaken the Western world since its repudiation of the Christian foundations of Western civilization. We should therefore not be surprised that Satan seeks to undermine faith and godly living through sexual temptation.

SEXUALITY AND REDEMPTION

If spirituality and sexuality are so closely linked, we should expect that God's great work of redemption through Christ should also relate to the sexual aspect of man. Indeed, this is the case, as may be seen in the following ways:

- One of the first things God did after the Fall was to cover the nakedness of Adam and Eve, which had now become a source of shame and temptation (Genesis 3:21). He does this, as many commentators have noted, by killing an animal. Even as early as this, God is teaching the lesson that there can be no remission of sin without the shedding of blood. From the very beginning of the history of sinful mankind, God clearly intends to redeem mankind, including his sexual nature.

- As we have already seen, the Bible pictures God's redemptive work on behalf of His people, delivering them from sin and corruption, in marital terms, with God being the Husband of Israel and Christ making the Church His Bride.[136]

- Parallels between human marital relationships and the spiritual relationship of God with His people, the most notable of which is found in Ephesians 5:22-33, show that redeemed human sexuality is intended to follow the example set by Christ while at the same time modeling that glorious relationship to the surrounding world.

---

[136] Many would also include here the Song of Solomon as a picture of the pure love of Christ for His Church; I would argue that such is not the primary function of this beautiful love poem, though it may be a secondary application.

EXTRAMARITAL SEX

The most obvious application of the Seventh Commandment is to sexual activity outside marriage. This may seem so obvious as not to require mentioning, but no ethical prohibitions are obvious in the modern world. We must thus consider precisely what God is here forbidding and why it is forbidden.

RELEVANT TERMINOLOGY

As is the case in contemporary society, the Bible uses a variety of words to describe illicit sexual activity, and each has its own shade of meaning and area of emphasis. We will examine a few of the more important terms used in Scripture.

- Adultery - The word actually used in the Seventh Commandment refers to sexual activity outside marriage by those who are married. This is explicitly forbidden because of the covenant bond that constitutes a marriage (Malachi 2:14). It also undermines the picture of God's relationship to His people that marriage is intended to portray.
- Fornication - The Hebrew word *zanah* and the Greek word *porneia*, from which we get our English word *pornography*, are both used more frequently than the word for adultery. Probably the main reason for this is that they have a wider semantic range, incorporating both adultery and sex outside marriage by unmarried people. Though this term is not used in the Seventh Commandment, the practice is forbidden in no uncertain terms (e.g., Matthew 15:19; Romans 1:29; I Corinthians 5:1; 6:18; Galatians 5:19; Ephesians 5:3; I Thessalonians 4:3).
- Prostitution - Some translations of the Bible sometimes render *zanah* and *porneia* as *harlotry* or *prostitution*. In fact, no distinct term exists in either Hebrew or Greek in the Bible to describe having sex for money. Thus, unlike many of the issues considered in this course, extramarital sex is one activity where motive is *not* a factor. Whether one is doing it for love or money is immaterial; sex outside marriage is still *wrong*.

PREMARITAL SEX

The prohibition of fornication certainly suffices to rule out premarital sex as well as extramarital sex, but we live in a world where premarital sex is not only condoned, but is often expected as a natural part of the maturation process, so we need to give it some special attention. Contemporary arguments include some of the following:

- Sex is essential to evolutionary progress, since in order for the fittest to survive, they must reproduce, so engaging in sex is simply doing what comes naturally as a healthy animal.
- Premarital sex is important as a proving ground; one must gain sexual experience, not only in order to learn what will please one's eventual life partner, but also to discover whether one's current cohabitant is sexually compatible, which is obviously necessary for a lasting relationship.
- Premarital sex is essential for social acceptance. Everyone is doing it, so why should you be different?

- Sex is a way to cultivate intimacy. How can you really know a person until you sleep with him or her?

The foolishness of such arguments may seem obvious on the surface for those whose standards come from Scripture rather than from the world, but in the environment in which today's young people live and breathe, they clearly have power, not only to convince before the fact, but also to rationalize behavior afterward. Some, however, would even go so far as to argue for the legitimacy, or at least the lesser severity, of premarital sex on the basis of Scripture itself. How might one argue such a thing?

- Premarital sex was not treated with the same severity in the Old Testament law as was adultery. While adultery was a capital offense (Leviticus 20:10), premarital sex was punished by marriage without the possibility of divorce (Exodus 22:16-17; Deuteronomy 22:28-29). Premarital sex was not subject to capital punishment because it did not, like adultery, involve the violation of a vow taken before God, but it was still a punishable offense, and therefore clearly pictured as *wrong*. In fact, the expectation that a woman would be a virgin when she married was so strong that one who deceived her prospective husband in this matter *was* subject to capital punishment (Deuteronomy 22:13-21) - a penalty that Joseph wished to spare Mary when he suspected her of premarital sex (Matthew 1:19).
- The fact that premarital sex was punished by marriage in the Old Testament raises another question: does this imply that sex in and of itself *constitutes* marriage? I Corinthians 6:16, which uses the language of Genesis 2:24 to describe the consequences of sleeping with a prostitute, would seem to point in this direction. Such an argument, however, ignores the public and covenantal aspect of marriage. Marriage is not simply an act performed by two people in the privacy of the bedroom or the back seat of a car, but involves vows taken before God and before human witnesses.
- The belief that sex constitutes marriage has led many to attempt to justify premarital sex by engaged couples - after all, if you're planning on getting married anyway, why wait for the ceremony to become one? In addition to the obvious practical problem that many engagements are broken off, one should note here that Scripture gives two options - marriage or abstinence (I Corinthians 7:9); no third alternative is acceptable in the eyes of God.

LESSER SEXUAL ACTIVITY

The Seventh Commandment extends beyond the realm of actual sexual intercourse, however. Jesus made this clear in the Sermon on the Mount when He equated lustful thoughts with adultery (Matthew 5:27-28). How does this connection affect our understanding of sexual activity short of intercourse, from holding hands to kissing to more intense activity? How should Christians approach the age-old question asked by teenagers everywhere, "How far should we go?" Note the following:

- Jesus began with thoughts, and so should we. In the same way that murder begins in the heart, so does adultery begin with lust. We should note that lust is not sexual desire in itself, because sexual desire within marriage is pure and beautiful, as the Song of Solomon illustrates. Instead, we should understand sexual lust as a desire that can only be lawfully fulfilled within marriage.[137]

- The typical response here is that, if "thinking it is as bad as doing it," then why not go ahead and do it, since the sin has been committed already? Though no one would argue such a thing except someone attempting to justify fulfilling his urges, we should note that, though all sins are in a sense equal before God in alienating a person from the Righteous One, not all sins have the same consequences. Though fornication is no more sinful than the lust that generates it, the consequences for the participants, as well as for others who may know about it or be affected by the relationship issues that result, are much more dire.

- How, then, is the Bible's treatment of lust helpful for teenagers wanting to know the appropriate boundaries for their relationships?[138] I think the best way of approaching this issue is to recognize that, not only do thoughts lead to actions, but actions also lead to thoughts. If lust is wrong, then actions that generate lust are also wrong. Young people who are exploring relationships with those of the opposite gender thus should be aware of what thoughts are being generated in their minds by the things they do. In short, if holding hands makes you think about jumping into bed, then don't hold hands! Note that Christians should be conscious, not only of the thoughts going through their own minds, but of the thoughts being created in the other person as well (cf. I Thessalonians 4:6). For example, a young woman may think her short skirt, low neckline, or tight jeans are cute and stylish but be unaware of quite how powerful an effect her attire is having on the visually-oriented males around her.

- Because one's thought life is such an important part of sexual purity, one should not anticipate a simple list of do's and don't's. What produces lustful thoughts at one stage of a relationship might not do so later. As a result, if one seeks to honor God in this matter, one must be brutally honest about one's own thoughts and desires, as well as showing true love for the other person by considering the responses he or she is experiencing.

BIRTH CONTROL

In the same way that the Sixth Commandment led us to a discussion of a variety of life-and-death issues, so the Seventh Commandment opens the door for considering a variety of issues associated with sex and marriage, beginning with birth control. We should note here is that, for most of the Church History, birth control has not been a controversial issue. There were two main reasons for this: first of all, artificial means of preventing pregnancy were either not available at

---

[137] Note that the term *lust* in the Bible goes beyond the realm of sex to include any illicit desire (cf. James 4:2).

[138] I've heard some truly absurd arguments on this one. Some have used the King James reading of I Corinthians 7:1, "It is good for a man not to touch a woman," to assert that holding hands is sin. The context of I Corinthians 7, however, clearly indicates that Paul has sexual intercourse in view. Genesis 20:6 and Proverbs 6:29 use similar euphemisms.

all or were of very questionable efficacy (e.g., herbal treatments of various kinds), and secondly, Christians were universally opposed to the use of those mechanisms that were available. Something that everyone considers wrong is not controversial.

In recent years, however, things have changed. The availability of reliable artificial birth control methods and altered societal conditions, such as a shift from a rural agricultural economy where children were economic assets to an urban or suburban one where high levels of education are needed, thus making children an economic liability, have combined to bring about widespread acceptance of birth control among many Christians, both evangelical and otherwise. Thus what was once non-controversial has become a matter of considerable disagreement among believers. The issue is complicated by the fact that the Bible does not once mention the subject, so we again find ourselves dependent on the application of biblical principle rather than on explicit biblical teaching.

Despite the existence of real controversy, a few uses of birth control should clearly be ruled out:

- Birth control outside marriage is clearly wrong. Contrary to what "safe sex" advocates would tell us, the use of birth control outside marriage is immoral because it facilitates what the Bible clearly condemns: extramarital sex. No one should be using birth control outside marriage because they should not be having sex outside marriage.[139]
- Birth control after conception is also obviously immoral. Many artificial applications that are marketed as methods of birth control are really abortifacients - rather than preventing the union of sperm and egg, they destroy the fertilized egg, usually by preventing implantation in the womb. While it is not the purpose of this course to go into depth about the technical distinctions among different forms of birth control, students should be aware that while contraceptives such as condoms, diaphragms, and various spermicides do not induce abortions, other "birth control" methods like the intrauterine device (IUD), birth control pills (which both seek to prevent ovulation and then prevent implantation of the fertilized egg if the first hormone fails), and the so-called "morning-after pill" are abortifacients, and thus forms of murder.

ARGUMENTS AGAINST BIRTH CONTROL

Having ruled out the obviously immoral uses of birth control, we need to give attention to the area where true controversy lies among Christians: What about birth control within marriage? We will start by considering the arguments of those who oppose birth control. As noted, this has been the prevailing view of the Church until the last century or so.

---

[139] The objection is always raised at this point about the use of birth control pills for medical reasons. However, if medication is being taken to regulate hormones and not to prevent pregnancy - if the purpose is not to allow for premarital sex without needing to fear the most obvious consequences - then that medication is not "birth control," but medicine.

- The first and most obvious argument presented by birth control opponents is taken from Genesis 1:28. They note that the first commandment God ever gave to man was to "be fruitful and multiply." Unquestionably, one of the purposes for which God instituted marriage was as a means of reproduction. Birth control advocates note, however, that this is about the only commandment of God that mankind has succeeded in keeping, to such an extent that overpopulation is a major concern in some parts of the world.[140] Furthermore, if God intended this command to apply to every individual rather than the human race as a whole, wouldn't celibacy be a sin? Wouldn't God have promoted (rather than grudgingly permitting) polygamy?

- The second argument against birth control is that children are viewed in Scripture as being a blessing from God (Psalm 127:3,5). After all, who would refuse one of God's blessings? Advocates of birth control note that the passage doesn't specify when one's "quiver is full," and that many of God's blessings can be less than beneficial if overindulged (food and drink being obvious examples).

- Thirdly, Scripture pictures childlessness as a curse in Scripture (Genesis 20:18; 29:31; I Samuel 1:1-11). If God punishes those He wishes to curse with childlessness, why should God's people seek that which is a mark of God's disfavor? Advocates note that not all childlessness is seen as a curse (Hannah, for instance, was not being punished), and that birth control may not always be used to allow for childlessness, but instead to limit the number of children.

- A popular argument against birth control, largely associated with the Roman Catholic Church, is that sex exists only for the purpose of procreation. Catholic authorities have argued that any sex act not open to procreation is in fact lustful, so that one could commit adultery even by having sex within marriage (see the papal encyclical *Humanae Vitae* issued by Pope Paul VI in 1968, which makes this very argument). The roots of this teaching lie deep within the fiber of Catholicism, going back to some who argued that the forbidden fruit in the Garden of Eden was really sexual intercourse, so that sex, even within marriage, should be viewed as a necessary evil essential to propagate the race. This view leads to advocating celibacy as the only path of true holiness and requiring it for priests, monks, and nuns. Scripture, however, does not teach that the only justification for sexual intercourse is procreation. It is also intended to express the oneness of husband and wife (Genesis 2:24) and to allow for the legitimate fulfillment of sexual drives (I Corinthians 7:2,9).[141] For the issue of celibacy, see below.

---

[140] Fears of overpopulation have been countered in recent years, however, by drastically declining birth rates, especially in developed countries. Many nations in Europe, along with China, face aging populations and a declining workforce unable to support the vast social safety net created by the Welfare State in the West and Maoism in China; in this respect, the United States is not far behind, with a birth rate only marginally above that needed to sustain a stable population.

[141] Some have noted that the argument that sex is intended only for procreation creates problems on logistical grounds as well. From a mathematical standpoint, a woman is fertile for a total of three years in her entire life (about three days each month, therefore ten percent of the time, for about thirty years between puberty and menopause). If God intended sex solely for the purpose of procreation, this was not a very efficient way of doing it.

- Another biblical argument often used against birth control is taken from Genesis 38:8-10. Here Onan is killed by God for refusing to impregnate his sister-in-law after the death of his brother. The essence of the argument is that God was displeased because Onan enjoyed the pleasures of sex without allowing for the possibility of pregnancy, and thus was punished severely for practicing a second millennium BC form of birth control. This interpretation fails to recognize that Onan was not punished for using a birth control technique, but for disobeying the law of levirate marriage (cf. Deuteronomy 25:5-10). Though this law had not yet been instituted, Judah clearly had something similar in mind, as did God. Thus Onan's problem was not that he did not desire to have children, but that he wanted no children who would interfere with his inheritance of more property from his father.

ARGUMENTS FOR BIRTH CONTROL

Arguments for birth control are much harder to develop, largely because artificial birth control was unknown in Bible times with the exception of certain herbal treatments, which Scripture never mentions. Those who advocate the use of birth control therefore base their justifications on the biblical principle of stewardship. If God intends us to care wisely for the resources He has provided, should not this have something to do with decisions concerning childbearing? Some of the situations where such arguments might be relevant include:

- Delaying the start of a family - Some argue that the difficulty of adjusting to married life is such that one's complete attention must be devoted to building a strong relationship with one's spouse before adding the further complication of children to the picture. Others justify the use of birth control for educational or financial reasons, arguing that a stable career and a solid financial base are important before bringing children into the family.
- Spacing children or limiting the size of the family - Some advocates of birth control in marriage note that wise use of one's resources requires careful planning with an eye toward what the family can afford and what the house can accommodate.
- Health purposes - Others note that consideration of the mother's health may require limiting the size of the family, or even choosing to have no children at all.

The response of opponents of birth control to each of these situations is the same. Where is your faith? Why should a couple decide for themselves what they can and cannot handle rather than trusting God, both to provide the children He wants to give, and then to provide the means to care for His good gifts? Furthermore, they rightly argue that many who practice birth control do so, not out of a concern for stewardship at all, but out of a selfish desire to maintain the lifestyle to which they have become accustomed without the inconvenience of children or the sacrifices of money and time needed to care for those God might send.

This question therefore is a difficult one about which to be dogmatic. While certain obvious cases can be eliminated, one must admit that stewardship is a legitimate teaching of Scripture, especially in the book of Proverbs. Engaging in sexual intercourse without considering the possible consequences is no more an act of faith than crossing the street blindfolded in the belief that God will care for His own. Who would not call irresponsible the actions of Nadya

Suleman, the so-called Octomom, who gave birth to octuplets in 2009 by in vitro fertilization despite being unmarried, on welfare, and already having six young children? Faith does not rule out wisdom, nor does the exercise of wisdom imply a lack of faith. Nonetheless, Christians should be cautious about advocating something that believers until the last century would never have even considered. The main concern here is that we let the values of the world shape our own - that because birth control is now widely accepted in society at large, Christians surely must find some way to justify its use in their own lives. That becomes a problem only when our motives are the same as those of the broader society - the emphasis on individualism and personal fulfillment, material prosperity, and pleasure-seeking as the primary goal of life. If, on the other hand, we sincerely seek to serve God in the best way possible with the resources that He has provided, we face little risk of falling into the pattern of the surrounding society.

SPECIAL CASES

Certain special cases must also be considered when discussing the issue of birth control. The first of these is childlessness. Even if a Christian married couple may choose as the path of wisdom the delay, spacing, or limitation of childbirths, may they ever legitimately choose childlessness? Here in my opinion the arguments against birth control carry more weight; there is a big difference between seeking to live wisely in bringing children into the world and choosing not to do so at all. God does "seek godly offspring" (Malachi 2:15). While some motives, such as health or the demands of ministry (see below) may justify such a choice, we must conclude that the normal trajectory of a marital relationship is intended to include children.[142]

Another special case involves the question of *permanent* birth control - sterilization. The issue now shifts from total birth control to irreversible birth control. Should a Christian woman ever have a tubal ligation? Should a Christian man ever get a vasectomy? Again, the issue of motivation looms large. Is the decision being made for health reasons, to avoid the inconvenience of regular birth control measures, to implement a final decision on family size, or to avoid children altogether? The motive matters. Furthermore, the fact that such a step is permanent ought to be taken into account.[143] The fact of the matter is that circumstances may change in the future. Health problems might not go away, but the family's situation could change for a wide variety of reasons. What, for instance, if a spouse dies, the survivor decides to remarry, and the new spouse wants children? Such decisions are often made for shallow reasons, and permanent solutions should not be sought for situations that might prove to be temporary.

Finally, what about celibacy? While some have been called to follow this path by God (Matthew 19:12) and Paul advocated it for the sake of Christian ministry (I Corinthians 7), Scripture pictures marriage and family as the normal path to be taken by most people (Genesis

---

[142] In recent years, I have gotten an increasing amount of opposition from students when making this point. "But what if I just don't want kids? Do I need a reason?" They simply can't understand why each individual should not have complete freedom to choose whether or not to bring children into the world. Such is the impact of the surrounding society on the Christian Church.

[143] Though today some surgical sterilization procedures can be reversed.

2:18). One should never view singleness as an inferior condition, however. Some have been called to a single life. We should note, of course, that the calling to a single life involves the call to celibacy. Sex is only to be practiced within the confines of marriage, so the single life is to be a life without sex (again, unlike the picture given in the popular culture today, where the single life is presented as a life full of all kinds of sexual opportunities and experimentation).

But if singleness, with its accompanying celibacy, is not to be viewed as an inferior lifestyle, neither is it to be viewed as a superior one. As noted above, the Catholic Church has long taught this, in the process requiring celibacy of all who would devote themselves to the ministry of the church on a full-time basis. The arguments in favor of this position, in addition to the flawed view of the origin and purpose of sex noted above, include the observation that Jesus never married along with a heavy emphasis on Paul's comments in I Corinthians 7. The problem, of course, with this argument is that Scripture speaks of those who would forbid marriage as departing from the faith (I Timothy 4:3). Furthermore, Peter, alleged to be the first Pope, clearly was married (Jesus healed his mother-in-law in Mark 1:29-31), as were the other apostles (I Corinthians 9:5). Paul was the exception rather than the rule. One should not be surprised that such an unnatural requirement produces an unusual preponderance of unnatural behavior that does nothing but dishonor the name of Christ.

DATING

Dating is a relatively recent phenomenon in Western cultures, and was unknown in Bible times. Throughout most of history and in many cultures today, marriages are arranged, usually by parents, are viewed as the union of two families, and are approached with financial and social considerations foremost, with little if any attention given to romantic attraction. Dating, however, has become a major part of the courtship process in the West in the last century or so, and must be addressed on the basis of biblical principles.[144] Note the following:

- While for some, dating is simply a way for friends to spend time together, often with other couples, for recreation or relaxation, the fact that it is typically the gateway to deeper relationships means it should be approached seriously. The first thing to keep in mind here is that, because virtually every marriage begins with a simple date, and because of the extent to which emotional involvement often draws people into deeper relationships, one should not date anyone with whom marriage could not be at least a possibility. For a Christian, this means that one should never date an unbeliever. "Missionary dating" is not a sound strategy; even if it occasionally brings about the conversion of the unbeliever, it much more often draws the believer away from his or her relationship with the Lord, and on occasion leads to a lifetime of unhappiness in violation of II Corinthians 6:14-18.

---

[144] We should note that, within the last decade or so, the practice of dating has been challenged on both ends of the spectrum. Some Christians have forsaken the practice through the impact of Josh Harris' influential book *I Kissed Dating Goodbye*, pursuing formal courtship instead, while on secular college campuses, "hooking up," involving casual sex with no effort to build a relationship at all, has replaced dating for some.

- One of the great dangers of dating is the temptation to engage in physical intimacy because of significant amounts of time spent alone as a couple. Thoughtful couples should avoid too much time alone by spending time together in the presence of others and planning activities that will help to avoid temptation. The principles enunciated under the first topic in this chapter concerning activities that stimulate lustful thoughts should always be kept in mind.

- Dating should be purposeful. If one truly loves another person, he or she will seek that person's spiritual growth and development. Christian couples who are seriously considering marriage should have devotions together and pray for one another and for their relationship regularly. They should seek to cultivate real honesty in their interactions with one another; if openness is not possible while courting, what basis is there for marriage?

- Pay special attention to matters of conflict resolution. If conflicts never arise, the two people involved clearly don't yet know one another well enough. When conflicts do arise, are they being handled biblically on both sides? This will say a lot about whether the two should pursue the relationship further.

- Two Christians who are seeking God's will in marriage should be active in serving the Lord together. If this is the real purpose for which God has left His people in this world, it should be the center of any relationship between believers. Does your dating life involve you in greater service for God, or does it hinder you from serving? The answer to the question will tell you quite a bit about the spiritual health of your relationship.

DIVORCE

Divorce is a painful reality that is increasingly prevalent in our world. One of the saddest aspects of this problem is that the increasing incidence of divorce among professing Christians. Many reasons may be cited for this, although most of these may be traced back to the influence of an increasingly secularized culture that places little value on marriage, encourages alternative living arrangements, and places personal fulfillment and happiness above commitment, self-sacrifice and putting others first. In any case, few Christians today have been untouched by divorce, either in their own families and churches or in others close to them.

While the world's approach to marriage, and therefore to divorce, is clearly unbiblical and immoral, we should also note that the subject is very controversial among Christians. Not all of those who sincerely seek to obey God in this matter agree on what the Bible teaches on the issue, so we will focus on Christian views of the subject of divorce rather than dealing with secular approaches to the issue.

THE PERMANENCE OF MARRIAGE

Scripture clearly teaches that marriage was instituted by God and is intended to be permanent (Genesis 2:24). This must be the foundation for any discussion of the Bible's teaching on divorce. As noted earlier in the section on oaths and vows, one who approaches marriage with the conviction of its permanence and a determination to fulfill the vows that are taken at the altar will be far less likely to seek the easy way out when difficulties and conflicts arise later. The fact that God intended marriage to be permanent also implies that any biblical provisions for divorce are exceptions rather than expressions of God's desire for human relationships.

OLD TESTAMENT TEACHING ON DIVORCE

The Old Testament has little to say on the subject. Perhaps the best-known passage addressing divorce is Deuteronomy 24:1-4. The passage deals with a situation where a man finds "some indecency" in his wife and divorces her. He is instructed in such cases to provide her with a legal document formalizing the divorce. Furthermore, we are told that, should her succeeding husband also find her to be wanting, she may not return to her first husband again and remarry him. Rabbinical scholars differed on the meaning of these verses, arguing largely about the meaning of *indecency*. Shammai and Hillel, two Jewish teachers who lived during the Intertestamental Period, carried on a long controversy that was continued by their followers. Shammai argued that indecency meant adultery, and that therefore marital unfaithfulness was the only legitimate basis for divorce. Hillel argued, with some justification, that because the law specified stoning for adultery, divorce would have been irrelevant in such circumstances, so indecency could have been practically anything that displeased the husband - if she burned his toast, she was toast. In any case, only the husband here has the right of divorce, and the only remarriage that is forbidden is remarriage to a previous spouse. We will look shortly at Jesus' explanation of this passage, but should note at this point that these verses never advocate divorce, but instead set up safeguards against the most egregious of wife-swapping practices, which sadly seem to have been prevalent among the Israelites of Moses' day.

Other Old Testament references include Leviticus 21:14, which forbids a priest to marry a divorced woman; Isaiah 50:1 and Jeremiah 3:8, which speak of the Lord divorcing faithless Israel because of her adulteries; and Malachi 2:16, where God says, "I hate divorce" (NIV),[145] in the context of castigating the unfaithfulness of the returning remnant to the wives of their youth. Here divorce again is not absolutely forbidden, but is viewed as limited to extreme situations, and those who lightly abuse it are condemned by God.

NEW TESTAMENT TEACHING ON DIVORCE

In the Gospels, Jesus addresses the issue in four passages (actually two parallel pairs). In Matthew 5:31-32, in the Sermon on the Mount, Jesus includes divorce in the list of subjects on which he contradicts rabbinical misinterpretations of the Old Testament law. He appears to be condemning the view of the Hillel school, which took a very liberal view of divorce, and allowing divorce only on the ground of marital unfaithfulness. The statement that one who divorces his wife for an illegitimate reason "makes her commit adultery" is a reflection of a culture where unmarried women who had no families to support them were forced to remarry in order to avoid winding up on the street, while the statement that "whoever marries a divorced woman commits adultery" indicates that the marriage bond is not truly broken by an illegitimate divorce, so that

---

[145] The English Standard Version translates the relevant words as "The man who hates and divorces..." The passage translated in this way is no less a condemnation of the divorces of convenience in which the Israelites were engaging.

subsequent remarriage would be adulterous. Luke 16:18 is even stronger in that it mentions no exception for infidelity.[146]

Matthew 19:3-9 and Mark 10:2-12 are accounts of the same incident. The Pharisees here are trying to draw Jesus into the debate still raging among the rabbis over the explanations of Deuteronomy 24 given by Shammai and Hillel. This constitutes a "test" in the sense that, no matter what position Jesus took, He was sure to alienate half of His audience. Jesus refuses to be baited into taking sides and begins where all should begin - with the Bible's statements about the permanence of marriage in Genesis 1:27 and 2:24 (note that the sequence of events in the conversation differs slightly in the two accounts). When they press Him further by citing the Deuteronomy 24 passage, Jesus does what only He, as the Author of Scripture, can do - He affirms that Deuteronomy 24 does not express moral law, but was intended to place limits on the worst expressions of human hardness of heart. In other words, it was a temporary expedient rather than a universally applicable moral dictum. Again, He affirms the exception for marital unfaithfulness (included in Matthew, but not in Mark). The teaching of Jesus thus leaves us with a repudiation of the easy divorce advocated by the school of Hillel, an assertion that divorce is permissible (but not required) in cases of marital infidelity,[147] and a warning that remarriage in cases of illegitimate divorce is itself adulterous.

Paul also addresses the issue in I Corinthians 7:10-15. Note that the discussion of divorce takes place in the broader context of a discourse on marriage, including Paul's defense of celibacy "in the present distress" (verse 26). Paul begins in verses 10-11 by telling Christian husbands and wives that they should not divorce one another (note that husbands and wives are addressed equally here, which was not the case in the Old Testament). This in no way invalidates the exception for adultery given by Jesus, but expresses the ideal of the permanence of marriage among Christians. In verses 12-15, Paul addresses a problem that would rarely have existed in Jesus' time a few decades earlier - the religiously mixed marriage. We should not view this situation as one in which Christians violated the prohibition voiced by Paul in his next letter to the church at Corinth about being unequally yoked; instead, we must recognize that, especially in the first generation of the church, many were converted who had unbelieving spouses. The question then arose, "If an unequal yoke is wrong, should a believer remain in such marriage?" Paul's response in verses 12-14 is an unequivocal affirmative - the believer should not seek to dissolve the marriage if the unbeliever is willing to continue in it because of the godly influence the believer brings into the home environment.[148] Should the unbeliever choose to dissolve the union,

---

[146] Those who argue that divorce is always sin typically begin with Luke 16:18 and argue that the permitted exceptions, even those made by Jesus, are really "because of the hardness of man's heart" and are not really a reflection of God's will.

[147] Note that this would have been a non-issue in the Old Testament, where stoning would have made the question of divorce moot in cases of adultery.

[148] The idea that a believing parent makes the children "holy" in the sense of bringing them into the covenant family of God is a stretch here, though it is often used by paedobaptists; such children are no more under the covenant than the unbelieving spouse is. The point is that Christian influence in the home has a salutary effect of setting them apart from the pagan world surrounding them.

however, divorce is permissible.[149] Paul thus adds a second exception to the one given by Jesus -
divorce is permissible when a Christian spouse is deserted by an unbeliever.[150]

WHAT ABOUT ABUSE?

What about cases of spousal abuse? Does this provide a third exception where divorce is
permissible - one the Bible fails to mention? Some argue that abuse constitutes "emotional
abandonment," and therefore fits under the umbrella of Paul's treatment in I Corinthians 7:10-15.
Sadly, many men who abuse their wives (or even wives who abuse their husbands) have no desire
to leave the marriage because they *like* beating up their spouses, therefore Paul's exception simply
doesn't fit in many cases. If emotional abandonment with no express desire to dissolve the
marriage on the part of the partner becomes a legitimate basis for divorce, the door is flung wide
open for divorce for almost any reason, since who could not make a case for emotional
abandonment in a marriage that has become distasteful? While legal remedies are available, all
recognize that the protections afforded by injunctions and such are extremely limited - too many
women are brutally beaten or even killed by men against whom they have been granted injunctions
or protection orders.

The church does have a role to play in situations where both spouses are professing
Christians. If one spouse is abusing the other, church discipline should be invoked. On the basis
of Matthew 18:15-18, a professing Christian who refuses to repent when brought before the
church is to be excommunicated as treated as an unbeliever, in which case the exception raised by
Paul in I Corinthians 7 would become relevant. In any case, the church has much to do to minister
to believers who are in troubled marriages for whatever reason.

POLYGAMY

One might legitimately wonder why this book includes a section on polygamy, which is
illegal in the United States and is thus, for all practical purposes, a dead issue. It is worth
considering for several reasons, however. The first is that, given the sexual permissiveness of the
age and the willingness to argue that "a family is whatever you define it to be," how long will it
be until statutes against polygamy are challenged successfully in the courts, as has been the case
with homosexuality? The second is that those who have practiced polygamy in the past, aside
from primitive peoples, have sought a biblical justification for doing so. A few examples of this
would include:

---

[149] As is remarriage - the word used to indicate that the believer is "not enslaved" in such cases is the
same one Paul uses in Romans 7:1-3 to indicate that a woman is bound to her husband while he lives, but after he
dies she is "not bound" and is free to remarry.

[150] The fact that this exception is prefaced by Paul's indication that he is speaking, not the Lord (verse 12)
does not in any way reduce its inspiration or authority; Paul is simply indicating that this is a question that Jesus
did not address.

- Islam - Muhammad and his followers cite the examples of the Patriarchs to defend their teaching that a man may have multiple wives, though the Bible never sets a limit of four, as does the Qur'an.

- Jan of Leyden, the leader of a group of radical Anabaptists who took over the town of Münster in the Netherlands around 1535, taught that God had restored the Kingdom of David, and that the rule of the saints would include the practice of polygamy. After a brief period of tyranny leading to starvation during a siege of the city, Jan was brutally executed along with many of his followers.

- John Humphrey Noyes, the founder of the Oneida Community in upstate New York in 1848, taught and practiced "complex marriage," in which Christians held their wives in common as well as their possessions. The result was a primitive experiment in eugenics that, for some unimaginable reason, the neighbors found objectionable. Eventually, the commune gave up the practice and settled down to the manufacture of silverware.

- The best-known example in recent years, of course, is Mormonism. Joseph Smith and Brigham Young taught and practiced polygamy, not only following the examples of the men of the Old Testament, but also based on the Mormon belief that marriage solemnized in a Mormon Temple lasted for time and eternity, and that such marriage was the only way that women could advance to godhood. The result was abundant sexual indulgence marketed as an act of mercy to women! Mormons repudiated the practice when a special revelation to the president of the church miraculously coincided with a Supreme Court decision preventing statehood for Utah as long as the Mormons practiced legalized polygamy. Today, only a few fringe groups in the deserts of the Southwest continue the practice, and apart from the occasional attention-grabbing incident, are generally left alone.

POLYGAMY IN THE BIBLE

Because of the biblical defense used by its practitioners past and present, a biblical response is necessary. After all, polygamy was practiced by great men of the faith, including Abraham, Jacob, David, and most notably Solomon. Note the following:

- Scripture clearly pictures monogamy as the norm. The family as instituted by God was monogamous (Genesis 2:18-24); note that *two* were to become one flesh, not *two or more*. Polygamy begins among the rebellious descendants of Cain (Genesis 4:19). Furthermore, the requirement of the New Testament that an elder be "the husband of one wife" (I Timothy 3:2) at least suggests, though the point may not be made definitively, that the toleration of polygamy, like that of open divorce, is to be viewed as due to "the hardness of men's hearts."[151]

- Polygamy was tolerated in the Old Testament, even to the extent of being recognized in the law (Exodus 21:10; Deuteronomy 21:10-14), though both of these passages refer to concubines - slaves in one case and captives in the other. Furthermore, the polygamous practices of the men noted above are never condemned by God.

---

[151] This is especially true when we note that the qualifications for church office are never intended to set church leaders apart from others, but simply describe the qualities of a consistent Christian. Elders are not distinguished from others because they alone are monogamous; all faithful Christians are expected to be.

- Polygamy was not considered to be adultery. Polygamous marriages were real marriages, subject to the same constraints as any other marriage. Nor was polygamy ever explicitly forbidden, though the qualifications for church leadership come close to doing so.
- On the practical level, polygamy caused nothing but trouble. Sarah was jealous of Hagar, Leah and Rachel squabbled frequently, Peninnah plagued Hannah, the sons of David's wives developed murderous rivalries, and Solomon built pagan temples outside Jerusalem to enable his wives to worship their gods, thus leading Israel down the path to idolatry. In not one circumstance is polygamy ever pictured as having positive consequences in the life of a family.

POLYGAMY AND MISSIONS

Polygamy is not a major issue in America today, though it may become so someday soon. It is, however, an issue among missionaries, especially those working in foreign cultures. Suppose a polygamist comes to salvation through exposure to the Gospel - what should he do? Because Scripture does recognize polygamous marriages as true marriages, one cannot legitimately argue that the man has committed adultery, and thus should divest himself of all wives except the first one on the ground that he is forcing those women to live in sin. In fact, such a divorce would be wrong because marital unfaithfulness has not occurred. On the other hand, no matter how deeply ingrained such a practice may be in the culture, such a man may not be permitted to serve as a leader in the church, no matter what his gifts or influence may be. Furthermore, the biblical ideal should form the basis for instruction that would lead to no further polygamous marriages being constructed. That, along with the examples set by church leaders who model godly marriages, should cause polygamy to die out within a generation, at least among Christians.

HOMOSEXUALITY

When we were examining the issue of birth control, we noted that the question had not been a matter of controversy among Christians until the last century or so because the practice was almost universally assumed to be wrong. When we arrive at the topic of homosexuality, this is even more true. No moral question could more clearly illustrate the tendency of the church to follow the world. The progression is a typical one - condemnation as sin followed by pity for maladjustment or sickness followed by acceptance as a difference for which one cannot be faulted followed by full inclusion and advocacy followed by the condemnation of any who oppose it. Here, however, the dramatic reversal has occurred in less than half a century.[152]

---

[152] The treatment of homosexuality in the medical community followed a parallel track. From the belief that homosexuality was a form of moral perversion, psychologists then argued that it was a form of mental illness, after which geneticists argued that it was a physical defect or genetic disease, which later came to be treated as a genetic difference rather than an abnormality. If it is simply a genetic difference and not a defect, it should be accepted, protected, and even promoted, and surely anyone who is not willing to do so must be the victim of some sort of psychological defect himself.

THE BIBLE'S TEACHING ON HOMOSEXUALITY

While homosexuality is only mentioned specifically in the Bible a few times, the references are so strong and clear that one should not be surprised that the issue has been a no-brainer for most of the Church's history. Note the following:

- Homosexuality is the sin for which Sodom and Gomorrah were destroyed by God in Genesis 19:4-8. The passage gave the name *sodomy* to this particular form of perversion.
- Homosexuality is condemned in Leviticus 18:22, and in Leviticus 20:13 is listed as a capital offense.
- Deuteronomy 23:17 forbids male cult prostitution, which was homosexual in nature. In I Kings 14:24, Rehoboam is condemned for allowing male cult prostitutes, while Asa (I Kings 15:22) and Jehoshaphat (I Kings 22:46) are commended for purging the land of them.
- In Romans 1:26-27, Paul describes homosexuality as the result of God giving sinful mankind over to the natural consequences of rebellion. Note that this is the only explicit biblical reference to lesbianism.
- I Corinthians 6:9-10 and I Timothy 1:9-10 include homosexuality in lists of behaviors contrary to sound doctrine and sufficient to exclude one from the Kingdom of God.
- II Peter 2:6,8 and Jude 7 both allude to homosexuality in their descriptions of the reason for the destruction of Sodom and Gomorrah.

"BIBLICAL" ARGUMENTS FOR HOMOSEXUALITY

Given the clarity of the Bible's teaching on the subject, how could we possibly have arrived at a situation where many churches quietly acquiesce in the acceptance of homosexuality, a few openly ordain practicing homosexual pastors,[153] and one church - the Metropolitan Community Church - was founded for the specific purpose of affirming and ministering to gays, lesbians, and the transgendered? The obvious reason is that these churches have long ago repudiated the inspiration, inerrancy, and authority of the Scriptures and have instead sought their moral foundation in the changing values of the surrounding culture. Yet the approach to the question by such churches goes beyond their rejection of the authority of the Bible. Ironically, the same people who reject the Bible also devote a tremendous amount of time and energy to arguing that the Bible really doesn't condemn homosexuality at all! Thus they both reject the Scriptures and reinterpret them to fit their preconceptions. How can such clear passages as those cited above possibly be "reinterpreted"? Note the following:

- The usual approach to Genesis 19 is to argue that God did not destroy Sodom and Gomorrah for homosexuality, but either for their lust for gang rape (this would explain the II Peter and Jude verses), or even more absurdly, for pride and lack of hospitality (Ezekiel 16:49 is often cited here).

---

[153] The list includes the United Church of Christ (1985), the Episcopal Church (2003), the Evangelical Lutheran Church in America (2009), and the Presbyterian Church - U.S.A. (2010).

- The passages in Leviticus are explained away as referring to homosexual cult prostitution rather than "normal" homosexual relationships. Note that this would cover the Deuteronomy and I Kings passages as well.

- Romans 1:26-27 is the most difficult to evade. The typical argument regards the *unnatural* behavior condemned in the passage as homosexual activity on the part of heterosexuals; after all, when homosexuals engage in homosexual activity, for them it is *natural*.

- The inclusion of homosexuality in the lists in the Pauline epistles is explained away by giving technical cultural explanations to the terms used and arguing that what is being described is simply not the same as the loving homosexual relationships that these churches accept and advocate.

- Such churches are not satisfied simply to give twisted interpretations of clear biblical passages in order to make them say exactly the opposite of what they obviously teach. They go even further, arguing that the Bible actually affirms loving homosexual relationships. The most frequently cited is that between David and Jonathan. The way the explanation goes is that in I Samuel 18:1-4, Jonathan loved David "as his own soul," and Saul took him into his household to provide a lover for his son; Jonathan even takes his clothes off in David's presence; later they go off into the field together (I Samuel 20:11) and kiss passionately (I Samuel 20:41). When Jonathan dies, David mourns him by affirming that his love for him was "extraordinary, surpassing the love of women" (II Samuel 1:26). To read sexual innuendo into the beautiful description of a friendship is in itself an abomination.

- Ruth and Naomi are abused in even worse fashion. Some homosexual apologists go so far as to argue that Ruth's beautiful affirmation of loyalty to Naomi in Ruth 1:16-17 was really a marriage vow (after all, the verses are often used in marriage vows in modern weddings!) in which the two became lesbian lovers. They seem to miss the point that the affirmation occurs in the context of a conversation about Ruth's future marital prospects, and that the story ends with Ruth happily married to Boaz and bearing the ancestor of both King David and the Messiah.

SECULAR DEFENSE OF HOMOSEXUALITY

Not all advocates for homosexuality twist the Bible, of course; most simply ignore it or condemn it as outdated, traditional at best, and bigoted at worst. Defenses of the practice come from other directions, some of which are blatantly contradictory.

- The "gay gene" theory - This is at the heart of the "I was born this way" approach. Scientists have postulated that homosexuality is genetic in origin, but the best-known efforts to substantiate this conclusion have been examples of junk science at its worst. Simon LeVay's 1991 study purporting to show structural differences in the brains of heterosexuals and homosexuals used a very small sample, produced ambiguous results, and has never been successfully replicated. A few years later, Dean Hamer claimed to have identified the gay gene in a genetic study of identical twins and siblings, at least one of whom was gay. He noted that, in a high percentage of identical twins who possessed the genetic marker in question, both were gay. The obvious problem here, of course, is that if homosexuality were genetic, the number should have been 100% instead of somewhere around half. Environmental factors have, on the other hand, proved to correlate much more effectively with homosexual orientation, including the absence of a strong father figure, a domineering mother, and childhood sexual abuse.

- Related to the gay gene theory is the evolutionary argument. Some apologists for homosexuality argue that homosexuality must be inborn because of the evidence of homosexual behavior in the animal kingdom. LeVay got involved in this debate as well, claiming that sexual behavior varies greatly among animals and that such behavior among creatures of the same gender is quite common (e.g., grooming practices among primates), though rarely reproductive in form and almost never exclusive (i.e., what would be called bisexual rather than homosexual orientation in humans). The anthropomorphism involved in such arguments is laughable (monkeys engaging in same-sex heavy petting?), but shows the extent to which advocates will go to undermine the argument that homosexuality is *unnatural*. One should also note that the evolutionary argument contradicts the fundamental tenet of Darwinism, which holds that the characteristics passed on to future generations are those that most readily contribute to the perpetuation of the species. If such a thing as a gay gene existed, the evolutionary process would have selected it *out* millions of years ago, since it inhibits reproduction rather than fostering it.
- The third argument often heard is based on individual freedom. Homosexuality is a personal choice, and neither the government nor anyone else has any right getting involved in what happens between consenting adults. No one seems to notice that the argument on the basis of personal choice directly contradicts the claim that "I was born this way."
- Related to this is the legal argument. Opposition to homosexuality is pictured as discrimination and bigotry, compared to the denial of equal rights to African-Americans, and subject to aggressive legal action. We live in a society where Christians increasingly struggle to uphold biblical values. Gays are seeking to use the courts to force, not only equal rights, but universal acceptance and affirmation, thus forcing their radical values on all who would differ from them. Some Christian adoption agencies have been forced to close their doors because they refused to place children with gay couples. Christian organizations that refuse to hire homosexuals have been threatened with loss of their tax-exempt status as non-profits; though none of these suits has yet been successful, the climate in our courts is such that a ruling along these lines may occur in the near future.

CHRISTIAN RESPONSE TO HOMOSEXUALITY

How, then, should Christians respond to homosexuality? Clearly, it must be treated as sin and perversion, but we should note that it is no more sinful, and therefore no more worthy of condemnation, than heterosexual sins such as adultery and fornication. Couples who choose to live together without benefit of marriage are "living in sin" whether they are of the same or different genders.[154] Note the following:

---

[154] Somewhat bizarrely, some advocates of gay marriage claim that it should be allowed so that homosexuals are *not* forced to "live in sin" when they really desire the legal status of married partners. Such an argument misses the point that perversion is perversion whether the law recognizes it nor not. Abortion does not cease to be murder just because the government says it is legal.

- Christians should not be seduced by the "gay gene" argument or any other claim that homosexuals cannot help themselves, thus their behavior should be accepted and protected. I Corinthians 6:11 completely demolishes any such claims when Paul speaks in the past tense of homosexuals who have been delivered from their sin by the saving grace of Christ. Scripture thus gives hope for change where the world offers none.
- Do not be seduced by the argument that "if two people truly love one another, how can that be wrong?" Jesus commanded His followers to love all people, but that doesn't mean one is free to sleep with them. The definition of love underlying such an argument is far from what the Bible teaches on the subject (see pages 21-24).
- "Love the sinner but hate the sin" is relevant here, even though, contrary to popular belief, the Bible does not contain the phrase. Jesus interacted and even ate with the vilest of sinners in His society, seeking to reach them with His message of salvation. Homosexuals are not to be treated as lepers, or as if their sin is far worse than the sins from which God has delivered all those who trust in His Son.
- Love does not mean acceptance of sinful behavior. The Church ought to reach out to all repentant sinners, but that should never include excusing their sin. It *certainly* does not include affirming their "alternative sexual orientation" or ordaining them to the ministry.

FEMINISM

As we continue to consider issues of sex and gender, we arrive at the question of the role of women. As noted in the introduction to this chapter, basic biblical teaching on the subject leads us to conclude that men and women are essentially equal before God, but have been given different roles to play in the divine economy. The foundational biblical principles that lead to this conclusion are vital to any attempt to understand the role of women in the family, the church, and the world. The following biblical passages are vital to the development of this understanding:

- Genesis 1:27, which teaches that man and woman were alike made in the image of God, supports the idea of the essential equality of men and women (and thus the duality of human gender says something very important about God Himself). Because men and women share the divine image, they are the same in essence.
- Galatians 3:28 teaches the spiritual equality of men and women. Though often used to contradict other clear biblical teachings on the relationship of the sexes, this passage decidedly affirms the spiritual oneness that unites all believers in a common salvation.

While the Bible clearly teaches male-female equality, it just as clearly teaches role differentiation. Note the following:

- Genesis 2:18-23 speaks of Eve being created as a "suitable helper" for Adam. That role differentiation is intended is underscored by Paul in his reference to the passage in I Timothy 2:13. Thus role differentiation is a part of the created order, and may not be explained away as the result of the Fall.
- While the Fall did not create gender distinctions, it did affect them adversely. Genesis 3:16 indicates that the harmonious relationship between man and woman was perverted by

sin so that, while the woman became dissatisfied with her role as a helper and wanted to rule the roost, man was tempted to abuse his God-given authority and become a tyrant. Note that I Timothy 2:14 sees this, too, as influencing a proper understanding of gender relations.

- Gender distinctions also are involved in the redemptive work of God in the lives of His people. Ephesians 5:22-33 shows that the husband's loving headship and the wife's willing submission are important, not only in following Christ's example, but also in providing a picture of the redemptive work of God to the watching world.

These ideas sound very strange indeed, and often offensive, to the society in which we live, which views any hint of role differentiation as a challenge to the very idea of equality. How, then, can the two be reconciled? Is female submission really shameful subservience, a mark of inferiority? Is male headship nothing more than the manifestation of an outdated patriarchal view of the world that is an insult to modern sensibilities? Not according to Scripture it isn't. The fact that role differentiation is compatible with essential equality can be seen nowhere more clearly than in the relationships among the members of the Godhead. As we already saw on page 156, intertrinitarian relationships are used as an example of the ways in which men and women relate to one another under the Headship of Christ. The fact that Christ always submitted to the will of His Father (e.g., Luke 22:42) in no way implies that He is inferior. The fact that the Father is the principal Creator, the Son the Redeemer, and the Holy Spirit the Sanctifier - different roles in the divine economy - does not remotely suggest that the members of the Trinity are less than equal, nor does the fact that the Father elects those who are to be saved, the Son redeems them, and the Spirit regenerates them.

WOMEN IN THE FAMILY

How, then, can these biblical teachings be applied to proper understanding of the role of women? As far as the role of the woman in the family is concerned, Ephesians 5 clearly teaches submission to her husband. The man is the head of the house, but this certainly does not restrict the wife to being a doormat, spending her entire life "barefoot and pregnant." The best evidence of this is found in Proverbs 31:10-31, where the noble wife is engaged in a wide variety of activities for the benefit of her family. Much of the outcry with regard to this biblical mandate today has to do largely with the rejection of the view of marriage and the family found in Scripture. If a family may be defined according to the preferences of the individuals involved, so that single parents, couples living together without benefit of marriage, and gay couples should be viewed as every bit as legitimate as the "traditional" family of one man and one woman, united in the bonds of matrimony, and their children, then clearly the idea of a designated role for women in the family becomes absurd. We should not be surprised that a rejection of biblical morality leads to a cycle where immorality breeds confusion, which in turn breeds more immorality. Is it any wonder that men and women today have no idea who they are or what their place in the world should be, and that so many, in their confusion, turn to forms of sexual experimentation, including but not restricted to homosexuality?

WOMEN IN THE CHURCH

With regard to a woman's role in the church, the Bible is very clear about male leadership. While the most obvious passage to address this subject is I Timothy 2:11-15, where women are explicitly forbidden to teach or exercise authority over men (the two basic functions of an elder - see I Timothy 5:17), we should note that the qualifications for elders and deacons in I Timothy 3:1-13 also assume male leadership ("the husband of one wife"). In practice, male leadership in the Church was also the pattern in the New Testament. Jesus' apostles were all men, as were the heads of the churches mentioned throughout the rest of the New Testament period. Furthermore, the submission of women in the church context is also brought out in passages like I Corinthians 11:4-12 and I Corinthians 14:34-35. Though these are difficult passages about the interpretation of which many disagree, they nonetheless do teach a place of submission for women. That the silence mandated here is not absolute may be seen in passages like I Corinthians 11:5 and I Timothy 2:8-10, where women are described as "praying and prophesying," and allusions to women teaching children (II Timothy 1:5) and other women (Titus 2:3-5).

Why, then, have so many churches begun to practice what the Bible explicitly forbids - the ordination of women to the ministry? Though the practice has greatly spread and accelerated since the rise of feminism in the nineteenth century, it goes back much further in the history of the Church.

- Heretical groups in the second and third centuries practiced the ordination of women. The most notable of these was the Montanists in the late second century. Montanus, who was convinced that the Kingdom of God was about to arrive on earth in the town of Pepuza in Asia Minor, began traveling with two "prophetesses," Priscilla and Maximilla, proclaiming his novel teachings. Various Gnostic groups in the same period also practiced the ordination of women; it is from the writings of such groups that modern scholars like Elaine Pagels, a professor at Princeton University, build their argument that the ordination of women was the original practice of the church, somehow ignoring the fact that the Church *repudiated* these teachings rather than affirming them.[155]
- Contrary to the constant criticism of the Church as a patriarchal dinosaur insisting on perpetuating the values of a long-forgotten age, the Christian Church liberated and elevated women in ways unknown in Roman society. To the Romans, women were little more than the possessions of their husbands, to be treated like so much property. The Church gave dignity where little had previously existed.
- Women priests were strictly forbidden throughout the history of Catholicism, as they are today. Convents and female religious orders gave ample opportunity for women to exercise leadership abilities among other women, though some medieval visionaries claimed authority for extrabiblical teachings in ways to which the Church obviously objected.
- With the rise of Protestantism during the Reformation, women generally still were forbidden to preach, though certain radical Anabaptist groups were exceptions to the rule.

---

[155] The same idea appears in Dan Brown's notorious novel *The Da Vinci Code*, mixed in with a variety of fanciful conspiracy theories.

Fringe groups like the Quakers, who have no ordained ministry at all, allow women to preach on the same basis as men.

- In the nineteenth century, the Salvation Army, though technically not a church, allowed men and women to preach on an equal basis. In fact, William Booth, the founder of the group, always claimed that his wife Catherine was a better preacher than he was.

- Nineteenth-century cults founded by women claiming prophetic gifts include the Seventh-Day Adventists, begun by Ellen G. White, and Christian Science, founded by Mary Baker Eddy.

- With the rise of Pentecostalism around 1900, many small independent churches arose, often founded and led by women who claimed divine inspiration. Women's ordination continues to be commonplace among Pentecostals today.

- The real influence of the feminist movement is not seen until the middle of the twentieth century, when mainline denominations began one after another to ordain women. Influenced by the surrounding culture in the same way we have already seen in regard to homosexuality, churches ignored biblical authority in order to conform to the "enlightened" ideas of the modern world. Rare is the liberal church today that does not ordain women, and the practice is increasingly penetrating the evangelical world.

We again must ask the question of how something that so blatantly contradicts the teaching of the Bible could become common practice among professing Christians. The answers are similar to what we already saw in the discussion of homosexuality above.

- Rejection of biblical authority is foundational here again, but not all who favor the ordination of women simply reject biblical teaching in order to do so. They then must explain the passages that so clearly teach the opposite of what they are advocating.

- The passages limiting a woman's role in the Church are explained away as the products of the culture of the day. If the Roman world was patriarchal, obviously no one raised in that kind of environment would be willing to accept female leadership, so the Church was forced to accommodate to the world in which it began.[156]

- Others, not as charitable, argue that the writers of the Bible and leaders of the Church were simply unenlightened Neanderthals who simply didn't know any better. Paul was a male chauvinist pig and Jesus was simply the victim of the limited, outdated view of His times.

- The typical response to Pauline passages forbidding female leadership and enjoining silence is that these were intended for a specific cultural situation rather than intended as general principles to be observed by the Church throughout history. Scholars theorize about women speaking out in the services in Ephesus and Corinth in totally unacceptable ways, then suggest that the behavior about which they have speculated (with no supporting evidence whatsoever) is what Paul must have been forbidding. The problem with such an argument is that Paul tells his readers the reasons behind the prohibition, deriving them clearly from the Creation and Fall (I Timothy 2:13-14) rather than from certain specific obnoxious behavior among the women in Timothy's congregation.

---

[156] Note that, while for the New Testament Church accommodation to society is seen as an unfortunate weakness, accommodation to the values of *modern* society is seen as wise, and indeed the right thing to do.

- Scholars also without justification impute leadership roles to New Testament women:
  - Phoebe - But when she is called a *diakonos* in Romans 16:1, the word used is the common word for *servant*, only used to describe a church office in a few passages like I Timothy 3:8-13 where the context makes its specific intent obvious.
  - The four daughters of Philip (Acts 21:8-9) - But we have already seen in I Corinthians 11:5 that prophesying is not tantamount to ordination or even leadership.
  - Priscilla (Acts 18:24-26) - When she, along with her husband, is said to teach Apollos, this is private conversation, not the authoritative teaching ministry of the Church.
  - Mary Magdalene - All that can be said about her is that she carried a message from the risen Christ to the apostles; anything further is derived from second or third century pseudepigraphal literature.
- Another approach that has been very popular involves confusing the woman's role in the Church with that in society. The following examples are often raised:
  - Deborah was a prophetess, but those who cite her example forget that she strongly criticized Barak for not assuming the leadership role that was rightly his, and that this role involved judging disputes and leading the people into battle rather than exercising spiritual authority.
  - Esther was a queen, but was entirely submissive to Mordecai when spiritual issues were involved.
  - Lydia, the businesswoman in Philippi who hosted the prayer meeting that served as Paul's entryway into the city (Acts 16:11-15), led a gathering that consisted only of women, which in no way violates biblical teaching.
- Another argument equates gifts with calling, claiming that, if a woman has been given gifts by God that enable her to lead and preach with authority, it would be wrong to forbid her to do so. Yet the Bible distinguishes between gifts and ministries; gifts may be used in a variety of ways that do not imply formal church office. Furthermore, if God says that women are not to participate in the ordained ministry of the Church, He would not contradict Himself by depriving the Church of service for which He had qualified one of His children. Those who claim such a calling, along with those who profess to recognize it, do so in direct disobedience to the Word of God, and therefore claim for themselves greater wisdom than God Himself.
- Some who argue for women's ordination do so on a practical basis - if men will not take up the task, should not women fill the need rather than allowing it to go unmet? Such an argument was often used in the heyday of European foreign missions. The problem with this approach is that, in order to honor and obey God, not only the ends, but also the means, must conform to Scripture.
- Finally, the implication of inferiority is brought up again here. Any attempt, we are told, to limit what women are able to do in the Church suggests that they are somehow inferior to men and is an insult to the dignity of God's perfect creation. We have already addressed this issue above, noting that the assertion that role differentiation implies inequality simply does not conform to what the Bible teaches.

WOMEN IN THE WORLD

What, then, about the role of women in society at large? If liberals err in using biblical examples like Deborah and Esther to argue for female leadership in the Church, evangelicals have too often erred by using biblical mandates forbidding female leadership in the Church to argue against leadership roles for women in the larger society. One of the most notorious examples of this kind of thinking occurred during the Protestant Reformation. John Knox, who was to become the greatest leader of the Reformation in Scotland, had early in his career observed the persecution Protestants in Europe were facing at the hands of female rulers like Mary Tudor ("Bloody Mary") in England and Queen Mother Catherine de Medici in France. When he was forced to flee to the Protestant haven in Geneva to avoid persecution in England, he published a book entitled *The First Blast of the Trumpet Against the Monstrous Regiment of Women*. He argued, as noted above, that women were to submit to male authority on all occasions, so the very existence of queens was unbiblical (after all, Esther had no authority, and the only queens of note in the history of Israel were Jezebel and Athaliah, of whom nothing good whatever might be said). John Calvin, the leader of the churches in Geneva, tried to talk him out of publishing his ideas, noting the distinction between leadership in the Church and leadership in society, but Knox would not listen. Unfortunately for him, in the time between the composition of the book and its publication, Mary Tudor died and was replaced by her Protestant half-sister Elizabeth, who was immediately convinced that Knox was speaking against her. The result was that Knox became *persona non grata* in England, unable to preach there for the rest of his life. Similar arguments have been raised about women in politics over the years.

Scripture therefore must lead us to the conclusion that any task undertaken by a woman in the larger society is appropriate as long as it does not impinge upon her primary responsibilities to her family (the same may be said of men, who should never let their jobs get in the way of family). The Bible does teach that women have a special role in bringing up children (I Timothy 5:10), though this in no way lessens the father's responsibility in child-raising. Too often those who have argued against a significant role for women in the workplace forget that, for most people in Bible times, especially in the Old Testament, father and mother both worked at home - going out in the morning to do one's job and returning in the evening was not common practice in an agricultural society. Not until the Industrial Revolution did the pattern so familiar to our cultural memories - that of the father going out each day to work while the mother stays at home with the children - really develop. The question of women working thus should be discussed in the context of the welfare of the children, along with the motives for such choices. Does the wife and mother want to work because she seeks her primary source of fulfillment outside of her family relationships? Is work sought in order to finance luxuries that the surrounding society tells us are necessary? Is work sought because women are told by the predominant culture that they are little more than slaves if they remain at home, submit to their husbands, and care for their children? Is work needed because of immoral choices, such as is often the case with single motherhood? Here motive matters, but we should never automatically conclude that the stay-at-home mom is the only biblical mandate.

PORNOGRAPHY

Any word the etymology of which means *writing about fornication* clearly describes immoral behavior. More than any topic dealt with so far in this chapter, this one would seem to be non-controversial simply because it is so clearly wrong. Why, then, bother to discuss it? We cannot ignore it for the following reasons:

- The Internet has made pornography more readily available than at any previous time in human history; the temptation has become more than many are able to resist.
- Readily-available portable technology has led to a plague of pornographic communication among teenagers.[157]
- Thirdly, Christians often wonder about the appropriate response to the plague of smut that seems to be engulfing us more fully every day.

PORNOGRAPHY AND THE LAW

Pornography is not easy to define. Supreme Court Justice Potter Stewart, when faced with an obscenity case involving a sex-filled movie, famously said, "I may not be able to define pornography, but I know it when I see it." While drawing lines may not be easy, the commonplace understanding of pornography involves explicit visual portrayals of sex with no redeeming social value. The difficulty of defining pornography should not prohibit the government from protecting people against such harmful material. Sadly, though, the law has been virtually impotent in it efforts to purge this virus from the realm of public consumption. What are the central issues involved in the legal battles over pornography?

- The First Amendment - The most prominent aspect of the debate stems from the First Amendment's guarantee of freedom of speech. Advocates argue that even obnoxious speech is protected by the Constitution - as Voltaire said, "I disapprove of what you say, but I will defend to the death your right to say it." Groups like Americans United for Separation of Church and State and the American Civil Liberties Union have consistently defended pornographers against attempts to enforce moral standards in the public sphere. Such an argument is ludicrous, of course, since the state does legitimately enforce laws against child pornography and prosecute obscene phone calls or the transmission of obscene materials through the mail. Television programs are still subject to some degree of censorship, though it is becoming less and less effective, and other kinds of speech are censored, from slander and libel to speech that violates national security to yelling "Fire!" in a crowded theater (oddly enough, such liberal interest groups have few scruples about censoring *religious* speech).
- Others have argued that legal battles against pornography are counterproductive, since all they do is publicize smut and make more people want to see what all the fuss is about. They maintain that if pornography were legalized, it would soon die of its own shallowness

---

[157] According to one study, 22% of teen girls and 18% of teen boys admit to sharing nude or semi-nude pictures of themselves with someone of the opposite sex.

and worthlessness. Furthermore, if it were legal, it could be regulated and taxed.[158]
Sadly, the human appetite for sin and perversion cannot be dulled so easily. As Paul tells
us in Romans 13:3-4, the government is responsible before God to punish the evil and
protect the good. Man, if left to his own devices, simply will not pursue the path of
righteousness.

PORNOGRAPHY AND SOCIETY

What, then, of the argument that pornography is a victimless crime?[159] Child pornography
clearly shows the folly of such an argument, but what about consenting adults? Several issues
surface here:

- Pornography exploits those who participate in producing it - primarily, though not
  exclusively, women. As a result, this has become a difficult issue for feminists. On the
  one hand, they rightly oppose the exploitation of women, but at the same time, they desire
  to maximize the freedom of women - to sell their bodies for the pleasure of others as well
  as to kill their babies. Too often, however, those who appear in pornographic media are
  the poor and the weak, runaways, drug addicts, and those trapped in modern slavery rings.
- Pornography objectifies women, treating them as things to be displayed for the pleasure
  of others rather than as people with value and dignity.
- Pornography separates sex from love as well as from marriage, taking something intended
  to be beautiful and making it ugly and bestial.
- Pornography is addictive to those who partake of it. It becomes a habit every bit as hard
  to break as drugs or alcohol.
- Pornography, despite many claims to the contrary, is related to sex crimes. Though
  purveyors of porn try to argue that it provides a safe outlet for sexual urges, perhaps in the
  process keeping some from acting out what they imagine in their minds, too many don't
  stop with looking. The rate of use of pornography among sex criminals is extremely high,
  bringing into question any argument that looking at it does no harm. After all, if no one
  was ever tempted to put into practice what pornography portrays, why do so many
  pornographers produce supposed "How To" videos and market their wares as date-night
  viewing?

PORNOGRAPHY AND THE CHRISTIAN

The big problem here is not so much involvement in the production or distribution of
pornographic materials, but the ease with which one may gain access to them. Even a generation
ago, pornography came in dirty magazines in plain brown wrappers that men and boys hid under
their mattresses. Today, it may be seen with the push of a few buttons on cable television or the
Internet. The ease with which highly-sexualized material may be accessed has rapidly lowered
the standards of many Christians as it has lowered the standards of the surrounding world. In the

---

[158] The same argument is made with regard to drugs such as marijuana.

[159] Note that the same argument is made with regard to prostitution.

middle of the twentieth century, many Christians would not even go to movies, arguing that the entire industry was corrupt and did not deserve the support of believers. The widespread access to television changed the situation a little, but the real change came with the advent of the VCR. Now, people could rent movies and watch them in their own homes, and no one would be the wiser. The opposition to moviegoing rapidly collapsed as a result. Should a Christian ever watch an R-rated movie? Few have scruples against doing so as a matter of principle anymore, and I am constantly appalled at the movies that are watched by my high school students. If this is what is going on at the level of popular discussion among friends, what is happening when the kids are alone in their rooms? What views of sex are being communicated by such filth? What kinds of fantasies are being implanted deeply into the minds of those who view pornography online? If looking at a woman lustfully is tantamount to committing adultery with her (Matthew 5:27-28), adultery is more commonplace among Christians than anyone would care to admit.

What is to be done? First of all, Christians should open their eyes to the consequences of the depths of moral depravity with which the surrounding society is flooded. If we don't recognize evil for what it is, we will not care to safeguard ourselves against it. Secondly, we should acknowledge the need for the self-control that comes only as a gift from the Spirit of God; we cannot fight the battle alone, but with the power of God, this temptation, too, can be overcome. Thirdly, we should note the consequences of pornography for marriage and family life. When fantasies become dominant, reality becomes unsatisfying, and this is not good for any marriage. Furthermore, when the perverted becomes the norm, how can any couple hope for a healthy and happy sexual relationship?

DANCING

Why should a discussion of dancing be included under the Seventh Commandment? From the Puritans to the revivalists of the Second Great Awakening to the Fundamentalists of the early twentieth century, Christians have opposed dancing because of its associations with sexual suggestion and sexual stimulation. Though such objections often seem old-fashioned and foolish in the modern climate, we need to give serious consideration to the application of biblical principles to what Christians for several centuries considered to be wrong.

Dancing is essentially a means of communication through bodily movement. The self-expression involved in dancing can be an art form (e.g., ballet), a means of social interaction, or even a form of worship. The Bible has much to say about dancing, though the context in Scripture often has little to do with the controversy faced by Christians in modern times.

DANCING IN THE BIBLE

Dancing is mentioned more than twenty-five times in Scripture; the references can be broken down into three basic categories:

- Dancing is often an expression of joy by an individual (Judges 11:34) or a group (Jeremiah 31:13; Judges 21:21; Ecclesiastes 3:4; Luke 15:25). This corresponds to the celebrations common to most cultures, where dancing is a normal part of festive gatherings. Such dances involve no implications of sexuality.

- Dancing in the Bible is often an expression of praise to God (Exodus 15:20; II Samuel 6:14; Psalm 30:11; 149:3; 150:4). This, unlike today's "praise dancing," did not typically take the form of a performance observed by worshipers, but was itself a form of worship on the part of the participants. This, too, involved none of the connections to sexuality that Christians in the past have found objectionable.[160]
- The Bible mentions the kind of sexualized dancing to which Christians of the past objected in a few places, including the orgiastic celebration following the setting up of the Golden Calf (Exodus 32:19) and the seductive dance performed by Salome before Herod Antipas that led to the death of John the Baptist (Matthew 14:6). No one should doubt that dancing can be immoral or that it can be used in the service of false gods.

DANCING AS ART

Artistic movements of the human body can indeed be beautiful, and are capable of demonstrating God-given gifts in ways that thrill and inspire. Artistic dance can tell a story or communicate ideas about the nature of man and the world. Any judgment of the morality of art involves an assessment both of the ideas that are being communicated and the ways those ideas are being expressed. Dance troupes like *Cirque du Soleil* are capable of doing beautiful things with their bodies that amaze and inspire, yet at the same time may communicate ideas about the world that are far from Christian. In addition, many of those today who use dance as an art form do so in ways that are blatantly immoral, displaying and moving the human body in ways that are openly sexual.

SOCIAL DANCING

This, of course, is the controversial question, though today it has become far less controversial in many Christian circles than it used to be. The current generation of Christian young people often cannot fathom why their elders ever found dance to be objectionable, though a mere glance at most music videos should make the answer obvious. Note the following:

- Social dancing means different things in different cultures. In Bible times, it was a communal expression of joy with no sexual component whatsoever, and such continued to be the case in many cultures throughout history and today as well.
- While group dancing has most often served as an expression of communal fellowship, couples dancing has much more frequently been associated with the expression of sexual desires.[161] The squeaky-clean movies of the 1940s and 1950s used dancing as a metaphor

---

[160] In II Samuel 6:14-23, when David danced in joyful worship before the Lord to celebrate the entry of the Ark of the Covenant into Jerusalem, his wife Michal was concerned that his dance was too highly sexualized, and criticized him on that basis. God, however, took David's part in the dispute, and Michal was barren for the rest of her days.

[161] Irish playwright George Bernard Shaw once defined dancing as "the vertical expression of a horizontal desire legalized by music."

for sex; this was well known to the viewers at the time, though often unrecognized by people who watch them today. If seventeenth-century Puritans and nineteenth-century revivalists found things like square dancing objectionably sexual,[162] how much more would they object to many of the openly sexual dances of today? While one may not be able to build an airtight argument against social dancing from Scripture - certainly the practice was common in Bible times - one should note that dancing as couples was not what the Scriptures had in mind. While social dancing may well be perfectly innocent recreation, it is nonetheless open to all kinds of temptations, to say nothing of openly sexual forms of expression that are all too common. Even public schools that host dances today must lay out rules for what kinds of clothing and what kinds of dancing will be permitted, and still have difficulty enforcing such limits. The bottom line must be, as we have seen so often, an assessment of the kinds of thoughts and desires that are being generated. Godliness or lust - that is the question.

---

[162] Methodist revival preacher Peter Cartwright described one of his successful revivals in the following words: "A beautiful, ruddy young lady walked very gracefully up to me, dropped a handsome courtesy, and pleasantly, with winning smiles, invited me out to take a dance with her.... I can hardly describe my thoughts or feelings on that occasion. However, in a moment I resolved on a desperate experiment. I rose as gracefully as I could.... We walked on the floor.... I then spoke to the fiddler to hold a moment, and added that for several years I had not undertaken any matter of importance without first asking the blessing of God upon it, and I now desired to ask the blessing of God upon this beautiful young lady and the whole company, that had shown such an act of politeness to a total stranger. Here I grasped the young lady's hand tightly ..., and then instantly dropped on my knees, and commenced praying with all the power of soul and body that I could command. The young lady tried to get loose from me, and I held her tight. Presently she fell on her knees. Some of the company kneeled, some stood, some fled, some sat still, all looked curious.... While I prayed, some wept, and wept aloud, and some cried for mercy. I rose from my knees and commenced an exhortation, after which I sang a hymn. The young lady who invited me on the floor lay prostrate, crying earnestly for mercy. I exhorted again, I sang and prayed nearly all night. About fifteen of that company professed religion, and one meeting lasted next day and next night, and as many more were peacefully converted. I organized a society, took thirty-two into the church, and sent them a preacher."

9

THE CHRISTIAN AND THE
SANCTITY OF PROPERTY

Exodus 20:15 - "You shall not steal."

The prohibition against stealing may seem straightforward enough, yet consideration of the underlying principles draws us into a discussion of the relationship of the Christian to material possessions. In our materialistic age, a biblical view of these things is especially important. At least three principles enunciated in Scripture provide the foundation for the commandment against stealing.

- The principle of ownership - If private property were not legitimate, stealing could not occur. In order for you to steal something from me, I must be able to make a valid claim that said object is *mine*.
- The principle of stewardship - While the Bible pictures ownership of material things as legitimate, it is never viewed as absolute. Everything I have ultimately comes from God and belongs to Him. He has given us dominion over the world He made (Genesis 1:28), and we are responsible for exercising that dominion in a way that honors Him. A *steward* is someone who cares for property belonging to another; we may not simply do as we please with the good gifts He has given us.
- The principle of love - Ephesians 4:28 indicates that the opposite of stealing is not keeping, but giving. We should never regard the right of private property as limiting our responsibility to meet the needs of those around us. Such provisions were built into the Old Testament law, including the practice of leaving grain in the fields for the poor to glean (Leviticus 19:9-10, cf. Ruth 2) and the provision for the return of land to its original owners during the Year of Jubilee (Leviticus 25:10).

These fundamental principles have implications for our personal lives as we deal with the material possessions with which we have been so abundantly blessed, as well as with our evaluation of larger issues like economic policy and economic systems, as we will see as we move through this chapter.

WEALTH

Most twenty-first century American Christians do not consider themselves to be wealthy, though we have more material possessions than any civilization in history. The consumer goods and conveniences that we enjoy in abundance would have appeared as fabulous wealth to earlier societies. Not only this, but Americans, even those described as poor among us, have more riches than three-quarters of the world's population.[163] Thus biblical teaching on wealth is important to those of us today who enjoy so much of it, even though we may take it for granted and fail to acknowledge how wealthy we really are.[164]

Two extreme views that have all too often been associated with Christianity have undermined a biblical view of wealth over the years. The first of these is what might be called the Gospel of Poverty - the idea that true holiness may only be found in the repudiation of material possessions. The second is the Gospel of Wealth - the idea that God wants His children to be rich, and that all one must do in order to gain material wealth is to ask for it with sufficient faith, and God has promised to provide it. Both of these approaches seriously pervert biblical teaching on the subject of wealth, but both also contain a grain of truth, as most false teachings do.

THE PROPRIETY OF WEALTH

The monastic ideal portrayed wealth in itself as evil. Monks were required to take a vow of poverty in which they repudiated all ownership of material possessions.[165] This idea has its roots, not in the Bible, but in Platonic philosophy and Greek dualism. The Greeks taught that spirit was good and matter was evil. When this notion worked its way into the Christian Church, the conclusion was that, in order to cultivate the life of the spirit, the life of the flesh must be suppressed and denied.[166] Such teaching is unbiblical, not only because it denies that the material things of this world are good gifts from God, but also because it promotes the idea of salvation by works - that one must by one's own effort gain salvation by means of painful penance.

---

[163] If you have clothing, food in a refrigerator, a roof over your head and a bed to sleep in, you are richer than 75% of the people on earth, and if your income exceeds $10,000, 86% of the world's people are poorer than you are. In fact, 53% of the world's population lives on less than two dollars per day.

[164] Short-term mission trips often benefit participants by giving them a clearer idea of just how rich they are in terms of this world's goods, and how those who have far less are often far more thankful to God for what they do have.

[165] Stories illustrating this practice are legion, from Anthony of Thebes, the first Christian monk, who heard a sermon on the Rich Young Ruler and concluded that, in order to follow Christ, he needed to sell all his possessions and go out and live in a cave in the wilderness, to Francis of Assisi, who stripped himself naked before his wealthy merchant father in order to repudiate the family fortune; Francis' followers later had a difficult time keeping clothes on his back because he insisted on giving his clothing to every naked beggar he met. The extent to which this teaching was taken is portrayed in Umberto Eco's novel *The Name of the Rose*, where monastic leaders and papal representatives stage a lengthy debate on the question of whether Christ owned the robe He wore.

[166] Denial of the flesh went so far in some monastic groups that they practiced flagellation - beating their backs with whips in order to purify their souls.

The Bible, however, does not condemn wealth. In fact, in the Old Testament God rewarded His people with prosperity when they obeyed His law (e.g., Deuteronomy 7:12-14).[167] God is a God who delights to give to His people in abundance rather than providing in a way that enables them barely to get by. To see wealth as sinful is thus to refuse to acknowledge the goodness of God to His creatures, and especially His people.

THE PERVERSITY OF WEALTH

The opposite extreme is also terribly harmful. The Prosperity Gospel has deceived many into basing their hopes of God's blessing on material things, then doubting God, or at least the validity of their own faith, when God does not deliver what the televangelist has promised.[168] Scripture, however, teaches that wealth, though it is a blessing from God, carries with it real dangers and temptations. Note the following:

- Jesus' conversation with the Rich Young Ruler (Matthew 19:16-22; Mark 10:17-22; Luke 18:18-23) is very instructive here. Though the young man claimed to have kept all the commandments (at least those involving man's relationship with other men), he clearly neglected the First and Tenth Commandments - putting God first and avoiding covetousness. When Jesus told him to sell all he had, give it to the poor, and follow Him, He was not enunciating a general principle, but was pinpointing that which was keeping the young man from God. The greatest temptation associated with wealth is that it becomes an idol, taking the place of God in one's life.

- The ensuing dialogue with the disciples is even more enlightening (Matthew 19:23-30; Mark 10:23-31; Luke 18:24-30). The disciples had obviously been influenced by the first-century version of the Gospel of Wealth in that they were convinced that wealth in itself was a mark of God's favor. As a result, when Jesus spoke about how hard it was for a rich man to enter the Kingdom of Heaven, they were astounded, and wondered whether anyone could be saved (if not one obviously blessed by God, then whom?). Jesus then notes that salvation, for the rich as for anyone else, is impossible by human effort,[169] and encourages the disciples that their sacrifice of material things would lead to treasure in heaven. This exchange indicates something of the importance of spiritual priorities over material ones.

---

[167] An interesting indication of the Bible's emphasis on God's abundant provision is the way the words *fat* and *fatness* are used in Scripture. Unlike in our society, which gives such terms negative connotations, they are positive terms in the Bible, speaking of health, abundance, and prosperity. God wants to bless His people with the *fat* of the land.

[168] An even worse abuse occurs, of course, when such so-called Gospel ministries become nothing more than money-making schemes for the evangelist. Too many supposed preachers of the Gospel have enriched themselves by cynically taking advantage of the hopes of the poor: "If you send even ten dollars to the address on the screen, God has promised to multiply it so that, by the power of God, you will soon receive $100 in return."

[169] The illustration of the camel passing through the eye of a needle does not refer, as many have said, to a small door in the gate of Jerusalem through which caravans could enter the city at night, but only if the camel was relieved of its burden of trade goods and the beast knelt down and crawled through the narrow opening; such a gate did not exist until the Middle Ages. Jesus is not talking about something difficult, but something impossible.

- Material wealth can tempt a person to seek his security in his possessions rather than in God (Luke 12:16-21). Who needs to depend on God when he has plenty of grain in his barns or plenty of money in the bank? A life of faith is a life of dependence, and anything that encourages us to depend on ourselves, our own accomplishments, or our own possessions is spiritually devastating, as the man in the parable discovered. Security can never be found in things, and may only be found in God.

- Wealth neither quells greed nor generates satisfaction. Solomon was absurdly wealthy, yet he found that his wealth did not bring satisfaction (Ecclesiastes 2:4-11). When wealth is the source of our satisfaction, we will always want more - happiness will always be right around the corner, with the acquisition of just one more thing or the securing of one more raise.[170]

HOW SHOULD WE LOOK AT WEALTH?

Given the need to avoid the two extremes into which Christians have often fallen, along with the indications that wealth is to be viewed as both a blessing and a potential snare, what attitude should the Christian take toward material possessions? Note the following:

- Wealth should not be part of the Christian's expectations for this life. I Corinthians 1:26-31 indicates that God has not chosen many who are prominent in terms of what the world values, whether it be power, status, or wealth. He does this for good reasons: so that His people may learn to trust Him rather than themselves, and so that others may be able to recognize that what is accomplished by the children of God in this world is not based on personal qualities or inherent abilities, but on God's grace.

- We should not seek wealth as an end in itself (Matthew 6:19-21). Earthly treasure doesn't last - "you can't take it with you" - but treasures in heaven do.

- We may seek wealth as a means for accomplishing spiritual good, as Jesus indicates in the parable He tells in Luke 16:1-9. The story about the dishonest steward is a difficult one, since both the owner of the property and Jesus seem to be praising an openly deceitful person. While the owner apparently is commending the shrewdness of the steward, not his dishonesty,[171] Jesus draws a somewhat different application - that material wealth should be used in such a way that those who benefitted from its use would welcome the benefactor in heaven with words of gratitude.

---

[170] Our culture, of course, promotes this mentality both through advertising and through the planned and often very rapid obsolescence of consumer goods. Clothing may not wear out, but it goes out of style. The worst culprit here is technology, where the latest gadget becomes outdated the minute it leaves the store. Many businesses depend for their profit margin on their ability to create dissatisfaction and discontent, then convince people that they will only be happy, popular, "on the cutting edge," if they have the latest thing.

[171] The key to understanding this parable is the fact that the steward had originally been cheating his master's customers by charging them interest, which Jewish merchants were not permitted to do, and writing the documents in such a way as to conceal what was being done, presumably with his master's connivance. When he finds that he is about to lose his job, he goes to his master's business associates and rewrites their bills to reflect *the true cost of the transaction*. What is his master to do? He can't really complain that his steward corrected dishonest mistakes. On the other hand, those who had gained from the steward's sudden burst of honesty would no doubt be grateful - perhaps grateful enough to hire him after he lost his present position.

- Wealth is not to be used as a source of power to oppress others. James 5:1-6 gives a clear warning against this, as do many of the Old Testament prophets. How many businesses today use wealth and power to take advantage of the poor?[172]

- If we are to use wealth for the glory of God, to what extent should a Christian indulge in luxuries? The implications of this raise questions about everyday decisions like when clothing, furnishings, appliances, and, yes, electronics ought to be replaced. Should they be discarded and replaced by new ones when they wear out or break, or when something more attractive becomes available? Do we really need the latest gadgets, the fanciest cars, the biggest houses, the most exotic vacations? Priorities become a very important consideration when one must make decisions about the godly use of wealth, and stewardship should always be kept in the forefront of our minds.

GIVING

As we have already seen, stewardship of material possessions implies the responsibility to care for those in need. But to whom should these gifts be given, and in what way?

THE NEEDY IN THE FAMILY

I Timothy 5:8 indicates that the primary responsibility to care for those in need lies with the family. The strong language used by Paul here - that one who fails to care for needy family members has denied the faith and is worse than an unbeliever - shows the importance of this matter. In a society where the Welfare State has assumed responsibility for the needs of some from cradle to grave, families often are quite willing to abdicate their God-give responsibility to the state. In Matthew 15:4-9, Jesus criticizes this mentality, noting that no one can turn away from needy family members and gain God's approval in the process.[173] In particular, this implies the responsibility to care for elderly parents should they face needs in their old age.

THE NEEDY IN THE CHURCH

Scripture teaches that Christians have the responsibility to support the work of God financially. In the Old Testament, the Israelites gave 23% of their income to support the work of God - an annual tithe for the Temple (Deuteronomy 12:5-7), an annual tithe for the priests and Levites (Numbers 18:21-24), and a triennial tithe to help the poor (Deuteronomy 14:28-29) - in addition to freewill offerings.[174] The idea that tithing means giving ten percent is thus a bit misleading, even though the word *tithe* means a tenth, because the Israelites gave not just one

---

[172] Check-cashing businesses and rent-to-buy outfits are notorious for preying on the poor and ignorant, but so are many multinational corporations, which often fail to pay their workers a living wage in order to maximize their profits.

[173] See page 76 for a more detailed discussion of this passage.

[174] Given the rates of taxation today, 23% sounds like a bargain!

tithe, but many. Of course, we must also remember that the tithes they were paying supported not only the church, but also the poor cared for by the government.[175] The idea communicated by the tithe is illustrated by the requirement to give the firstfruits to God (e.g., Exodus 23:19; Leviticus 23:9-14; Deuteronomy 12:6). The point is not that ten percent of what I have belongs to God and the rest belongs to me, but that *everything* belongs to God, and the firstfruits, as representatives of the whole, indicate an acknowledgment that nothing I own is really mine in any absolute sense, but is a gracious provision of God.[176]

What about the New Testament? While tithes are never explicitly mentioned in the New Testament apart from descriptions of Pharisaical self-righteousness (Luke 11:42; 18:12) and Old Testament practices (Hebrews 7:4-10), giving is addressed. We are told that it is to be sacrificial (II Corinthians 8:1-7), joyful (II Corinthians 9:6-7), and proportional (I Corinthians 16:2). This money is to be used for the support of those who minister the Gospel (I Corinthians 9:6-14; Galatians 6:6-10; I Timothy 5:17-18[177]) and for the care of those who are in need (Acts 4:31-35; I Corinthians 16:1-3; I Timothy 5:3-16), especially widows and orphans who have no families to care for them.

THE NEEDY IN THE WORLD

I Timothy 5 implies an order of priority with regard to the care for the poor. The primary responsibility for the poor lies with the family of the needy person, and the church is then responsible to care for those who have no families to support them. Presumably, the state, on the Old Testament model, would then be responsible to provide a safety net only for those who have no family or church to care for them rather than becoming the first resort of those who are in need, as is so often the case today. A few comments should be made on this issue as well before we finish this topic:

- Christian compassion has often been a means of opening doors for the Gospel among those who are unsaved. Jesus Himself often ministered to the physical needs of those who up to that point had demonstrated no faith in Him, and the results sometimes produced faith and sometimes did not. To separate care for the world's needy from the communication of the Gospel, however, is to do something that differs little from the work of secular social service agencies. Meeting physical needs has no ultimate value if spiritual needs are ignored.
- We should also recognize the danger of using the meeting of material needs as a means of opening a door for the Gospel, however. Missionaries in China often sought to minister

---

[175] We should not conclude, of course, that these tithes were all that Israelites had to pay. Kings did, as kings so often do, levied taxes for all kinds of things, including wars and building projects (see I Kings 12:6-11).

[176] Note that the requirement that firstborn children needed to be redeemed (Exodus 13:11-13; Numbers 3) underscores this same point - that children ultimately belong to God, and not to their parents.

[177] The "double honor" referred to in this passage clearly indicates from the following verse that Paul means that elders are to be paid by the churches they serve (presumably he is referring to those who serve in full-time ministry) - they deserve material support as well as respect for their labors.

to starving Chinese peasants by distributing rice to any who asked for it. The Chinese, with their strong sense of courtesy, would often profess Christianity out of gratitude for the gifts they had been given. The missionaries soon found, however, that these "rice Christians" were simply adding Jesus to the long list of gods to whom they prayed. People who come to Christ because their physical needs are being met do not always undergo true conversions, though some who have first met Christ in this way later become true believers.

- Another question that arises has to do with whether Christians should give of their wealth to non-Christian relief agencies. Should Christians give to the Red Cross, the American Cancer Society, or umbrella organizations like United Way, which distribute money to a variety of charities with whom they are affiliated? While such organizations are able to meet some needs that are not addressed by Christian charities and some are worthy in their level of accountability and the nature of the help provided, many have philosophies that Christians cannot or should not support, such as the promotion of abortion or birth control outside of marriage. Christians thus should be very cautious about giving to non-Christian charities without thoroughly examining them first to see what they actually do with the money they receive.

GAMBLING

When one considers the appropriate use of material possessions, the issue of gambling frequently arises. Is gambling immoral, contrary to the law of God? Though some have argued for its legitimacy, most Christians throughout the years have asserted that gambling is unethical.

WHAT IS GAMBLING?

Gambling involves risking something of value, usually money, on the outcome of a chance event. Examples include lotteries, raffles, sports betting pools, casino games like slot machines and roulette, a wide variety of card games, and the sorts of activities with which carnival booths entice the gullible.

ARGUMENTS FOR GAMBLING

Those who have sought to defend the practice have argued both from Scripture and on the basis of more practical considerations:

- From a biblical perspective, advocates have noted the frequent use of casting of lots in Scripture. While most references to this in the Bible did not involve money (John 19:24 is the exception, and can hardly be used as a positive argument), they did involve taking significant risks on what was tantamount to flipping a coin. In most cases, decision-making was involved (e.g., Leviticus 16:8-10; Numbers 26:55-56; I Chronicles 24:5; 25:8; Nehemiah 11:1; Acts 1:21-26). In fact, the casting of lots was a means of ascertaining the will of God for issues like going into battle, dividing land, and choosing among individuals for a certain task. The weakness of this argument, however, is that these examples have nothing at all to do with gambling as it is practiced today with the exception of the soldiers gambling for Jesus' cloak while He was dying on the Cross.

- Gambling advocates also argue that it is innocent fun as long as a person controls his expenditures. What is the difference, they ask, between spending a hundred dollars for dinner and a show and gaining a similar amount of enjoyment from spending a few hours in a casino after having placed a hundred-dollar limit on yourself?
- Some defend forms of gambling as providing funds for a good cause. What of state lotteries that "benefit senior citizens" or church-run bingo games that help support a school or a building project?

ARGUMENTS AGAINST GAMBLING

Arguments presented by Christians against gambling are grounded in a variety of biblical principles, some of which we have already considered elsewhere.

- The biblical casting of lots when God commands it has nothing to do with gambling because He determines the outcome and speaks to His people in the process. Furthermore, the only example of the casting of lots that *does* involve gambling is a decidedly negative one.
- Gambling is bad stewardship of God's money. Gamblers lose far more often than they win, so Christians who gamble are guilty of throwing away God's money for neither a constructive purpose nor a worthwhile return. Waste is sin, whether of time or money (see page 71).
- Even if the gambler wins, this provides no justification for the practice.[178] Gambling is a zero-sum game in which, in order for someone to win, someone else must lose. Most often, the gambling establishment wins while most of the players lose. Furthermore, those who lose are often those who can least afford to do so. Gambling establishments, including state lotteries, prey on the poor who unrealistically place all their hope for a better life on one more roll of the dice or one more lottery ticket. Those who win at gambling establishments thus bear partial responsibility for the bitter consequences of gambling in the lives and families of the poor.
- Gambling involves a perverted view of the sovereignty of God. There really is no such thing as chance in God's world (Proverbs 16:33), but one who gambles in order to make money is trusting "luck" instead of trusting God.
- Gambling is an attempt to get something for nothing. God wants us to labor for our bread; one who seeks to avoid that labor through games of chance is wasting his time as well as his money.
- Gambling is addictive. Too many sad stories of ruined lives start with someone just spending a few dollars on the slot machines. Even if someone were to cite I Corinthians 6:12 to argue that gambling is "lawful," he would be hard-pressed to defend it as "helpful," and it certainly carries with it the danger of enslavement.

---

[178] A few years ago, a professing Christian won thirty million dollars in the Powerball lottery, and promptly announced that he would give three million dollars to his church.

- Gambling destroys marriages, breaks up families, and impoverishes further those who can least afford it. Casinos love the "high rollers," but most of their patrons are senior citizens and the poor who take advantage of free bus trips to spend a day at the slots. Even the rich, who seemingly can afford to throw money away, can be destroyed by gambling.[179]
- If someone wants to do something that will benefit senior citizens, he can give a donation to a ministry carrying out charitable work among them. Such a justification is merely an excuse for feeding one's lust for material gain.

GAMBLING AND THE STOCK MARKET

Some Christians have sought to justify participation in lotteries and casino gambling by arguing that many Christians are involved in the stock market. Is not this gambling as well? The key difference here is that one who puts money in the stock market is buying something - part of a company that is seeking to make a profit for its stockholders. Investing in the stock market is not seeking something for nothing, nor is it a zero-sum game where in order for someone to win, someone else must lose. Certainly one who invests money in stocks is taking a risk, but that is true of almost all expenditures. One should seek to invest wisely, but one must ultimately trust God rather than the economy for his security, especially in these uncertain economic times. Note, however, that one should give much greater scrutiny to playing the market through practices such as day trading, which comes much closer to gambling rather than investing.

GAMBLING AND THE CHURCH

Some churches use forms of gambling like raffles and bingo games to raise money for the work of the church. This is wrong for a number of reasons:

- God's work should be supported by God's people through tithes and offerings, given in faith that God will provide for His ministry. "Plundering the Egyptians" (Exodus 12:35-36) is no excuse for fleecing unbelievers for the benefit of God's work.
- Worthy ends do not justify unrighteous means. In order for something to be pleasing to God, both the ends and the means must be according to His law.
- Such practices by churches set a bad example for people in the congregation, especially young people, as well as giving a negative impression to the surrounding community.

INSTRUMENTS OF GAMBLING

Among the extrabiblical practices banned by American fundamentalists in the nineteenth and twentieth centuries was the use of the instruments of gambling. Because of the dangers and vices associated with gambling, Christians were told that they should not play any game involving

---

[179] One notable example would be baseball star Pete Rose, whose gambling addiction got him banned from the game, excluded from the Hall of Fame, ate up the millions he made from his athletic pursuits, and ruined his relationship with his family.

dice or face cards.[180] However, just because something is used for evil purposes does not make it evil in itself. Those who crucified Christ cast lots for His tunic (John 19:24), but the early Church had no problem with casting lots to choose the man to replace Judas as one of the Twelve (Acts 1:21-26). The only restriction that is legitimate here is if the use of such things causes a stumblingblock for someone else. That which wounds the conscience of a weak brother should not be done in his presence (see pages 19-21).

BUSINESS ETHICS

In the business world, the temptations to steal are very great and take many forms. While we don't have the time to go into this vast subject in any detail, a few examples should suffice to illustrate the point.

STEALING BY CUSTOMERS

Shoplifting by customers, whether by sneaking a small item into one's pocket without paying for it or by changing price tags in order to get something for a lower cost, is the most obvious form of stealing from businesses.[181] Sadly, many people seek to justify shoplifting by arguing that a big company would never miss something so small, or even claiming that big corporations are ripping their customers off all the time by their price-gouging, so they deserve to have the tables turned.[182] The size or amount is irrelevant, of course, as is the behavior of the corporation. Stealing is stealing, no matter what the amount or from whom.

STEALING BY EMPLOYEES

Stealing by employees, not shoplifting by customers, is the greatest cause of "shrinkage" with which most stores must cope. Whether removing merchandise, taking money out of the till, or using company property, even things as small as paper clips or Post-it notes, for non-business purposes, the employee is stealing. An increasing problem in this area involves the misuse of business computers, whether for playing computer games, checking personal e-mail, or viewing pornography. This new form of employee theft, a much more sophisticated way of wasting time,

---

[180] Some Christian colleges made their students sign a pledge that they would not use such things while they were students at the school. What was the result? The students played *Uno* and *Rook* instead - card games that are very similar to familiar games using face cards, but without the "evil" implements.

[181] The cost of shoplifting worldwide was estimated in a recent study to be in the neighborhood of three billion dollars per year.

[182] Anglican priest Father Tim Jones, of St. Lawrence parish in York, England, argued in a sermon on December 23, 2009, that shoplifting was justified as a last resort for the poor as long as they stole from large chain stores rather than family-run business and as long as they took only what they needed. Needless to say, the sermon caused a considerable uproar and went viral online.

is often difficult to detect.[183]   Much more extensive forms of stealing from employers involve things like embezzlement and padding expense accounts, though we should note that not working diligently is also a kind of theft..

STEALING BY EMPLOYERS

Employers are not immune from the temptation to steal, either, and often the more power one has, the more opportunity presents itself to do evil to others. A few examples:

- Cheating other companies with which they do business by deceptive marketing practices, misleading language in contracts, or failing to deliver what had been promised in a timely fashion.
- Stealing from employees through unfair labor practices, substandard wages, or unjustified layoffs.[184]
- Stealing from the public by producing goods of inferior quality at inflated prices. The widespread practice of planned obsolescence is a notorious example of this way of making a profit by deliberately producing something that is intended to break or become outdated in a short period of time.
- Deceptive advertising claims are a constant problem. Advertisers have gotten such a reputation for misleading people that few take their claims seriously any more. While *caveat emptor* may still be the prevailing principle, Christian businessmen should never conduct business with the public in a way that requires the buyer to beware.

ECONOMIC SYSTEMS

In the introduction to this chapter, we noted that three fundamental biblical principles underlie the application of the Eighth Commandment - the legitimacy of private property, the stewardship of material goods as coming from God and belonging to Him, and the responsibility to use material goods to help those in need. In the last section of the chapter, we will consider how the major economic systems that have dominated human history measure up to these three foundational ideas. Not surprisingly, no humanly-devised system fits the biblical pattern perfectly.

---

[183] Note that most companies have policies regarding these practices, and some are permitted within certain limitations.

[184] The question of moving operations abroad in search of cheaper labor is a complex question. Just because the wages paid foreign workers are far below those given to Americans does not mean they are necessarily unfair given the cost of living in the places where the workers live. Business mergers are also complex. Sometimes they lead to greater efficiency, which is a good thing, but sometimes they accomplish nothing more than padding the pockets of those high in the pecking order, while producing nothing of benefit to the public and depriving loyal and hard-working employees of their means of supporting their families.

FEUDALISM

The first economic system we will consider is feudalism, the economic system of the Middle Ages. In the feudal system, all land theoretically belonged to the king, who then parceled it out among his vassals in return for certain tax payments and military obligations. These in turn had vassals of their own. At the bottom of the totem pole were the serfs, who owned no land and were completely under the authority of their lord. They were allowed to work one or two days per week on small parcels of land for their own benefit, but were forced to work the rest of the time on their lord's lands without compensation. They also paid fees for the use of the lord's mills and other facilities and were required to fight for him in case of war.

- Ownership - Few in the feudal system had much that they could really call their own; everything belonged to the lord to whom they owed fealty.
- Stewardship - Since the feudal system existed in the time of Christendom, when Europe was viewed as the material manifestation of the Kingdom of God on earth, much lipservice was paid to God's sovereignty over the land. In practice, however, the lords of the manor did as they pleased, frequently in defiance of the often-weak kings. The kings, in turn, feuded with the Catholic Church over issues like lay investiture, which involved the question of who appointed church officers - the Pope, their spiritual lord, or the king or emperor, their feudal lord?[185] If someone were to do so much as suggest that control of land should rest with the godly rather than with the powerful, big trouble would ensue.[186]
- Love - Little concern was shown for the needs of the poor in the feudal system. About the only people who made any effort to care for those in need were the monks.

MERCANTILISM

Mercantilism arose in connection with the Age of Exploration. The basic idea here is that the state should control trade for its own benefit. Colonies were to be used as sources of raw materials, for which kings granted monopolies to state-run trading companies like the British East India Company. These raw materials were then processed in the mother country and sold as

---

[185] The infamous battle in the eleventh century between Pope Gregory VII and Holy Roman Emperor Henry IV over lay investiture shows how little concern for the sovereign rule of God entered into the behavior of either popes or kings.

[186] John Wycliffe, best known today as the first translator of the Bible into English, first came to the attention of the public over this issue. He argued that dominion over land would be given by God to the godly, and since the English nobles were displaying greater godliness in the fourteenth century than the leaders of the Church, which at this time had two popes (soon to become three) who were energetically anathematizing one another and excommunicating one another's followers, his idea gained traction, especially among the nobles, who protected him from the Pope's attempts to silence him. When some English peasants got the idea that they were holier than the nobles, however, they started a bloody revolution (Wat Tyler's rebellion in 1381) to seize the land for themselves. This cost Wycliffe his support from the nobility, and he was forced into retirement. The Pope got the last laugh when, forty-five years after Wycliffe died, he ordered his body exhumed and burned and the ashes thrown into the river.

finished goods in the colonies, which served as a protected market.[187] High tariffs were also erected against goods from other nations. Mercantilism also involved the promotion of home-grown industries, including stealing skilled workers from other nations and forbidding their own to leave the country, and the encouragement of cottage industry where raw materials could be turned into finished goods (the Industrial Revolution had not yet begun).

- Ownership - Government domination of trade, while greatly increasing the wealth of the traders and merchants, nonetheless placed the greatest emphasis on the prosperity of the state rather than the prosperity of individuals.[188] The government did encourage the accumulation of wealth, but insisted that overall economic control remain in its own hands.
- Stewardship - Aside from the practice of sending missionaries to newly-conquered lands, God had very little to do with this. Increasing secularism in the state and in the business world meant that stewardship was rarely a consideration.[189]
- Love - How did the mercantile system care for the poor? The interest of governments in accumulating national wealth meant that the population should be put to work to the largest extent possible. Often, this was accomplished by draconian laws against idleness, such as the English Poor Law, which forced all who were not working into poorhouses, where conditions were so dreadful that any job would be preferable to remaining there.

CAPITALISM

Capitalism was a product of Enlightenment humanism, with its emphasis on man as "the measure of all things." The greatest exponent of the system was Adam Smith, whose *Wealth of Nations* was published in 1776. Smith argued that the mercantile system with its strict government controls was detrimental to the accumulation of both personal and national wealth, and instead argued for a system of *laissez faire* in which the government would keep its nose out of business affairs. According to Smith, if each man pursued his "enlightened self-interest," all would benefit.[190] Capitalism dominated European economies for about a century, the golden age of classical liberalism, when free trade was the rule rather than government-enforced tariffs.[191]

---

[187] This system was one of the big complaints of the citizens of the American colonies; the Boston Tea Party was a vivid demonstration of the colonists' opposition to the East India Company's monopoly on tea.

[188] Some of those who gained the greatest wealth from the era of mercantilism were freelancers who defied or ignored government controls. The Pitt family, later to produce two Prime Ministers of England, initially gained its wealth by freebooting in India, circumventing the monopoly of the British East India Company.

[189] One possible exception here might be the Dutch Calvinists, who saw the Cultural Mandate (Genesis 1:28) as the basis of their economic endeavors, and thus saw God as the source of their wealth and the ultimate reason for seeking it.

[190] The charge of selfishness was leveled in Smith's own day, and he countered this by arguing that any enlightened businessman would recognize that he would prosper more in the long run if he treated his workers well than if he abused them.

[191] The high point of *laissez faire* in Britain was the repeal of the Corn Laws, a series of tariffs on imported grain, by Parliament in 1846.

- Ownership - This is obviously the strength of the capitalist system. Government has no right to deprive citizens of property that they have rightfully earned.[192]

- Stewardship - Nothing about capitalism overtly promotes stewardship, though Smith certainly would have argued that taking good care of your property would be the natural consequence of enlightened self-interest.[193]   God does not play an important role in this picture.

- Love - The poor do not tend to fare well under laissez-faire capitalism, at least in theory, contrary to Smith's insistence that enlightened self-interest would lead to treating workers well.[194] In practice, however, despite the abuses of the Industrial Revolution, during which many industrialists cared nothing for long-term interests and instead pursued immediate profits with little care for any who were hurt along the way, the poor tended to do rather well under capitalist systems. One reason for this is that the idea that "a high tide lifts all boats" turned out to be true to some extent in the nineteenth century. The standard of living of the poorest in industrialized countries rose significantly, though not to the same degree as that of the middle class and wealthy. Secondly, those who benefitted most from unfettered capitalism were often given to great deeds of benevolence. "Robber Barons" in the United States such as Rockefeller, Carnegie, and J.P. Morgan used much of their wealth for the public good, though the accumulation of that wealth justified the pejorative term by which they came to be known.

SOCIALISM

Socialism arose in the middle of the nineteenth century as a reaction against the unfettered capitalism of the Industrial Revolution. If capitalism traced its philosophical roots to the Enlightenment, socialism was influenced by Romanticism, which saw industry as destroying man's bond with Nature. Socialism came in many forms, from the Utopian Socialists in mid-century France to the Marxists that we will consider in the next section. If capitalism emphasized private ownership of the means of production, socialism argued that state ownership of the means of production would produce a more just society by distributing the wealth of the nation more equitably. Utopians, with their high view of human nature, argued that communal arrangements where work and profits were shared by all would produce an ideal society. Examples of Utopian Socialism included Charles Fourier and his phalansteries (planned communities of 1620 people

---

[192] One of the seventeenth-century forerunners of classical liberalism in the political realm was John Locke, who saw the right of property as the most fundamental of all human rights. His formulation of this belief stated that man's God-given inalienable rights included "life, liberty, and property" - a phrase later stolen by Thomas Jefferson, tweaked slightly, and incorporated into the Declaration of Independence as "life, liberty, and the pursuit of happiness."

[193] Benjamin Franklin's assertion that "a penny saved is a penny earned" is relevant here.

[194] Economic theorist David Ricardo enunciated what became known as the Iron Law of Wages, in which he argued that giving the poor workers in the factories and mines higher wages would do them absolutely no good, since, if given more money, they would simply have more children, leaving them in the same depths of poverty as before.

with varying job skills),[195] Manchester industrialist Robert Owen, who built a planned community for his workers,[196] and Claude Henri de Rouvroy, Comte de Saint Simon, a French nobleman who advocated a centrally-planned economy in the hands of great industrialists.[197] Utopian Socialism, in short, has been often tried, but always found wanting in practice.

Probably the form of socialism most familiar to modern students is the Welfare State, where the government levies taxes in order to control the economy for the benefit of workers and the poor. Beginning with the rise of labor unions and legislation passed to remedy the worst injustices of the Industrial Revolution, growing substantially with the planned economies during World War I that controlled industry for the benefit of the war effort, expanding substantially during the Great Depression with high tariffs and provisions for the unemployed and elderly, and finally dominating Europe today while it grows apace in the United States, the Welfare State is not pure socialism, but uses government intervention characteristic of socialism to regulate and harness the markets and business enterprises.[198]

- Ownership - Socialism seeks the common good by refusing to trust the individual's pursuit of "enlightened self-interest." Instead, the government must control business in order to promote the welfare of the individual. The result is that what I have is not ultimately my own, but is under the control of the state to one extent or another, depending on the version of socialism of which we are speaking.
- Stewardship - To the extent that Utopian Socialism was influenced by the Romantic movement, it tended to oppose industry and favor getting back to nature; the utopian communities in the early part of the nineteenth century in the United States were almost exclusively agrarian in their original formulations, though some, like those at Oneida and Amana, became industrial concerns. The pantheism of Romanticism meant that Nature itself was the motivation for stewardship rather than responsibility to God, however.
- Love - If private property is the strength of capitalism, care for the poor is, at least in theory, the strength of socialism. Whether speaking of planned communities or the Welfare State, government provisions for those in need, whether they are sick, elderly, or unemployed, has been a central concern. Despite the fact that much good has been done in this area, however, government control has also turned out to have its downside. Care for the poor has often destroyed any motivation to improve one's lot and created an

---

[195] The French never pulled this off, but a short-lived experiment along these lines was tried in America at Brook Farm, organized by Transcendentalist George Ripley, which lasted from 1841-1847.

[196] When his unorthodox religious views became unpopular in England, he founded a utopian community at New Harmony, Indiana, which also was very short-lived.

[197] After the Revolution of 1848, his ideas were put into practice in modified form with the creation of National Workshops, intended to provide work for the poor and unemployed on government projects like roads and bridges. Far more unemployed workers showed up than the system was able to accommodate, however, leading to riots in the streets of Paris, with the military cutting down the rioters by the thousand.

[198] This modified application of socialist principles to a capitalist economy explains both why President Barack Obama is called a socialist by his opponents and why he is able to deny being so.

underclass that is completely dependent on government largess. On the other side of the picture, the high taxes associated with the Welfare State have tended to inhibit initiative, causing economies to stagnate.

COMMUNISM

Communism is a term used to describe a version of socialism first proposed by Karl Marx and Friedrich Engels in 1848 in *The Communist Manifesto* and later developed more fully by Marx in *Das Kapital*. Marx borrowed G.W.F. Hegel's dialectical view of history, in which a dominant idea, called the *thesis*, gives rise to an opposing view, the *antithesis*, leading to a struggle between the two ideas. The result is some form of compromise, the *synthesis*, which becomes the new prevailing thesis, after which the process continues indefinitely. Marx applied this view to his own version of economic determinism, viewing the dialectic as representing conflict, not between ideas, but between social classes. In his view, the medieval conflict between the nobility and the peasantry gave rise to the middle class, which became dominant, only to give rise to the proletariat - the working poor, with whom conflict was inevitable. Unlike Hegel, however, Marx didn't see the process as going on indefinitely, but saw it leading to the dictatorship of the proletariat and a classless society. The necessity of violent class conflict demonstrated the extent to which Marx was influenced by Darwin, whose "Nature red in tooth and claw" he applied to social classes, while the belief in a classless society showed how much Marx was, despite his vehement denials, a utopian. He also strongly opposed religion in general and Christianity in particular, arguing that it was "the opiate of the masses," a tool of the bourgeoisie to keep the proletariat in their place by focusing their attention on eventual bliss in heaven if they passively accepted the suffering that was their lot in this life.[199]

- Ownership - Flatly denied by communists, who argued that all belonged to the state, favoring the good of the collective over the good of the individual.[200]
- Stewardship - Any atheistic system will obviously care nothing for accountability to God. Even in a secular context, the extent to which communist rulers were concerned for the care of the earth became visible after the fall of European communism, when scientists saw that the levels of pollution in industrial cities in Eastern Europe were seriously dangerous to human life.
- Love - Supposedly the great strength of communism, with its maxim, "From each according to his ability, to each according to his need," this simply has not turned out to be true in practice. Not only do we have the evidence of the massacres already cited, but we should also note that communist boasts of full employment, free medical care, free education, and shared prosperity for all have wound up looking instead like forced labor,

---

[199] Pure Marxism, of course, has never really been implemented, any more than pure capitalism has. Marx's dictatorship *of* the proletariat somehow never seemed to advance beyond Lenin's dictatorship *for* the proletariat by the Party elite.

[200] Lenin, with his massacres during the civil war following the Bolshevik Revolution, Stalin with his mass murders of the *kulaks*, the prosperous Russian peasants, during the implementation of the first Five-Year Plan, and Mao, with his slaughter of millions during the Cultural Revolution in China demonstrated how little communism values, not only private property, but even the life of the individual.

poor and inaccessible medical care, education only for the elite, and long lines in every city and town to get bread and cheese, while basic consumer goods are beyond the reach of all but Party insiders.[201]

But what of those who claim that Scripture promotes communism in the early part of the book of Acts (Acts 2:44-45; 4:34-37)? Did not the members of the Early Church share all things in common and give to any who had need? Did not the apostles, and later the first deacons, distribute food to the poor so that no one was in want? To call this communism is a travesty. As the incident with Ananias and Sapphira makes clear, the entire system was voluntary, not mandated by the government. Furthermore, it was practiced among Christians rather than by the entire society. Most tellingly, it was temporary. Though Christians collected offerings for the needs of the poor in later years, we find no evidence of such collective living arrangements after Acts 6:1-6.

WHAT ECONOMIC SYSTEM IS PORTRAYED IN SCRIPTURE?

Needless to say, all man-made economic systems fall short of the biblical model. Capitalism, while emphasizing the dignity of man, tends to ignore the depravity of man - "enlightened self-interest" assumes that human nature is inherently benevolent. Socialism and communism, on the other hand, tend to ascribe virtue to the state that no man-made organization can possibly possess. Why should the rulers act for the common good if individual businessmen and workers can't be trusted to do so? The corruption endemic in socialist and communist systems shows that rulers are every bit as susceptible to sin and temptation as the members of the bourgeoisie or the proletariat. Communism, of course, is the worst of all because of its overt atheism and its denial of human dignity. On the other hand, the economic system we find in the Old Testament was designed for a theocracy, so it is unrealistic for us to expect to be able to duplicate it in the secular states in which we live today. This does not mean, of course, that the principles on which it is based should not influence our evaluation of and advocacy for the economic policies of the society in which we live.

---

[201] The reality of life under communism is one of the main reasons why communist states have been closed societies. The rulers had no desire for their people to know how the other half lived in the supposedly degenerate world of capitalism.

10

THE CHRISTIAN AND THE SANCTITY OF TRUTH

Exodus 20:16 - "You shall not bear false witness against your neighbor."

In an age of moral relativism, truth is often a casualty. If people deny that truth exists, what compulsion do they feel to adhere to it? Words become nothing more than tools of power, ways of controlling others and getting what we want. In such an environment, the importance of the Christian as truth-teller becomes all that much more important. A person of integrity stands out in a world where those in positions of power have none, and where the man on the street is accustomed to treating truth as something infinitely malleable for his own benefit. Why should a Christian be a truthful person?

TRUTH AND THE CHARACTER OF GOD

The Bible teaches us that God is Truth (John 14:6) and that it is impossible for Him to lie (Hebrews 6:18). If biblical morality means bringing one's life into conformity to the character of God (Matthew 5:48), there is no room for lying in the life of the believer. Truth, in fact, may be defined as that which conforms to the character of God. Whatever is of God is truth, and whatever is not is a lie.

TRUTH AND THE WITNESS-BEARER

The idea of bearing witness in the Ninth Commandment speaks narrowly of testimony given in court - one is not to swear falsely in a way detrimental to one's neighbor. Like all the other commandments, however, this one goes far beyond the setting of the courtroom. Whenever one speaks, one bears witness, especially if one claims the name of Christ for his own. Even beyond this, "actions speak louder than words," so one's actions also bear witness - a person's testimony to God before the world is formed, not only by godly speech, but also by godly actions. We also recognize that actions can deceive as well as words; such deception is also condemned by this commandment.

TRUTH AND MY NEIGHBOR

Jesus' insistence in the Parable of the Good Samaritan that everyone is my neighbor provides another reason why this commandment should be seen as going beyond the formal courtroom setting. Truth may not be limited to those I like or whose cause I wish to advance; we are not free to deceive even our worst enemies. Why is this the case?

- Lying is the opposite of love because it destroys relationships rather than building them. If I lie to someone, even allegedly for his or her own good, he or she will soon learn not to trust me, and our relationship will be ruined. Good relationships are built on trust, and trust is undermined by lying. If a friend or loved one lies to you, you will naturally be skeptical of anything he says thereafter; if a student cheats in my class, I will always wonder about the legitimacy of other grades the student has gotten.
- Lying denies the image of God in my neighbor. When I lie to someone, especially if I profess to do so "for his own good," I deny that individual the right of responsible decision-making. In a sense, I play God for that person, insisting that I know better what is good for him than he does himself. Worse yet, by playing God and insisting that lying to him is what is for his own good, I am implying that I know better than *God*, who commanded His creatures not to lie, what is better in that particular situation. Who among us can bear such a burden of omniscience?
- Lying also shows a lack of personal trust in God. People lie out of fear or out of a desire to get something they want, and in the process fail to trust God to protect them and provide for them.

LYING

Building on the principles enunciated above, we need to give more time to the question of lying. One of the most startling aspects of my experience in teaching Ethics is the number of prominent, respected Christian writers on the subject who have defended lying under certain circumstances. If they are serious about faithfulness to Scripture, and the people with whom I have conversed on this subject are, they must defend their willingness to justify lying on biblical grounds. Admittedly, much of the debate here comes down to a matter of definition. What constitutes a lie and what doesn't? While the principles of the Bible are clear on this subject, a number of difficult passages involving specific historical incidents muddy the waters enough to raise questions about what exactly constitutes a lie.

QUESTIONABLE INCIDENTS IN SCRIPTURE

The following incidents raise questions about the practice of lying. Are these lies? If not, why not? If they are, does that mean that lying is sometimes justifiable? If so, under what circumstances?

- In Genesis, Moses records three incidents in which Abraham (Genesis 12:10-20; 20:1-18) and Isaac (Genesis 26:6-11) lie about their wives, claiming them to be their sisters.[202] Though God did not punish Abraham or Isaac, or even rebuke them, their attempts to

---

[202] The fact that Sarah was Abraham's half-sister and Rebekah was Isaac's cousin doesn't help much; the intent in all cases clearly was to deceive.

preserve their lives in a way that showed lack of faith in God nearly led to disastrous consequences, and certainly did harm to the innocent rulers who were victimized by their lies. The patriarchs here were wrong despite the lack of censure from God.

- In Genesis 27:1-30, Rebekah and Jacob collaborate to deceive Isaac and gain for Jacob the blessing that was to come to Esau. Though God used this deception for His own purposes, it may not be justified on those grounds. In fact, it destroyed the family - Jacob was forced to flee, Rebekah never saw her beloved son again, and relationships between Jacob and his brother Esau (and their descendants) were poisoned forever despite the brief reconciliation in Genesis 33. Just because God uses something to bring about His will does not mean that the action in itself was virtuous.

- In Exodus 1:17-21, the Hebrew midwives appear to lie to Pharaoh about the circumstances under which Hebrew babies were being born in order to explain why they had not followed his orders to kill all the male children. This, like the one that follows, is used to support the idea that lying in order to save life is justifiable, which is further bolstered by the strong commendation they receive from God for their actions. The open question here, of course, is whether or not they were indeed lying. Could their words to Pharaoh have been true - a way in which God delivered them from the dilemma in which Pharaoh had placed them?

- Joshua 2:5 relates the most famous incident in Scripture used to condone lying: the falsehood told by Rahab to protect the Israelite spies. The lie is overt, and in no way can be minimized or explained away.[203] What makes matters worse, of course, is that Rahab is rewarded for her deed, and then praised in the New Testament (Hebrews 11:31; James 2:25). The most common argument derived from this passage is that lying is justifiable in order to save life.[204] But note carefully that the action for which she is praised is protecting the spies - what the rulers of Jericho would have called treason. In both New Testament passages, this is seen as an act of faith; because she trusted in the true God, she threw in her lot with His people rather than with the pagans who were under God's judgment. In other words, she recognized a higher loyalty, and acted accordingly - "we ought to obey God rather than men." Her lie is never praised, though some would argue that it is inseparable from the act of treason since it was the means by which she protected the spies, but it is her faith on which the later passages concentrate.

- Joshua's military strategy at Ai in Joshua 8:3-29 is often presented as a justifiable lie. It unquestionably involved deception, but here we must argue that it does not constitute a lie because it fits within the accepted conventions of warfare.[205] This sort of military strategy

---

[203] This doesn't mean that some haven't tried to do so. The most common justification is that "all is fair in love and war," so that the conventions of warfare justify deceiving the enemy, making what Rahab did not really a lie because she had thrown in her lot with Israel (see next passage).

[204] Note the comments on the protection of Jews from Nazi persecutors in connection with the discussion of Situation Ethics on page 10.

[205] This does *not* mean that "all is fair in love and war." War operates within moral constraints, as we discussed on pages 109-111 in elaborating on the Just War Theory. An example of these moral constraints can be seen in the chapter following the one in question, when Joshua shows integrity even after being deceived by the Gibeonites.

is no more a lie than the use of the hidden ball trick in baseball or a play action pass in football.

- Another interesting example that is often used in connection with the lie of Rahab is the deception practiced by Samuel in I Samuel 16:1-5. What Samuel says to the elders of Bethlehem is technically true, but it is also clearly meant to deceive. Samuel is seeking to save his own neck, as well as that of David, since he has a clearer idea than anyone in David's family would have of Saul's true character. However we assess his action, what he did is clearly right simply because he was following God's command in doing so. Does this mean that what he spoke was not a lie, or that the passage provides an example of justifiable lying? Advocates of lying to save life would argue the latter, but for a distinction between lying and concealing the truth, see the discussion below.
- The final example we will consider here involves the words spoken by Elisha to the Aramean army at Dothan (II Kings 6:19). But did Elisha in fact lie to the Arameans when he brought them to the king of Israel, who was the enemy they sought? They may have thought they wanted Elisha in Dothan, but in fact their ultimate goal was the Israelite king in Samaria, the capital. He knew better what they sought than they did, since they were merely following the orders of an enraged ruler who had been foiled time and again by the revelations of his troop movements by Elisha to the king of Israel.

SINCERE FALSEHOOD

What if someone passes on false information that he believes to be true? Obviously this is not lying per se, since the speaker has no desire to deceive and lacks the knowledge that would enable him to evaluate his own words accurately. However, if all false statements defame the character of God, it remains a serious matter. The possibility of speaking falsehood in ignorance should cause the Christian to be very careful about what he affirms. Wise speech is prudent speech, and a Christian should accompany with appropriate qualifiers any statement about which he is less than certain. Humility in the face of our own fallibility honors God, who alone possesses all knowledge and speaks all truth. Careless speech, on the other hand, dishonors the Lord and harms others.

CONCEALING THE TRUTH

The example of Samuel in Bethlehem given above raises the question of concealing the truth. Must we tell all we know to anyone who asks? What if the person who asks the question has no right to the information being demanded? While I may legitimately refuse to divulge information to someone who has no right to that knowledge, I may not do so by means of falsehood. While I may say, "I'm not at liberty to share that information," I may not say "I don't know" if I do, nor may I lie simply to bring the conversation to an end.

What, then, is the bottom line with regard to lying? The character of God must be the determinative factor. One who seeks to be truly godly may not engage in falsehood, though he need not reveal all he knows to anyone who asks. When one fears that speaking the truth will have damaging consequences, one must trust God and obey His command, leaving the consequences to Him. Especially where lives are at stake, the choice is never between lying or bringing about someone's death; God has promised that He will always provide a way of escape that does not involve sin (I Corinthians 10:13).

ADVERTISING

The decision to include advertising under the Ninth Commandment is somewhat arbitrary in the sense that the abuses associated with modern marketing practices manage to break at least half of the Ten Commandments. Advertisers use behavior modification techniques to influence potential customers, stimulate lust by using sex to sell almost anything imaginable, lie by making false claims that enable merchants to obtain unjust gain from their customers, and stimulate covetousness. Note that I didn't even attempt to address the ways in which advertisers violate the first table of the Decalogue. In any case, the topic is addressed here because advertisers are widely known to practice deceit.[206]

HYPOCRISY

The term *hypocrisy* appears often in Scripture, especially in the Gospels, where Jesus, in His interactions with the religious leaders of the day, accuses them of practicing it. The term comes from classical Greek theater. Plays were staged in outdoor amphitheaters, leaving audiences at a great distance from the actors. In order to enable the viewers to distinguish one character from another, the actors carried huge masks (these also helped to amplify the actors' voices so they could be heard at a great distance). These actors were called *hypocrites* - those who wore masks. Thus the term came to be applied to anyone who was pretending to be something he was not.[207] Thus Jesus accused the Pharisees of pretending to obey God while they were really serving only themselves by manipulating God's law for their own convenience. Sadly, the essence of much advertising today is hypocrisy in this sense of the word. How do advertisers work very hard to give the impression that their products are things other than what they are in reality or otherwise deceive consumers?

FALSE CLAIMS

Many advertisers pretend to be something they are not by making false, or at least misleading, claims. Statistics and surveys, often commissioned by the manufacturer of the product, can effectively be used to give an impression of authenticity to the claims being made for

---

[206] The 1990 movie comedy *Crazy People* plays on this reputation by portraying the inmates of an insane asylum who inadvertently get involved in writing copy for ads. They tell the simple and straightforward truth because they lack the subtlety to deceive, and their ads become wildly popular with the public.

[207] This must be carefully distinguished from someone who *tries* to be something he is not. While this is often foolish because it is an exercise in futility or shows lack of self-confidence, it can also be commendable; someone who tries to improve his character, for instance, should be praised rather than criticized.

the product.[208] Though laws have sought in many cases to minimize the ability of advertisers to make false claims, they have often succeeded in accomplishing little more than requiring disclaimers, which are either read so quickly or written in such small print that they have little impact.[209] False claims are also often made through comparisons with similar products made by other companies. Most of these are highly selective, and again tend to be based on tests run by or sponsored by the manufacturer.[210]

FALSE ASSOCIATIONS

One of the favorite tricks used by advertisers to mislead customers is that of associating a product with a basic human drive with which it has no inherent connection.[211] Advertisers take advantage of human desires for success by filming endorsement ads with famous people, the desire for popularity by showing youthful, beautiful, happy people using their product, the desire for sexual fulfillment (Will a certain brand of toothpaste really improve your sex life?), and the desire for the esteem of others ("Be the first one on your block . . ."). Again, students can think of many examples of these deceptive tactics. Awareness of these techniques, and the logical fallacies and dishonest manipulations involved, will make us less susceptible to false advertising. The important thing to remember here is that not only must Christians be aware so they are not deceived, but they must also consider the values that are being used to advertise many products. Are these values ones that Christians should hold, or is susceptibility to such things an indication of love of the world? Furthermore, Christians who are involved in selling goods or services to the public should be very careful not to use dishonest marketing methods. The fact that everyone does these things is no excuse; Christians should stand for, and stand out for, integrity in such matters.

---

[208] Many examples could be cited here (this becomes an enjoyable exercise for students, who can rattle off a large number of them with ease, sadly demonstrating how much time they spend watching television). One common one was the commercial that made the claim, "Four out of five dentists surveyed recommend sugarless gum for their patients who chew gum." If you analyze this statement, it is simple common sense; the only surprise is that *only* eighty percent of dentists would make this recommendation. The commercial, however, uses the obvious in a way that makes it sound like dentists are endorsing the product in question.

[209] The major exception to this is advertising for drug companies. Anyone who watches the Hallmark Channel or any other outlet that caters to senior citizens is familiar with the rapidly-read long list of disclaimers associated with patent medicines advertised on such programs, including warnings against possible shortness of breath, nausea, dizziness, bleeding, depression, and *death* (on rare occasions, of course)!

[210] Have you ever noticed that almost every car on the road has been named "Car of the Year" by *somebody*?

[211] Note that this is a form of behavioral conditioning; like Pavlov's dogs that learned to associate the ringing of a bell with food, advertisers try to connect their products with strong values held by their target audiences.

FICTION

The issue of fiction arises in this chapter because it involves falsehood for artistic or literary purposes. Some Christians over the years have argued that fiction is of no value because it does not speak the truth, and that serious believers should not waste their time with that which is not true. What about this criticism? Should fiction be classified as false witness?

THE CREATIVE IMAGINATION

Creativity is an aspect of the image of God in man. God is a Creator, and has given His creatures the capacity to create beauty as well. When human beings produce works of art, they reflect in a dim way the initial creative act of God Himself. Fiction clearly cannot be classified as a form of misrepresentation per se because Jesus used fiction in His parables.[212] While this is true, do some forms of fiction run the risk of bearing false witness?

HISTORICAL NOVELS AND DRAMA

These forms of writing almost always involve some degree of fiction, either in heightening the drama or in filling in the gaps. In addition, such efforts cannot avoid interpreting the facts provided by history.[213] In such situations, authors rarely are able to avoid distortion, and are often tempted to twist the facts to arrive at descriptions congenial to the purposes of the novel or play. Examples of such distortions abound: Kenneth Roberts, who wrote novels of the American Revolution, portrayed Benedict Arnold as a misunderstood hero; John Osborne's twisted play *Luther* pictures the protagonist as vulgar and mean-spirited, and argues that the Reformation was largely caused by a persistent case of indigestion; Leon Uris' dramatic account of the founding of the state of Israel in *Exodus* takes considerable liberties, though he tends to do better than most in his pictures of historical people and events; Shakespeare's portrayals of historical figures like Julius Caesar, Mark Antony and the conspirators, Henry V, Richard III, and other English kings are far from the truth, yet have done much to shape public consciousness; Charles Dickens' account of the French Revolution in *A Tale of Two Cities* gives a wildly distorted picture of that epoch-making event. The main issue here is that readers must not mistake fiction for truth. As long as they understand the role of dramatic license, they can guard against believing that what they are reading or seeing is true to the way in which events actually occurred. Not many readers, however, have the motivation to research such things, and are thus easily misled. The impact of such fiction on public opinion can be seen in the extent to which Americans' perceptions of the Puritans have been shaped by Arthur Miller's play *The Crucible*, which is horribly inaccurate, and how most people tend to view the Scopes Trial through the lens of Lawrence and Lee's *Inherit the Wind*, which makes fundamentalists look like ignorant, bigoted buffoons. Both plays possess the veneer of authenticity, both present skewed perspectives of the events themselves and misleading portrayals of key characters, yet both have played a major role in shaping public opinion

---

[212] Jotham's fable in Judges 9:8-15 and Ezekiel's allegories in Ezekiel 16 and 23 are examples of fiction in the Old Testament.

[213] This is also true, of course, of historical writing itself, which is always selective and interpretive.

concerning the events in question. False witness is thus a legitimate problem when dealing with historical fiction, either in novels or on stage.[214]

BIBLICAL NOVELS AND DRAMATIZATIONS

If the problem of false impressions and their consequences is significant when dealing with historical fiction, how much more is it true when dealing with biblical narratives? Secular attempts to deal with Bible stories are notoriously speculative and unreliable, though they sadly tend to influence the opinions of the general public. Cecil B. DeMille's portrayal of the events surrounding the Exodus in *The Ten Commandments* clearly misses the point in many particulars despite its earnestness, while others like Martin Scorsese's *The Last Temptation of Christ* are pure blasphemy. But what of creative efforts produced by professing Christians, such as Lloyd Douglas' novel *The Robe*, Lew Wallace's *Ben Hur*, and Mel Gibson's film *The Passion of the Christ*? Here distortion is unavoidable because Scripture never gives us narratives of sufficient length or detail to fill two hours or more of film or several hundred pages of a novel.[215] Misrepresenting biblical truth by adding to God's revelation is a serious matter (Revelation 22:18), especially because of the harm that can be done to the way readers and viewers understand and apply the Word. How much more is this true of attempts to portray the Son of God, which can never avoid deception and will always in some way mislead those who read them or see them?

GOSSIP

Gossip is a seemingly-minor sin that can create major turmoil in any group of people. It involves situations in which the person to whom one is speaking does not have the right to the information being shared; he or she is neither part of the problem nor part of the solution.

BIBLICAL TEACHING ON GOSSIP

The book of Proverbs contains a number of verses that speak of the evils of gossip, along with other passages in Scripture. Note the following:

- Solomon recognized how strong the temptation to listen to gossip is - "The words of a whisperer are like delicious morsels; they go down into the inner parts of the body" (Proverbs 18:8; note that Proverbs 26:22 is identical).
- The wise king warns against associating with gossips - "Whoever goes about slandering reveals secrets; therefore do not associate with a simple babbler" (Proverbs 20:19).
- Proverbs 11:13 contrasts the gossip with a person who is able to keep a confidence - "Whoever goes about slandering reveals secrets, but he who is trustworthy in spirit keeps a thing covered."

---

[214] The same, of course, is true of television shows and movies that present stories "based on real events" or real characters.

[215] See the discussion of images in the church on page 42.

- Gossip leads to quarrels among friends; it is the fuel that feeds the fire - "For lack of wood the fire goes out, and where there is no whisperer, quarreling ceases" (Proverbs 26:20).
- The consequence is broken relationships - "A dishonest man spreads strife, and a whisperer separates close friends" (Proverbs 16:28).
- Even the law recognized the evil of gossip - "You shall not go around as a slanderer among your people" (Leviticus 19:16).
- Gossip appears in several lists of sinful behavior in Paul's epistles (Romans 1:29; II Corinthians 12:20).
- Paul warned that young widows, if supported by the church, could easily fall into this sin (I Timothy 5:13).

WHY IS GOSSIP WRONG?

While gossip may not always be lying in the sense that it is untruthful, it is always malicious speech, if not in intent, certainly in practice.

- Gossip is almost always false witness because of the "Whisper Down the Lane" effect - stories passed from one person to another are often distorted, even if the speaker lacks malicious intent, which certainly cannot be taken for granted. Gossip is typically characterized by exaggeration, misinformation, and partial truth.
- Gossip violates clear biblical teaching about dealing with offenses. Matthew 18:15-18 lays out the proper procedure, which begins with going directly to the person involved. Notice that nowhere in the passage is information communicated to another party without the concerned person being present or having been addressed first.
- Gossip is inherently unfair because the person who is the topic of conversation is not there to defend himself or explain the matter in question.

WHAT RESULTS FROM GOSSIP?

In the warnings noted above, we see some of the consequences of gossip, which include the following:

- Gossip destroys friendships and ruins relationships. One who spreads rumors not only sets the stage for a broken relationship between him and the person in question, but also alienates others who may be involved in the situation. How many people have begun to avoid one who had once been a friend because of something they heard from someone else?
- Gossip destroys the unity and harmony of groups. Such activity is commonplace in teenage cliques, but it is devastating in churches. How many churches over the years have actually split because of unbridled gossip?
- Gossip ruins reputations. People who are targets of malicious (or even sometimes innocent) gossip can have their reputations ruined, sometimes without ever understanding the cause of the disfavor they experience.[216]

---

[216] In Shakespeare's play *Othello*, the malicious gossip spread by Iago ruins Cassio's reputation in the eyes of his commanding officer, then destroys Othello's marriage, eventually causing him to murder his wife.

The procedure laid out in Matthew 18:15-18 thus is of great practical importance in maintaining the unity of the body of Christ and in enabling God's people to show love for one another.

CHEATING

In a 2001 survey of 4500 high school students, 97% admitted to cheating in some form on their schoolwork, whether by copying homework, looking at a friend's paper during a test, or plagiarizing a paper. Cheating has become much easier with the advent of the Internet, where term papers can be purchased on websites designed to encourage plagiarism, and cell phones that allow information to be stored easily, looked at surreptitiously, and texted to friends in other parts of the room while escaping notice. The Bible says little about school, and nothing about cheating per se, yet biblical principles clearly apply, and indicate that cheating is a serious matter indeed. As with our discussion of advertising, cheating could be addressed under a number of the commandments.

CHEATING IS STEALING

How does the cheater steal? He steals answers from a fellow student or from another source, but he also steals credit - a grade he has not earned. Cheating is a misuse of intellectual property. Just because cheating is easy, and just because everybody does it (e.g., downloading music from websites that allow this to be done without proper payment to the copyright owner), does not make it right.

CHEATING IS LYING

Cheating involves lying to the teacher by claiming to know something you don't know, but also involves lying to the world by getting a grade that is not a true reflection of your knowledge or achievement. Anyone who consults a cheater's records is being deceived about that person's ability and knowledge.

CHEATING HURTS PEOPLE

People seek to justify cheating in a number of ways, but one of the most absurd is to argue that it is ultimately harmless - that no one is really hurt by it. One the contrary, many people are hurt by cheating.

- God is slandered by the conduct of one made in His image. The cheater gives a false picture of his Creator, and a Christian who cheats bears false witness about his Redeemer.
- Cheating hurts the cheater. The very person who is attempting to benefit from the practice is often the one who is hurt the most. As with all lying, cheating embroils the cheater in perpetual deception. Furthermore, the knowledge that should have been gained and was not may one day be needed, and may not be easy to regain. In addition, if cheating should be discovered, the reputation of the cheater is often harmed irreparably because trust is destroyed.

- Cheating on schoolwork hurts the teacher. Teachers want to be able to trust their students, and finding that they are not able to do so is painful. Furthermore, the teacher is always tempted to wonder whether what has been discovered is merely the tip of the iceberg. Furthermore, cheating shows disrespect for the teacher because the student fails to appreciate the knowledge the teacher has worked so hard to impart.
- Cheating hurts other students. The academic environment is always to some extent competitive, so that students who cheat undermine the standing of those who earn their grades honestly. The cheater also places a moral burden on those who are aware of what he is doing, since he forces them to reveal his behavior or share his guilt.

CHEATING IS NEVER JUSTIFIABLE

People who cheat give all kinds of justifications for doing so. They argue that the requirements are unreasonable, that they can't hope to keep up with others unless they cheat since "everyone is doing it," that they didn't have enough time to complete the assignment, that the examples of people in the public eye show that cheating is acceptable in order to get ahead, that pressures from parents to get good grades or to get into the "best" colleges make cheating attractive, or even that they are too lazy to do all the work required. None of these reasons is an acceptable one; in simple terms, cheating is sin, an affront to God and man.

We should note, of course, that while cheating in school has been the main concern of this section, cheating in other areas of life is widespread - in the business world, on tax returns, and in marriage. One whose heart becomes hardened to the point where he believes cheating to be justifiable is not likely to stop when he gets out of school; the practice can destroy his entire life, his reputation, and the lives of those who are close to him.

11

THE CHRISTIAN AND THE
SANCTITY OF CONTENTMENT

Exodus 20:17 - "You shall not covet your neighbor's house; you shall not covet your neighbor's wife, or his male servant, or his female servant, or his ox, or his donkey, or anything that is your neighbor's."

The Tenth Commandment lacks the inherent interest value of some of the others, which lead to discussions of controversial social issues. This in no way minimizes its importance, however. In fact, Paul confessed that the Tenth Commandment played an important role in his conversion (Romans 7:7). The reason for this is that unlike the other commandments that overtly address outward behavior, it points directly toward the attitudes of the heart, which is the real root of man's rebellion against God.[217] While Paul, as a good Pharisee, could claim to have kept the commandments, at least to his own satisfaction, this one caught him short, for who can claim innocence in the face of this examination of the heart?

THE TENTH COMMANDMENT AS A SUMMARY

The fact that the Tenth Commandment addresses the heart makes it in a sense a summary of the Decalogue. We have seen often that Jesus, in the Sermon on the Mount in the latter part of Matthew 5, digs behind questions of outward behavior to reveal matters of the heart. Because actions stem from attitudes, coveting lies at the root of rebellion, murder, adultery, stealing, and lying.[218] This is also true of the rejection of divine authority in favor of personal autonomy that underlies violation of the first four commandments.

COVETOUSNESS AND ENVY

Covetousness and envy go hand in hand, though the two have slightly different meanings. The first refers to the things one desires, even if those "things" are people who are being treated

---

[217] Genesis 3:6 pictures covetousness as the source of the Fall of Man; Eve saw and wanted before she took and ate.

[218] Buddha had some sense of this truth when he said that "all suffering comes from desire." Unfortunately, his method for dealing with these desires - following the Eightfold Path of self-denial - was woefully inadequate. One cannot get rid of covetousness simply through self-discipline.

as objects, while the second refers to people who have what you want. Covetousness, even if harbored secretly in the heart and never revealed, can destroy human relationships. If I covet what you have, even if I never say or do anything about it, I will soon begin to envy you, which is bound to influence my behavior toward you (James 4:1-5).[219] Paul pictures covetousness as contrary to love of neighbor in Romans 13:9, and envy is something that love explicitly does not do in I Corinthians 13:4.[220]

COVETOUSNESS AND CONTENTMENT

Covetousness and contentment are mutually exclusive. As we give up the former, God gives us the latter. Paul had mastered this grace (Philippians 4:11-13), and had found the freedom that comes from not being dependent on circumstances in order to find happiness.[221] In Luke 12:15, Jesus saw covetousness as the root of the request for Him to settle a quarrel between two brothers. This led Him to tell the Parable of the Rich Fool, which shows that covetousness produces a perpetual lack of contentment; the possession of more and more things will simply not make a person happy, but will produce misery instead. One who seeks contentment in his possessions will become obsessed with them - increasing them, protecting them from decay and theft, keeping ahead of his neighbor; such a person never has enough, and thus is never content.

SUCCESS

One would think that someone who considers himself successful is less likely to covet what he does not have. But as we have already seen, when one defines success in material terms - wealth, possessions, fame, popularity - one never seems to have enough. As a result, we must arrive at a true definition of success if we hope to escape the snare of covetousness.

SUCCESS IN GOD'S SIGHT

One who wishes to be successful in the sight of God must recognize that God defines success very differently than the world does. Success for the Christian is determined much more by who we are than by what we do or what we have. One important passage that speaks to this issue is II Peter 1:3-11. The qualities listed here keep one from being "ineffective or unfruitful" so that he will "never fall." One who lacks them, however, is "so nearsighted that he is blind."

---

[219] The story of Achan clearly shows the destructiveness of covetousness. He saw the forbidden objects, which led him to covet them and then take them (Joshua 7:20-21). This resulted not only in death for him and his family, but in military defeat for Israel as well.

[220] One of the real dangers that Scripture recognizes is the temptation to envy the wicked because of their prosperity and worldly success and power (Psalm 73:3; Proverbs 3:31; 23:17).

[221] The entire fourth chapter of Philippians is an excellent meditation on this subject (see especially verses 4, 6-13, 18-19). Note that verse 13, which is so often taken out of context, does not refer to strength to do things like get good grades on tests or win athletic contests, but to be content regardless of circumstances, which may include suffering and failure from a human perspective.

Note that the qualities listed in verses 5-7 build upon one another; this is not merely a list, but a sequence, where each is to be added to the one before. This does not imply, of course, that those later in the list are not to be sought until the earlier ones are mastered. Instead, we should understand that each quality is inadequate unless it is supplemented by those that follow. How do these character qualities produce a successful life as God defines the term?

- Faith - Peter assumes faith as the starting point for success in life. One who has never been transformed by the grace of God and the power of the Holy Spirit cannot hope to live a successful life.

- Virtue - The word used here refers to moral excellence or moral fiber; one who possesses virtue is able to stand firm and live out in practice the faith he professes. Hananiah, Mishael, and Azariah, the young Jewish men in Daniel 3 who stood firm when faced with the gaping maw of the fiery furnace if they did not succumb to the demand for idol worship, are good examples of this. Without this moral excellence, faith is worthless (James 2:14-26), as may be seen in the case of Demas (II Timothy 4:10), who forsook the ministry because of the lure of the world. Moral excellence is a quality of the successful life in thought (Philippians 4:8) and word (Ephesians 4:15,29) as well as deed.

- Knowledge - In the Bible, knowledge is practical. It is not simply a mass of information stored in the brain, but also the wisdom to use that information in a beneficial way. The good intentions associated with virtue must be channeled rightly, according to God's revealed will; this was the wisdom that Solomon asked of God in I Kings 3:16-28. However, a person may be morally vigorous, but unless he channels that desire according to revealed truth, he will fail. This was the case with Samson, whose zeal for the Lord and faith were obvious, but who cared too little for the constraints of God's law, and as a result turned his energies in all sorts of harmful directions.[222]

- Self-control - This is the quality of being able to rein in one's desires and appetites, as Joseph did when tempted by Potiphar's wife (Genesis 39). One who fails to add this discipline, which has its source in the Spirit of God (Galatians 5:22-23), to wisdom and knowledge will end up as a failure. Solomon, perhaps the best illustration of this, is cited in Scripture as a positive example of wisdom, but his lack of self-control (cf. I Kings 11:1-13) led to the regrets expressed near the end of his life in the book of Ecclesiastes.

- Steadfastness - The word here, also translated in other versions of Scripture as *patience* or *perseverance*, literally means "to remain under" - in common parlance, to hang in there, particularly under difficult circumstances. In Scripture, Job is explicitly singled out as one who possessed this quality (James 5:11). On the other hand, a person may possess self-control, but if he cannot stand up under pressure from others or from circumstances, he will ultimately fail. Aaron, when he made the Golden Calf under pressure from the people in Exodus 32:1-4, is a good example of one who lacked steadfastness, though he evidently possessed self-control in his personal life.

---

[222] The same might be said of Othello in Shakespeare's play, whose moral zeal made him an easy prey for the villain Iago because he did not exercise that zeal according to knowledge. Thus, after killing his wife Desdemona and right before he commits suicide, he describes himself as "one who loved not wisely, but too well."

- Godliness - While we usually use this word to refer to outward behavior that conforms to the law of God, the basic idea in this passage relates more to an inner attitude of reverence or piety; the issue therefore is behavior toward God rather than behavior in the sight of other people. Outstanding among the many examples of this quality found in Scripture is Isaiah, when he finds himself before the throne of God in his Temple vision in Isaiah 6. He displays reverence before God as he falls on his face in God's presence and acknowledges his sin and his inability. On the other hand, Scripture also provides us with an example of one who persevered, but whose lack of reverence before God cost him dearly. Uzzah, trusted with the task of transporting the Ark of the Covenant, was clearly a man who sought to serve the Lord and was zealous for His glory. His lack of reverence, demonstrated by touching the Ark in order to keep it from falling off the cart, cost him his life (II Samuel 6:1-7).

- Brotherly affection - The Greek word here is *philadelphia*, denoting love for others (see page 22). If one truly loves God, he will also love the brethren (I John 2:9). The love of David and Jonathan for one another shows how godliness works its way out in love for others; Jonathan certainly had good reason to hate or fear David, but his love for the Lord overflowed into love for his friend as well. We can see godliness as well in the love Joseph shows to his brothers when he forgives them after all they had done to him. Those who claim to love God but are unable to love their brothers bring great shame to the name of Christ, whether one speaks of biological kinship (the enmity between Jacob and Esau comes readily to mind) or spiritual bonds (e.g., Euodias and Syntyche in Philippians 4:2-3).

- Love - This is *agape* (see page 22), the love of I Corinthians 13 as well as the love of God for His children; this selflessness is the capstone of the successful Christian life. One who possesses all the qualities listed by Peter but lacks love needs to repent, as did the Ephesian church in Revelation 2:1-7.

Of what does success then consist from a biblical perspective? Success comes not only from cultivating these qualities through the work of the Spirit in one's life, but also by seeking to increase in each of these characteristics throughout one's life as a Christian. If one possesses these evidences of God's grace, success in material terms will be of little importance, and coveting the things of this world will seem preposterous.

SETTING PRIORITIES

The cultivation of the qualities that constitute success in the Christian life also involves setting godly priorities. Jesus, in Matthew 6:33, notes that one who wishes to be successful in this life must put the Kingdom of God first, leaving the provision of the things so often associated with worldly success in the hands of God. If we really believe that God cares for His children and gives them all they need, we need not be preoccupied with such things, but instead give our time and attention to cultivating and living out those traits that define success in terms of Kingdom values.

FORMING GOOD HABITS

Most of the things we do are done by habit. Our patterns of life are largely unconscious, developed over many years, and become more and more fixed the longer we live.[223] Because of this, one must strive to develop good life patterns. Just because something is done habitually does not mean we are excused from responsibility for that action. Habits do not begin as habits, but as conscious actions that become habitual through constant repetition.[224] Breaking bad habits and forming good ones are not two different processes, but really two sides of the same activity. Bad habits will never be broken until they are *replaced*. In order to stop doing something, you can't simply grit your teeth and struggle to refrain - you need to do something else instead.[225] This is reflected in the biblical "put off/put on" pattern (Colossians 3:9-10); God always provides the positive behavior that He intends to replace the negative behavior that is to be shunned.

BECOMING MORE LIKE CHRIST

Ultimately, success is defined as become more like Christ (Matthew 5:48). Paul speaks of following the example of Christ in passages like Philippians 2:5-11 and Philippians 3:7-14, as does Peter in I Peter 2:21-25. This is what success looks like, and such pursuits leave no room for coveting the things of this world.

COMMITMENT

When Paul speaks of the role of the Tenth Commandment in his own conversion in Romans 7:7-9, he makes a strange connection between the commandment and death. He notes that his understanding of the Tenth Commandment caused him to die. What did he mean by this? When someone looks into his own heart and sees the sin there, he dies in the sense of holding out no hope of acceptance before God. The commandment, in a sense, killed him, at least in terms of his own perceptions of his spiritual state. On the other hand, this death, when it leads a person to turn to Christ as it did with Paul, leads to a new life (Galatians 2:20). Dying with Christ and being raised again with Him produces a life of commitment rather than one of covetousness. What does such death involve?

DEATH TO SIN

In Romans 6:1-13, Paul speaks of the kind of death that results in new life. He uses baptism as an example, since it symbolizes one's identification with the death and resurrection of Christ as one goes under the water and is brought up again. Death to sin has strong ethical

---

[223] Thus the expression, "You can't teach an old dog new tricks."

[224] I have a poster on my classroom wall containing a quotation from Aristotle: "We are what we repeatedly do. Excellence, then, is not an act but a habit."

[225] This is why people who are trying to quit smoking often begin to chew gum.

implications, including deliverance from the penalty of sins committed as well as the original sin with which one is born, deliverance from the power of sin, so that the Christian is no longer a slave to his sinful nature, but rather a slave to righteousness, and a glorious hope of eventual deliverance from the presence of sin altogether when one enters the presence of God in Heaven. Though the Christian cannot avoid sin altogether in this life (I John 1:8), sin is no longer the default mode; rather, righteousness has become standard operating procedure as a result of the grace of God and the sanctifying work of the Holy Spirit. Christians sin, yes, but such behavior is fundamentally incongruous - it is as incongruous for a Christian to sin as it is for a corpse to breathe.

DEATH TO SELF

Matthew 16:24-26 contains one of the great paradoxes of Jesus' preaching ministry, where He talks about the need to lose one's life in order to find it. "Taking up one's cross" is not bearing a burden, but going to one's death. What does this loss of life, this denial of self, mean? Death to self does not mean the kind of self-denial sought by monks who lived in caves in the desert, depriving themselves of all but the minimum of food and clothing and of virtually all human contact in order to cultivate holiness, nor do the words of Jesus to the Rich Young Ruler when He told him to sell all he had and give it to the poor (Matthew 19:21) define it.[226] Instead, death to self means that our desires - the things that we "covet" - should be brought into line with God's desires. Under those circumstances, God has promised to give us all that our hearts desire (Psalm 37:4; Matthew 7:7-11)!

DEATH TO SATAN

Satan is the implacable enemy of the believer, doing everything in his power to destroy one's effectiveness for Christ (I Peter 5:8). Yet the truth is that Satan, like the sinful nature to which he appeals, can have no power over one who is dead in Christ and alive with Him. The power of Satan can be successfully resisted by one who is dead to his appeals and blandishments. The truth of the Word (cf. Matthew 4:1-11) and the power of the Spirit (I John 4:4) can enable the Christian to resist Satan so effectively that he will flee from a power that he is unable to overcome (James 4:7).

---

[226] Nor does it mean, as many Christians tend to think, that if they submit to God's will in their lives He will make them do the worst thing they could imagine; submitting one's will to the will of God does not mean that God will make us do whatever we hate the most. It does mean that the Christian who has died to self will come to love whatever God's will for his life happens to be.

CONCLUSION

What, then, is the conclusion of the matter? We should note the following in seeking to summarize the ideas of this book:

- Right living is defined by God, not only because He has the right to dictate how His creatures should live, but also because we have been made in His image and are intended to reflect His character, which is the foundation of biblical ethics.
- The world in which we live and the people among whom we live are in rebellion against God, and therefore should never be the standard by which we measure right and wrong. In fact, we can generally assume that, apart from the operation of common grace, the values of the society around us will be ungodly.
- Salvation is not the result of godly living, but its cause. People are not saved because they live good lives; instead, they live good lives because they are saved. Only the Holy Spirit can transform a rebel determined to follow his own selfish desires into a child of God whose greatest desire is to be like Jesus.
- Like salvation itself, moral living is the result of the grace of God at work in the life of the believer. One who lives uprightly can claim no credit for "being good," but instead recognizes that all the glory for whatever goodness one may possess and demonstrate must be given to God, who alone can produce attitudes and behavior that are totally contrary to fallen human nature.
- Godly living is to be pursued by anyone who names the name of Christ. Not only every word and every deed, but even every thought is to be taken captive in the desire to obey Jesus and honor Him (II Corinthians 10:5).

SCRIPTURE INDEX